Claudia Derichs, Susanne Kreitz-Sandberg (eds.)

Gender Dynamics and Globalisation

Gender-Diskussion

Band 6

LIT

GENDER DYNAMICS AND GLOBALISATION

Perspectives on Japan within Asia

edited by

Claudia Derichs and Susanne Kreitz-Sandberg

LIT

Gedruckt auf alterungsbeständigem Werkdruckpapier entsprechend
ANSI Z3948   DIN ISO 9706

Wir danken der Vereinigung für Sozialwissenschaftliche Japanforschung
(VSJF) und Frau Patricia Dorner für ihre vielfältige Unterstützung

Bibliographic information published by the Deutsche Nationalbibliothek
The Deutsche Nationalbibliothek lists this publication in the Deutsche
Nationalbibliografie; detailed bibliographic data are available in the Internet at
http://dnb.d-nb.de.

ISBN 978-3-8258-9761-1

A catalogue record for this book is available from the British Library

© LIT VERLAG Dr. W. Hopf Berlin 2007
Auslieferung/Verlagskontakt:
Fresnostr. 2   48159 Münster
Tel. +49 (0)251–62 03 20   Fax +49 (0)251–23 19 72
e-Mail: lit@lit-verlag.de   http://www.lit-verlag.de

Distributed in the UK by: Global Book Marketing, 99B Wallis Rd, London, E9 5LN
Phone: +44 (0) 20 8533 5800 – Fax: +44 (0) 1600 775 663
http://www.centralbooks.co.uk/acatalog/search.html

Distributed in North America by:

Transaction Publishers
New Brunswick (U.S.A.) and London (U.K.)

Transaction Publishers
Rutgers University
35 Berrue Circle
Piscataway, NJ 08854

Phone: +1 (732) 445 - 2280
Fax: + 1 (732) 445 - 3138
for orders (U. S. only):
toll free (888) 999 - 6778
e-mail:
orders@transactionspub.com

Contents

Contents

Gender Dynamics and Globalization
Perspectives on Japan within Asia

Claudia Derichs

The importance of integrating gender as an analytical category into social scientific research has been stressed by feminist scholars the world over. This volume addresses gender as a category that cuts across any field of social, political, and economic organization. It takes into account the dynamics that have been sparked off by an increasingly respectful attitude in many countries towards principles of gender equity, gender mainstreaming, or women's rights. After the United Nation's Decade of Women (1975–85), World Conferences like the International Conference on Population and Development in Cairo (1994) and the Fourth World Conference on Women in Beijing (1995) provided a global foundation for national and sub-national initiatives targeting at the empowerment of women. The globalization of women's issues – and gender issues in a more capacious sense – has triggered many a national initiative and has left its traces in various shapes, some of which are introduced and discussed in this volume. While Japan takes centre stage in each contribution, the perspective is not limited to the country's territorial borders. Rather, Japan's location within Asia leads to a transnational and comparative perspective that enables the reader to put "the Japanese situation" into relation.

In her introductory chapter, Ilse Lenz traces the history of the concept of gender in modern Japan (since 1868). By identifying a hegemonic national gender order during the country's modernization, Lenz underlines that an analysis of this order requires the acknowledgement of an intersectionality of elements that are formative for individual and collective identities – for instance class or ethnicity. An integration of such formative notions helps to explain historical developments (here: the change of gender order) in a much more accurate manner than concentrating exclusively on a single core notion (as, for example, gender). Applying this fresh approach, Lenz carves out three sub-periods of Japanese modernization which have been crucial for changes in the national gender order: civil national modernization, organized national modernization, and reflexive modernization. Since Lenz's chapter covers the whole period of Japan's modernization, it provides an excellent synopsis of the evolution and progression of the concept of gender in this country.

The subsequent articles in this volume comprise a selection of papers from an international conference on Gender Dynamics in Japan and Asia, held in November 2004 at the Japanese-German Center Berlin (JDZB). The conference recruited speakers from several European and Asian countries. Their common denominator was the application of a gender-sensitive perspective on issues such as national identity, the changing appeal of role models, legacies of a misogynous past, gendered education policies, female imaging in the media, or working women's networks. The transnational dimension was highlighted by comparisons drawn between Japan and other countries of the region such as China and South Korea. We have selected a group of articles for this volume which attend to

- concepts of gender and gendered identities; and
- actors within gendered spaces of society.

Given the fact that the two sections overlap in some of the contributions, we have structured the chapters according to their central argument, i.e. whether it is concept-oriented or actor-oriented. The topical scope of all these chapters brings gender as an omnipresent mode of social organisation into our minds. It is the intention of all contributors to address aspects of Japanese social reality which have hitherto got detracted from the mainstream of gender studies on Japan. The chapters of the first section discuss conceptual terms like 'gender free', 'gender identity', and 'masculinity'. In chapter 2, Michiko Mae addresses the paradigm shift that has taken place in Japanese gender studies. Mae examines this shift by analysing the cultural meaning of a fixed gender order for Japan's modernization, and by relating the premises of this gender order to the 1999 Basic Law for a Gender-equal Society. The term *gender-free*, which was coined in the process of formulating stipulations for a gender-equal society, indicates the development of a mindset that enables both men and women 'to develop a multitude of ways of living, regardless of gender distinctions and roles determined by society and culture.' (Mae) Although this term was used in circles and movements striving for gender equality, it did not enter the text of the 1999 Basic Law, apparently because conservative forces feared the negation of any gender differences by employing it. The gender free concept, says Mae, overcomes the boundaries of a culturally determined gender order. It is directed towards a cross-border transculturality and opens up 'new ways of thinking and acting for the individual.' The Japanese women's movement clearly follows this direction, but it has to gain more mileage in order to convince the cautious and the doubtful of the positive effects of a gender free mindset.

In chapter 3, Annette Schad-Seifert shifts the view to men's studies and provides an in-depth analysis of the consequences of the male breadwinner model that was cultivated in a peculiar manner throughout the high-growth period of the post-war Japanese economy. Principles such as lifetime employment or a seniority based reward system exerted a strong influence on the building of an 'ideal type' – in the Weberian sense – of the male breadwinner. 'A male school graduate could expect to join a company, rise through the corporate ladder and receive a continuously growing salary,' Schad-Seifert summarises a typical part of a salary man's (*sararīman*) biography. Whereas this outlook on a seemingly carefree life appealed to many male Japanese for some decades, the 1990s put this model increasingly into question. The young generation developed different ideas of how they want to live. Changing attitudes towards life and work became particularly expressed through a new type of an 'unsteady', non-lifetime worker called *furītā*. Together with the phenomenon of *furītā*, a men's liberation movement emerged and more young Japanese males began to critically reflect on the dominant models of gender identities. Schad-Seifert explores various kinds of 'new' masculinities and the dynamics they have deployed within the corporate world, the media, and academia. Because of the changes in employment structures, alternative lifestyles are becoming an option, at least for the young generation.

In the second section of the volume, the authors relate to actors who are actively or passively involved in the enhancement of the protection of women's rights, the discourse on controversial topics like the 'comfort women', but also the imaging of Korean women in the Japanese media. In a chapter that traces the policy outputs in the context of women's rights, Hiromi Tanaka and Mihee Hong describe the implementation processes of the Convention on the Elimination of All Forms of Discrimination against Women (CEDAW) in Japan and South Korea. CEDAW was adopted by the United Nations General Assembly as early as 1979, and has since then become ratified by 165 countries. The fact of the convention's ratification, however, blurs the oftentimes bitter struggles of women's organisations and women's movements to make sure that its proper implementation will follow suit. Taking a comparative approach, Tanaka and Hong gauge the adoption of CEDAW by the Japanese and South Korean administrations, its effect on gender relations in the two societies, and the mutual influence of implementation procedures. Both countries ratified CEDAW in the 1980s. Tanaka and Hong depict the similarities in the process leading to this ratification and emphasise the role of the respective national women's movements on the one hand, and the relevance of what is referred to in the literature as 'Women's Policy Machinery' on the other hand. In terms of mutual influence, the adoption of South Korea's Equal Employment Law is raised as an example for the impact of Japanese feminist policy formation on policy-making in the neighbouring country. But both authors also point out different political and historic conditions in the two countries that should not be neglected in the comparison of national policy-making, policy formation, and implementation.

The impact of international conventions like CEDAW or events like the Fourth World Conference on Women in Beijing 1995 is not always tangible on the spot. It is rather the result of norms and standards that have trickled down to the micro-cosmos of social organisation, where they appear in various shapes such as codes of conduct, corporate regulations, or recommendations for interaction. At this point, Maria Baier (chapter 5) takes up the issue and illustrates how huge corporations are eventually pressured to abide by internationally defined standards and nationally enacted legislation on their shopfloor. Picking up the court case against sexual discrimination in wages and promotions at Sumitomo, Baier illustrates how much support discriminated female employees need in order to achieve gender justice at the workplace. In this regard, Baier portraits the Working Women's Network in Osaka as an influential actor in effecting Japan's Equal Employment Opportunity Law, which may be considered as an offspring of CEDAW on the national level. The Working Women's Network was founded in 1995 as a support group for women who face discrimination at work. It is, accordingly, staffed by lawyers, scholars, female workers and would-be plaintiffs of sex discrimination suits against private Japanese companies. In her very dense and detailed mapping of the network's activities, its struggle, its successes as well as its current problems, Baier plots a line that links the international and the national level of feminist advocacy work.

Chapter 6 is committed to a dark spot of Japanese modern history, namely the issue of the so-called comfort women who were forced to serve as sex slaves during the second world war. Ulrike Woehr provides a discourse analysis of the public and intellectual debate of this issue, covering primarily the 1990s, i.e. when the topic received particular press coverage in the Japanese media. The majority of published newspaper articles on the forced prostitution issue show a revisionist Japanese view which outweighs the self-critical perspective. This has led to maneuvering the public view towards an opinion that holds the former sex slaves as women whose business it was to sell their bodies. In contrast to the coverage in the mainstream print media, the intellectual discourse tackled the comfort women issue from a much more critical and, on the Japanese side, self-critical angle. Woehr gives a painstakingly researched account of the contrasting positions taken by leading female intellectuals of Japanese and non-Japanese origin. The questions that have been raised since it was pointed out that the communities of women forced to serve the army as sex slaves included Japanese nationals as well, have by no means been answered. The topic has, it seems, been linked even stronger than other topics of feminist interest to a debate on nationalism (in both Japan and Korea). Woehr thus identifies two straits of the discourse on Japanese 'comfort women' that need reconsideration: 'First, Japanese victims of militarised sexual violence are discussed in isolation, that is, without clarifying their (unequal) relationship to other women victimised by the Japanese army. While similarities are emphasised, differences are neglected. Second, Japanese women are only looked upon as victims, and not from the perspective of their active and, often, patriotically inspired support of the war and the colonial system.' The 'comfort women' debate has without doubt evoked some fresh and thought-provoking ideas within the Japanese feminist discourse.

In the next cluster of chapters, Wolfram Manzenreiter and Susanne Kreitz-Sandberg analyse several features, intentions, outcomes and results of gender segregation and gender-specific treatment in the field of education. In chapter 7, Manzenreiter claims that physical education in Japan leads to a (re-)production of what Bourdieu calls 'body regimes' – defining them 'as mindsets of orientation which are incorporated into the (physical) body, consciously as well as unconsciously, by the members of a social community.' The 'rule' of body regimes becomes noticeable in the shapes of male and female bodies (muscles as a signifier of male physical strength, for instance), gestures, body movements and the like. Body regimes are subject to conventionally accepted norms, which are, in turn, transmitted in formal physical education and other institutionalized forums of physical training. Manzenreiter gives numerous examples of practices in schools, sport clubs and the like which proof a more or less strategic construction of femininities and masculinities in contemporary Japan. He traces them back to institutions in pre-war Japan that sought to enforce specific ideals of masculinity, and thereby proves a certain historical continuity in gendering sportive activities, particularly with regard to reproducing masculinities. Although globalization and social change have brought forward new perspectives on the participation of both sexes in sport activities, the influence of entrenched body regimes remains strong. 'The school as a social institution proves to be incapable of establishing counter-trends to the hegemonic body regimes,' says Manzenreiter, indicating that female subordination and male domination prevail.

Susanne Kreitz-Sandberg's findings match those of Manzenreiter with regard to primary school education. Kreitz-Sandberg reviews secondary data of a case study at a primary school in Japan, which shows that once established patterns of gender segregation and a standardisation of gender roles are still forming big obstacles to a flexible and gender free operation of equity-oriented projects. Kreitz-Sandberg compares this Japanese study with results of a case study from the Philippines. The data reveal that both in the Philippines and in Japan, school teachers are actively engaged in projects to raise awareness for the importance of equality between the sexes. Many teachers, however, admit the limits their activities face because of the conservative social environment they are working in. This became more obvious in Japan than in the Philippine school projects.

In the final thematic chapter, Hilaria Goessmann examines the ways in which gender and ethnicity are dealt with in Japanese TV dramas. Her case in point is a TV drama aired in 2002 with the title 'Kankoku no obachan wa erai!' (Korean Aunties Are Admirable!). The female Korean characters in this drama function as role models for Japanese woman, Goessmann finds. They care for their family rather than for their individual professional career, and reject individual self-fulfillment. Emotional relations between men and women are 'pure' in a more or less romantic sense, and love affairs often occur between Japanese women and Korean men. While these have become common features of TV dramas with Korean protagonists, the trend still requires some explanation. Goessmann suggests that the loading of the Korean characters with positive social values is related to a nostalgia or retro trend in Japan, which becomes most obvious in the presentation of gender relations. According to Goessmann, 'the gender relations are idealized because they are seen to represent "good old Japan".' How long this trend will prevail in Japanese TV dramas is open to speculation. Recalling Michiko Mae's discussion of the gender free concept in chapter 1, the prospect of implanting a gender free mindset into Japanese media productions seems still distant.

Susanne Kreitz-Sandberg concludes the volume with a compilation of the central results of the preceding contributions. In this volume, authors and editors alike did not want to elaborate on the women's and men's movements in Japan, on the role of women in Japanese society, on the 'modern girl' or else. This has been done by many others to whom we owe our thanks for providing us with highly valuable information. The new approach we have taken here lies in giving space to male- *and* female-dominated terrains of Japanese society which have been examined extensively by scholars all around the world, but which still lack a gender-sensitive explanation – at least to a considerable extent. We have chosen spaces of discourse and action that, we feel, deserve closer attention from the field of gender studies. We are led by the conviction that the application of a gender perspective is not only helpful, but unconditionally necessary in order to understand and analyze social, political, and economic change in contemporary Japan. Guided by this shared understanding of the category of gender, both authors and editors hope to offer some interesting and innovative perspectives on Japan within Asia.

Concepts

of Gender and Gendered Identities

Gender at the Crossroads – Modernisation and the Changing National Gender Order in Japan

Ilse Lenz

1 Rooting 'Gender' in Japan

Gender has been a key paradigm (Ōsawa 2003: 7) for structuring modern Japanese society: Whereas men and women shared their work, their meals and often even their bath in rural folk culture until the late 19th century, in modern Japan men and women were considered fundamentally different and lived in separate spheres. Male workers went to the factory, housewives went to the supermarket, to the schools as PTAs and increasingly to the local education centres and town councils. In other words, modern Japanese society is character-ised by a marked gender dualism and a separation of female and male spheres. And this gender dualism legitimated a deeply rooted gender inequality in work, family and politics (Lenz/Mae 1997).[1]

However, gender as a key category of social science has taken roots in Japan only in the 1990ies (cf. Inoue et al. 1994). The wave of feminist and new approaches in social sci-ence after 1990 coined the term gender in order to overcome a limited view on women as a disadvantaged 'deficit group' (cf. Ōsawa 1994). In contrast, the concept of gender inte-grates the view on men *and* women and renders visible the social and cultural differences between them but also the fact that their positions are interrelated in systems of social ine-quality: In this view for example, the low wage of women part time workers is interrelated to the high wage of male core workers (and again to their positions as main earners versus main unpaid caregivers in the household) (Ōsawa 1994, 2000).

From the mid 1990ies the debate turned to the *social construction of gender*: Gender was seen as rooted in modern cultural discourses which inscribe biological differences (and resulting cultural social norms) into *persons* following a rigid *gender dualism*: Everyone must be classified into one of the two legitimate 'sexes'; persons must be male or female and a 'third space in-between' is outlawed. This rigidity is especially remarkable in East Asian societies – also in Japan – where traditional culture played with inter-gender as in the Peking opera, the kabuki drama and at a more basic level the concepts of the blending of male and female symbols in folk religions (Robertson 1998).

The debate around The Basic Law for a Gender-equal Society (1999) reflects these various dimensions of 'gender'. In 1995, the prominent feminist sociologist Chizuko Ueno reframed the international discussion on the social construction of gender for the Japanese debate following especially Christine Delphy. She proposed that gender as a social con-struction does not derive from 'sex' as a biological fact, but rather precedes it. It signifies the line that divides human society into men and women, i.e. gender is differentiation itself; moreover, gender relations are stratified and they constitute asymmetric power relations

11

(Ōsawa 2003: 9; Ueno 1995). Thus gender is seen as a cultural representation of difference *and* as a basic organising principle of inequality.

But gender in this context also implicitly involves the concept of the 'freedom from gender' as a repressive norm which prescribes male or female roles irrespective of individual thinking, likings and needs. In the words of the Basic Law for a Gender-equal Society the gender-equal society is 'a society where both women and men shall be given equal opportunities to participate voluntarily in activities in all fields as equal partners in the society, and shall be able to enjoy political, economic, social and cultural benefits equally as well as to share responsibilities... [Its formation shall be] promoted based on respect for the human rights of women and men, including: respect for the dignity of men and women as individuals' (1999, art 2.1., 3). Gender is strongly connoted with respect for human rights and individual capacity in contrast to the collective norms of femininity and masculinity in Japanese modernisation.

In this sense, gender as a concept combines three dimensions:

- It is an organisational principle of classification and knowledge. Persons and things like grey suits or pink blouses or kimonos or even babydress are inscribed with symbolic gender representations. Gender is a key axis of the symbolic order as Mary Douglas has shown (1966). In the hegemonic symbolic gender order, conformism is exacted. For example in Japanese enterprises, for a long time men used to be imagined as corporate warriors (in grey suits) and women as tea servers and flowers in the workplace.
- It is an organisational principle of power relations and the division of labour. Gender as an organisational principle does not necessarily lead to hierarchies. It can structure symmetric or asymmetric relationships (Lenz/Luig 1990). But in modern capitalist societies, it organised the unequal gender division of labour and the marginalisation of women in politics and decision making (Lenz 1995).
- It forms part of the site of identity formation in which persons develop identities and become embodied subjects (Giddens), persons who live with their head, their heart and their bodies and who develop agency. Gender studies transcend the narrow focus of homo economicus or sociologicus who lives just in his head (Folbre 2001) and integrate the perspectives on the body, emotions and rationalities. To come back to the example of male core workers and part time tea pourers: These male workers are represented as rational core organisation members – disembodied in their grey suits – whereas women serving tea stand for the body and its needs.

A large and fascinating body of literature has evolved on these dimensions of gender in Japan which unfortunately due to space cannot be discussed here. The debate on intersectionality i.e. the interdependence of gender, class and ethnicity is still at the beginning, however. I think that the importance of integrating gender, class and ethnicity may become more obvious in the future as migration is growing, class divisions become visible again and the mainstream vision of Japan as a middle class-society is slowly vanishing. The hot debate on the 'society with disparities' (*kakusa shakai*)[2] can be read as an indication for a growing importance of class.

So I want to make short observations: Ironically, gender has become rooted in Japanese social science at the very moment when the national hegemonic gender order is being questioned and changed. In this moment, the concept of gender alone will not be sufficient to analyse the historical development and change of this national hegemonic gender order, but rather an intersectionality approach is needed in which gender, class and ethnicity are integrated.

2　The Three Stages of Modernization and the Hegemonic National Gender Order

In the following I want to argue that gender in the sense of intersectionality is a useful category (Scott 1988) to analyse modernisation in Japan. Also, I propose that a national hegemonic gender order[3] was formed in the first stages of modernisation which is now being contested and changing in its third 'reflexive' stage: Main factors are socio-economic forces like the change to a knowledge-intensive service society and globalisation, as well as the increasing respect for individual needs and the influence of the women's movement. I assume that the ideological rigidity with which present neoconservative forces in the LDP and social groups push for upholding this national hegemonic gender order will not solve Japan's internal present problems and may contribute to isolating it in East Asia.

Let me first sketch some lines for a comparative approach to modernisation in Japan.[4] My understanding of modernisation is indebted to the concept of 'multiple modernities'[5] for which Japan is a key case. In an interdependent world system, modernisations take multiple paths. In their course, cultural and social forms from international and local contexts can be selected and integrated in flexible ways and thus new forms of synthesis will emerge. Women's movements were highly committed to creating, selecting and to culturally adapting international concepts like 'motherhood protection' in the first wave or 'work-life-balance' in contemporary Japan.

I also refer to and enlarge the concepts of reflexive modernization. The key authors like Ulrich Beck assumed that modernization in classical industrial societies proceeds in two stages from the simple to the reflexive phase of individualisation and globalisation (Beck 1986). I would like to propose three stages of modernization for classical industrial societies:[6] The first stage of civil national modernisation, the second stage of organised national modernisation and the third present stage of reflexive modernisation. My argument is that the national hegemonic gender order is shaped during the first and second phases. It is eroding and changing during the third phase of reflexive modernisation.

3　Civil National Modernisation and the Foundation of the Modern Gender Order

The first stage is civil national modernisation. The nation emerges as the key concept of social organisation and it is constituted by its members, the 'national people'.[7] The somewhat awkward term of 'civil' points to the new shape of society in the modern nation: The people constitute the civil society which is basically founded on universal concepts of humanity which are accorded to the members of the nation: They are seen as 'men' (and later as persons) and part of the national community. In Meiji Japan (1868–1912), this community was framed by the neopatriarchal family state with the emperor at its apex and the emerging political and economic public sphere in the family state was defined as the domain of men. Women's demands for voting and political participation were negated until 1945. Gender structured political participation overriding ethnicity: In the Japanese family state under the emperor, after 1925 the vote was given to Japanese men and male Korean residents in Japan who were seen as their 'younger brothers', but refused to all women irrespective of ethnicity.

The modern principles of potentially universal humanity stand in contradiction to the new hierarchical forms of differentiation in modern nations. Some groups (mainly men from the upper strata) were fully included in political, economic and social citizenship, while others such as the poor, peasants, workers and women, were marginalised or excluded. The lines of the modern constellation of internal inclusion/exclusion were thus redrawn in the processes of sociocultural development.

The structuring of exclusion and marginalization by class and by gender worked in different ways, however. Class was based on the unequal *socio-economic distribution of resources and authority*. Gender, however, was constructed along modern discourses of *natural difference and gender dualism*. The scientific discourses proclaimed that women are biologically destined to be mothers. Cultural discourses naturalised 'national culture' in asserting that the 'beautiful customs' since 'times immemorial' had established 'Japanese motherhood and feminity'. The constructs of quasi natural gender difference legitimated the national hegemonic gender order (Connell 1994; Lenz 2005) and its internal boundary drawings. These boundaries where complex and fluctuating in a time of upward social mobility between elite men (and their wives), the rising middle strata with their new division of labour between salary men and their modern good (house-)wives and wise mothers and the vast majority of the working men and working women.

The nation as an imagined community also legitimated the drawing of external boundaries between the 'Japanese people' and for example the other peoples in East Asia. In Japan after 1868, the 'escape from Asia' proclaimed by Fukuzawa Yukichi was expressed in the Japanese hegemonic gender culture: It was constructed by claiming proximity to the Western hegemonic gender culture which was imposed as a standard of civilisation and by demarcation from Chinese or Korean gender relations. The Japanese women's movements would have to face the problem how to relate to women and women's movements in East Asia.

Also, during the first stage of national civil modernisation the fundamental modern institutions were introduced and established: the disembedded market, capitalist industrial production based on the free labour market, the modern family with its gender dualism and modern science and technology. The naturalised gender dualism legitimated the differential access to and the hierarchies in these institutions. Whereas the majority of the new factory workers in the spinning and textile industries were female, in the family state ideology their work was linked to domestic roles: They were supposed to earn wages either as daughters to support the parental farm or as future brides to earn their dowry. Contrary to social reality, the public field of work and economy was classified as male sphere. The modern corporate household, the *ie*, was defined as the sphere of male authority of the household head and of female care work.

Modern natural and social sciences developed in almost complete exclusion of women until about 1945 when they could enter general universities (Krämer 2006). Pedagogy, sociology and medical science contributed to construct the image of the chaste wife and mother (*ryōsai kenbo*) and in their national mainstream legitimated the antibirth control and antiabortion laws to control national reproductive behaviour (Frühstück 2003). Thus women had no voice in the scientific reflection and evaluation of national modernisation and they could only gain voices as writers and intellectuals.

4   Organised National Modernisation

The second phase can be termed as organised national modernisation (cf. Lenz 2005; Wagner 1995; Krämer 2006). In Japan this includes the institutionalisation of the welfare state, Toyotism and the modern *my-home* family with its gender-polarised division of labour. Democratisation was concurrent with the organisational society in which large male centred organisations like employer's associations and trade unions negotiated on the ways of social change and the development of the welfare state. The welfare systems and the labour market were oriented towards the 'male breadwinner' and the housewife and children had no access to independent social security (Ōsawa 1994; Kimoto 1995).

In the 1950s large enterprises instituted the 'three sacred goods of 'Japanese personal management' for their male core workers: secure employment, continual on-the-job training for and upwards promotion along a scale of related jobs. Thus they built up a well skilled loyal and flexible core workforce who saw the enterprise as their work community or common destiny (*unmei kyōdōtai*). In the same period, many firms made agreements with their trade unions in which included 'early pensioning' for women, in fact after either marriage or childbearing or in some cases after reaching the age of 30. Access to life long independent wage work for a living wage was constricted for women. The later recruitment as part time worker without employment rights from the late 1960s aimed at married women and was shaped as supplementary work for housewives who were supposed to rely on the main male breadwinner.

The nuclear family was idealised and privatised as the 'my-home family' but increasingly subsumed under capitalist enterprise society: Women took over housework and everyday familial decision-making as the men were recruited for the production front of the corporations. The family was symbolically celebrated as the 'happiness of women'. The naturalisation of gender dualism makes this sexual division of labour appear 'self-evident' and beyond doubt. The modern gender dualism may even have increased its absolute and fundamental character due to this conflation of 'women's nature', 'women's role' and 'women's happiness' in the vision of the Japanese middle class society. Former differences according to age, social position or ethnicity were retreating for some time. Thus gender dualism serves as an organising principle naturalising legitimation of social inequality and hierarchies in the evolving welfare state.

In contrast to gender, class was receding as a symbolic principle of conflict; in Japan after the phase of high growth a large majority perceive themselves as middleclass. The national project after 1970 was affirmed in global economic success, giving recognition to the nation as an imagined community. Existing class differences as enduring lower class status or poverty in special urban and larger rural areas tended to become invisible. The same goes for culturally or ethnically discriminated groups as Koreans living in Japan or *burakumin*.

In organised national modernization, gender was a key organisational principle structuring the hegemonic national gender order and the enterprise society emerging from the 1950ies. It built on social systems and structures from the first phase as on the patriarchal household (*ie*) or women's exclusion from politics, but changed and reorganised them: The 'my-home family' of the industrial couple with the male breadwinner and the housewife behind the production front evolved from the *ie* and transcended it, as it became a space for house-wives and mothers (cf. Lenz 2005).

Gender was emphasized while class was receding. Ethnicity was ingrained in the hegemonic gender order in a double way: Japanese ethnicity was homogenized and highly valued by conservative political leaders and mass media and linked to a supposedly unique Japanese culture. Homogenisation and Nipponism worked to legitimate the national (gender) order as unique, incomparable and closed against international challenges. But emphasizing Japanese culture and ethnicity also legitimated the marginalisation and exclusion of minorities as Koreans living in Japan, *Burakumin* or migrant workers. It contributed to the closing of the Japanese public mind towards East Asia which can be observed in parts of the political elites and the mass media.[8] It is interesting, that the Japanese women's movement has counteracted these tendencies by international networking and joining NGO coalitions in East Asia (cf. Lenz 2005).

5 Social Forces for Changing or Conserving the Hegemonic Gender Order in Reflexive Modernization

The third present phase is reflexive modernization which is connected to globalization, new international knowledge systems and value changes. It embraces changes of social systems and structures from the first *and* second phases (for example the remnants of the *ie* and the my-home family) (cf. Lenz 2005). Thus it contributes to eroding the national hegemonic gender order. This order has proved dysfunctional as it contributed to the demographic crisis with the rapidly receding birth rate and drastically ageing population and blocked using the highly qualified female workforce according to their wishes and potential.

As globalisation and structural change to tertiary, often flexible employment are driving forces of reflexive modernisation, reflexive modernisation is often experienced as insecurity and flexibilisation. Thus the change of the hegemonic gender order is seen as threatening the interests of male core workers and levelling their position with the flexibilised mostly female employment. Rigid social systems are eroded, but it is a crucial challenge to develop new visions for social integration based on more balance, participation and equality. The Japanese women's movement has contributed new ideas and stepping stones towards more domestic and international equality (Lenz 2000a; Lenz/Mae 2007; Inoue 1994).

The conservative political leaders under Abe Shinzō and the extreme rightist groups now aim for a restoration of the national hegemonic gender order in its postwar form and in more radical versions for the abolishment of gender equality in the Japanese constitution (Kimura 2005). Whereas the Basic Law for a Gender-equal Society (1999) proposed solutions for the demographic, economic and participation issues of present Japan (cf. Ōsawa 2003), the neoconservative approaches lack these realistic goals: Evocations of the national gender order of the past in rapid social change will have little potential for solving present and future problems. They do follow the formula of combining neoliberal deregulation with neopatriarchal stabilisation of the family and some recourse to the family state in the sense of a warm emotional national community under a patrimonial benevolent ruler.

Little attention has been paid to the growing gap and isolation of the Japanese conservative backlash to the gender democratic trend in East Asia. In 1997, South Korea has passed a stronger Equal Employment Opportunity Law than Japan and in China women play a strong role in the economy. In South East Asian countries with their high economic female activity, the Look East policy never was considered from its gendered content. The US neoconservatives, however, follow a comparable project of neoliberal deregulation, neopatriarchal family and religious nationalism.

In reflexive modernisation, the future appears open and contingent to a certain degree. A new hegemonic gender order may emerge in which global and national hegemonic discourses are combined, military androcentric violence is employed for conflict resolution and the boundary lines of gender, ethnicity and class are deepening. In other scenarios, global gender governance centering around the UN and regional organisations like the EU can be negotiated in globalisation and linked to national reforms for gender equality. But instead of modern biological destiny, gender now is seen as an issue of history and change which is crucial to reflexive modernisation.

Notes

[1] This essay summarises some results of long comparative gender research on Japan. As the literature used is comprehensive and cannot be enumerated in this context, I beg for leave for including only literature directly quoted; cf. also Lenz/Mae 1997; Lenz/Mae/Klose 2000; Lenz 2000a,b, 2005, 2007.

[2] Cf. Tachibanaki 1998; Yamada 2004; I want to thank Annette Schad-Seifert for information on this point.

[3] For the concept of the national hegemonic gender order cf. Lenz 2000c, 2005.

[4] For the research literature used and a comparative discussion with modernisation in Germany please cf. Lenz 2005.

[5] Cf. Eisenstadt 2003; I want to thank Steffi Richter for advice and discussion in this context.

[6] As modernisation is contingent and shaped by the sociocultural context as well as by the world system, my phase model is only oriented towards the classical modernisation of industrial nations starting from the 19th century. China as well as South Korea for example have a different trajectory. The similarity of the Japanese and the German cases which both started from a 'late comer'- perspective is highly interesting (cf. Lenz 2005).

[7] The meaning of 'people' may fluctuate between the 'imperial subject' (*shimin*), the 'national people' (*kokumin*) or 'citizen' (*shimin*) according to the historical and cultural contexts; for the integration of international concepts into Japanese social thinking and social science cf. Ishida 2001.

[8] The most prominent example is the repeated praying at Yasukuni shrine by the Japanese prime ministers in the last years which shows neglect and lack of understanding towards the memories and feelings of governments and the majority of the population in China and South Korea.

Ilse Lenz

References

Beck, Ulrich (1986): *Risikogesellschaft.* Frankfurt: Suhrkamp.
Beck, Ulrich/Giddens, Antony/Lash, Scott (1994): *Reflexive Modernization: Politics, Tradition and Aesthetics in the Modern Social Order.* Cambridge: Polity Press.
Connell, Robert (1994): *Masculinities.* Berkeley et al.: University of California Press.
Douglas, Mary (1966): *Purity and Danger. An Analysis of Concepts of Pollution and Taboo.* New York: Praeger.
Eisenstadt, S.N. (2003): *Comparative Civilizations and Multiple Modernities.* 2 vol. Leiden, Boston: Brill.
Folbre, Nancy (2001): *The Invisible Heart. Economics and Family Values.* New York.
Frühstück, Sabine (2003): *Colonizing Sex: Sexology and Social Control in Modern Japan.* Berkeley et al.: University of California Press.
Inoue, Teruko et. al. (eds.) (1994): *Nihon no fueminizumu.* [Feminism in Japan]. 7 vol. Tokyo: Iwanami.
Ishida, Takeshi (2001): *Die Entdeckung der Gesellschaft. Der Weg der Sozialwissenschaften in Japan.* Frankfurt a.M.
Kimoto, Kimiko (1995): *Kazoku jendā kigyō shakai.* [Family, gender and enterprise society]. Tokyo: Minerva shobo.
Kimura, Ryōko (2005): *Jendā furī toraburu. Bashingu genshō o kensho suru.* [Trouble with gender-free. Analysing the backlash phenomenon] Tokyo: Hakutakusha.
Krämer, Martin (2006): *Neubeginn unter US-amerikanischer Besatzung? Hochschulreform in Japan zwischen Kontinuität und Diskontinuität 1919—1952.* Berlin: Akademie-Verlag.
Lenz, Ilse (1995): Geschlecht, Herrschaft und internationale Ungleichheit. In: Becker-Schmidt, Regina/Knapp, Gudrun Axeli (eds.) (1995): *Das Geschlechterverhältnis als Gegenstand der Sozialwissenschaften.* Frankfurt, New York, pp. 19–47.
Lenz, Ilse (2000a): What does the women´s movement do, when it moves? Kommunikation und Organisation in der neuen japanischen Frauenbewegung. In: Lenz/Mae/Klose pp. 95–132.
Lenz, Ilse (2000b): Politische Modernisierung und Frauenbewegungen in Japan und Deutschland. Zum Versuch einer vergleichenden Perspektive. In: Pigulla, Andreas et al. (eds.): *Ostasien verstehen. Peter Weber-Schäfer zu Ehren. Festschrift aus Anlaß seiner Emeritierung.* Bochumer Jahrbuch für Ostasienforschung, 23, pp. 217–231.
Lenz, Ilse (2000c): Gender und Globalisierung: Neue Horizonte? In: Cottmann, Angelika et al. (eds.): *Das undisziplinierte Geschlecht. Frauen- und Geschlechterforschung – Einblick und Ausblick.* Opladen, pp. 221–247.
Lenz, Ilse (2005): Internationalisierung, nationale Entwicklung und reflexive Modernisierung: Deutschland und Japan im Vergleich. In: Kössler, Reinhart/Kumitz, Daniel/Schultz, Ulrike (eds.): *Gesellschaftstheorie und Provokationen der Moderne.* Münster, pp. 60 –72.
Lenz, Ilse/Luig, Ute (1990): *Frauenmacht ohne Herrschaft. Geschlechterverhältnisse in nichtpatriarchalischen Gesellschaften.* Berlin. 2. Aufl. 1995. Frankfurt a. M.
Lenz, Ilse/Mae, Michiko (eds.) (1997): *Getrennte Welten, gemeinsame Moderne? Geschlechterverhältnisse in Japan.* Opladen 1997.
Lenz, Ilse/Mae, Michiko/Klose, Karin (eds.) (2000): *Frauenbewegungen weltweit. Aufbrüche, Kontinuitäten, Veränderungen.* Opladen 2000.
Lenz, Ilse/Mae Michiko (eds.) (2007): *Quellensammlung zur Neuen Frauenbewegung in Japan.* Wiesbaden.
Ōsawa, Mari (1994): The Gender Revolution in Social Science. In: *Social Science Japan,* 2, pp. 24–25.

Ōsawa, Mari (2000): Government Approaches to Gender Equality in the mid-1990s. In: *Social Science Japan Journal*, Vol. 3, 1, pp. 3–21.

Ōsawa, Mari (2003): Japanese Government Approaches to Gender Equality since the mid-1990s. Wayne State University. Occasional Paper Series Nr. 9.

Robertson, Jennifer (1998): *Takarazuka: Sexual Politics and Popular Culture in Modern Japa*n. Berkeley: University of California Press.

Scott, Joan Wallach (1988): Gender: A Useful Category of Historical Analysis. In: Scott, Joan Wallach: *Gender and the Politics of History*. Columbia, New York 1988, pp. 28–50.

Tachibanaki, Toshiaki (1998): *Nihon no keizai kakusa: Shotoku to shisan kara kangaeru*. Tokyo: Iwanami shoten

Ueno, Chizuko (1995): Sai no Seijigaku. [The politics of difference]. In: Iwanami Kōza Gendai Shakaigaku. [Iwanami Lectures on Contemporary Sociology]. 11, *Jendā no Shakaigaku* [The Sociology of Gender]. Tokyo: Iwanami Shoten, 1995, pp. 1–26.

Wagner, Peter (1993): *A Sociology of Modernity: Liberty and Discipline*. New York: Routledge.

Yamada, Masahiro (2004): *Kibō-kakusa-shakai: 'make-gumi' no zetsubōkan ga Nihon o hikisaku*. [Society of expectation gaps: The despair of the 'losers' is tearing Japan apart]. Tokyo: Chikuma shobō .

From Culturality to Transculturality
The Paradigm Shift in Cultural and Gender Studies

Michiko Mae

1   Introduction

The changes taking place in Japanese society and culture nowadays reflected in the changing relationship between sexes; also manifest themselves on a cultural level in the transition from culturality to transculturality. The transformational process that took place in Japan in the first phase of its modernisation, on the other hand, was rooted in the nexus formed by the nation and a nationally and culturally determined gender order. Nowadays, in the age of globalisation, there are several signs pointing to the dissolution of this nexus. The present paper looks into the enormous impact of the 1999 Basic Law for a Gender-equal Society (Japanese: *Danjo kyōdō sankaku shakai kihonhō*), which was meant to initiate the change of the gender concept based on gender roles and lead to a gender-free concept. This law indicates a paradigm shift in gender studies. The heated discussions and debates around this law make overt and clarify the significance of gender order for the stability and legitimation of Japanese society and culture in the first phase of modernisation. They also come to show why the gender-free concept can become instrumental for the further development of civil society in Japan.

The phrase 'from culturality to transculturality' best characterises, from a cultural point of view, the Japanese modernisation process from its beginnings in the 19th century to the present day. Both the development of modern culture and the development of gender relations are related to the shift from the nation-state to globalisation. The first phase of modernisation was marked by the nexus between *nation* building, national *culture*, and nationally and culturally determined *gender* order. This nexus is dissolving in the age of globalisation and individualisation; nowadays we are in a critical phase of transformation in which culturality and transculturality, on the one hand, and re-gendering and de-gendering, on the other, clash with one another. This is especially true of Japanese society but it characterises the situation in other western countries as well.

Women's movements and their international connections are essential to a transnational civil society which begins to mould itself in the context of 'globalisation from the bottom up'. Inequality, discrimination and marginalisation cannot be regarded within national cultural borders any longer. They have become part of a transnational discourse about women's rights, human rights, democratisation, etc. which promotes equality and the recognition of differences. Women's movements include more and more transnational and transcultural discourses and strategies, international statements and regulations, etc. in their local and national preoccupations with hegemonic national gender relations. In this way, more and more transnational networks and organisations have been founded since the turning point of the international women's movement in the 1980s, in which both global and culturally contextualised approaches are interwoven. Cultural difference is acknowledged and respected and can be seen in connection with the universal claims of human rights, i.e. in a global context.

2   The Basic Law for a Gender-equal Society

The connection between international processes and their implementation on a local and national level influenced the incorporation of the resolutions of the Beijing *World Conference on Women* into the 1999 'Basic Law for a Gender-equal Society'. This was made possible due to intensive lobbying from the mid 1990s on. This law bears the rather long title *Danjo kyōdō sankaku shakai kihonhō*, which means *ad litteram*: 'Basic law for a society in which both men and women can and should participate equally.'[1] Its official English translation is: 'The Basic Law for a Gender-equal Society'. The procedure leading to this law was very unusual for the Japanese administrative system. Information was provided regularly to the population, opinions of citizens and experts were taken into account, NGOs were consulted and experts in social and gender policy such as Ōsawa Mari were called in. This was all due to the fact that the procedure was a novelty for the Japanese bureaucracy.

Some quotations selected from the preamble of the Participation Law illustrate the character of this law:

> Considering respect for individuals and equality under the law expressly stipulated under the Constitution, steady progress has been made in Japan through a number of efforts toward the realization of genuine equality between women and men together with efforts taken by the international community. However, even greater effort is required.
>
> At the same time, to respond to the rapid changes occurring in Japan's socioeconomic situation, [...] it has become a matter of urgent importance to realize a Gender-equal Society in which men and women respect the other's human rights and share their responsibilities, and every citizen is able to fully exercise their individuality and abilities regardless of gender.
>
> In light of this situation, it is vital to position the realization of a Gender-equal Society as a top-priority task in determining the framework of 21st-century Japan, and implement policies related to promotion of formation of a Gender-equal Society in all fields.[2]

These quotations give the impression that the introduction of the Participation Law has been a significant step in the development of civil society in Japan. And indeed, many women in Japan optimistically began to hope that the policy developed along these lines would prove irreversible.[3] However, a strong conservative movement has emerged in recent years whose activities have hindered the implementation of the Participation Law in several prefectures, cities and communities.[4] Indeed, the formulation 'gender-equal participation' (*danjo kyōdō sankaku*) had been criticized as an imprecise formulation of compromise by women committed to the cause, even before the beginning of the actual legislation procedure. The main criticism by feminists was that the law did not use the precise term 'equality' (*byōdō*), which made its text less pointed and progressive than they wished it to be. The conservatives had until then criticized the term 'equality' (*byōdō*) for being too radical even though it is embedded in the 1947 Japanese Constitution.[5] On the other hand, they criticized the term 'gender-equal participation' (*danjo kyōdō sankaku*), for completely different reasons. Their argument was rather contradictory in itself: They contended that the term 'equality' (*byōdō*) could be understood in the sense of 'equal rights for men and women according to gender differences,' but the term 'gender-equal participation' (*danjo kyōdō sankaku*) was unacceptable. The reason for their rejection of the term was their fear that the term 'gender-equal participation' entailed the gender-free concept which they understood as a fundamental negation of gender differences.

3   The Gender-free Concept and Its Criticism

The Prime Minister's Office founded an advisory council in 1994. The council drafted a 'Concept of a Gender-equal Participation Society' (*danjo kyōdō sankaku shakai vijon*) in 1996, which, following Ōsawa, stipulated that one of the aims of the realization of a Participation society was the 'liberation from gender', i.e. from socially and culturally shaped gender differences; in Japanese: *shakaiteki bunkateki ni keisei sareta seibetsu.* Ōsawa, who was a member of the council, reported that the term 'gender' which was little known in Japanese society would not be used in the text. Still, despite this compromise, the aim of the law remained clear due to the use of the expression 'regardless of gender' (*seibetsu ni kakawari naku*) in several parts of the text (Ōsawa 2002c:80-83).

The term gender-free[6] is a Japanese-English neologism which was coined in Japan. It designates a way of thinking according to which men and women should be able to develop a multitude of ways of living, regardless of gender distinctions and roles determined by society and culture. The term was first used in a booklet issued by the Tokyo Women's Foundation (*Tokyo Josei Zaidan*) in 1995. The term does not appear either in official law texts, such as the Participation Law, or in scholarly works. It emerged from the activities of the movement for equal status and it is employed in the practical work of many regional participation offices and centres, and in schools. Most frequently, it appears in connection with kindergartens and child education and it refers to the possibilities of educating children in a gender-free manner and the necessity to do so (Tachi 1999; see also Kreitz-Sandberg in this volume).

The controversial debates about the Participation Law, on the Internet, for instance, are revealing especially with regard to those statements which most powerfully attack feminist advocates of Participation and the gender-free concept. For example, critics reproach representatives of the gender-free concept with hiding behind a strange Japanese-English term which the Japanese population cannot understand.[7] If they really wanted to abolish gender differences and transform the Japanese into neutral beings, then they should call themselves 'the group of those who wish to abolish gender difference' (*seisa teppaigumi*) or 'unisex committee' (*unisex suishin iinkai*). Other arguments brought against the gender-free activists are that since 1995 some schoolteachers began to introduce mixed name lists, not to separate boys from girls in sports, to exchange men's and women's parts in theatrical productions in schools, to teach combat sports to girls and sewing and cooking to boys, not to require different colours of satchels for boys and girls, etc. Even more, critics say, these changes happen without regard to the schoolchildren's wishes and feelings. The author Nakagawa claims that human beings can only develop a higher personality if they are able to identify themselves clearly as either men or women. Gender difference is a universal principle of humankind, and, consequently, it is only through the natural combination of the paternal and maternal principles that families can be founded and children can receive proper education. Should this natural order be destroyed [by the dissolution of the male and female principles; my comment], then the family would collapse, normal personality would be disturbed, men and women, devoid of gender awareness, would not be able to develop normal sexual behaviour, the population would decline, the foundations of national consciousness and the sense of belonging would collapse, and, eventually, society would disintegrate. In other words, should one want to destroy society, one would not need a revolution. It would be enough to destroy the gender order. According to the critic's view the eradication of gender order would have the same effects as a violent revolution.

It is indeed true that such statements sound ridiculous and cannot be taken for more than a parody. However, arguments of this kind are supported by extremely tenacious groups of critics and massive resistance campaigns, which is why they cannot be ignored.[8] The procedures for the implementation of the Participation Law and the implementation regulations of the different prefectures and communities have been used as a battlefield on which the parties involved fight for the leading principle of the Participation Law. In the following, I shall describe the emergence and development of the Participation Law, on the one hand, and the opposition movement, on the other, in more detail, in order to illustrate the intentions of this law more clearly.

4   The Process of Development and the Aims of the Participation Law

The Japanese Participation Law represents a change of paradigm from women's policy to gender policy, which is the most significant turning point in the new Japanese women's movement since the end of the 1960s. After the Second World War, the new Japanese Constitution of 1947 guaranteed individual dignity (§ 13) and equal rights for men and women (§ 14). The most important rights for the equality of men and women are universal franchise (§ 44), freedom of choice of profession (§ 22), individual dignity and equal domestic rights for men and women (§ 24) as well as the right to education (§ 26). Before the new Constitution came into effect, Japanese women did not have equal political rights. Since the UN World Conference on Women voted for the World Plan of Action in 1975, Japan has also taken several measures in its women's policy which are in line with the World Plan of Action. The first plan of action in Japan was initiated in 1977; in 1985 Japan ratified the UN Anti-Sex Discrimination Law; in its wake, Japan announced the Equal Employment Opportunity Law in 1985, which came into effect a year later and was amended in 1999. The legislation passed and measures taken until the 1990s could be grouped under the heading *women's policy,* the aim of which was to abolish discrimination against women by creating and supporting women's equality with men. At the Fourth UN World Conference on Women in Peking in 1995 another World Plan of Action was ratified which promoted *gender mainstreaming* in all political and social fields. Consequently, each country was obliged to create a national central organisation for the promotion of *gender mainstreaming*. In 1975, Japan founded 'The Centre for Planning and Promoting Women's Issues' (*fujin mondai kikaku suishin honbu*) which changed its name to 'The Centre for Gender-equal Participation' (*danjo kyōdō sankaku suishin honbu*) in 1994. Its president was the Prime Minister himself, and all ministers automatically became members. The already mentioned advisory council 'Advisory Council for Gender-equal Participation' (*danjo kyōdō sankaku shingikai*), with its seat located directly in the Prime Minister's Offices, was commissioned to develop a plan for a 'gender-equal society' and delivered its results in its report 'Concept of a Gender-equal Society' (*danjo kyōdō sankaku shakai vijon*). A new legal 'Advisory Council for a Gender-equal Participation' (*danjo kyōdō sankaku shingikai*) was founded in 1997 and its mission was to prepare the Participation Law. The council considered a large spectrum of opinions, canvassed from regional public and private organisations and from the population,[9] which were provided by its sub-commission in its report. The final result was presented to Prime Minister Obuchi in November 1998. This formed the basis of the draft bill of February 1999 which was agreed upon in the cabinet. The Upper House passed it unanimously with some amendments after several discussions in May 1999. The Lower House went through a similar procedure and also voted for it unanimously. Subsequently, the law became the 17th Basic Law of the country on June 15 of the same year.

There were intensive discussions on several levels of the legislation procedure regarding the designation of the law as 'Gender-equal Society Law' (*Sankaku shakai kihonhō*). I have already presented the perspective of the women who were involved in this debate. Furuhashi Genrokurō, member of the advisory council, offers an insight into the controversial debates that took place in the advisory council. He summarized the discussions and reported that the council deliberated whether to use the generally unknown and therefore incomprehensible expression 'gender-equal paticipation' (*danjo kyōdō sankaku*), or to use the notion of 'equal status' (*danjo byōdō*) instead (Furuhashi 2002:100ff.). They discussed whether or not it would be appropriate to make explicit the inequality between men and women which actually exists in Japanese society, and whether they should posit the realization of equality as the main goal of the law. Some argued against this idea, saying that the Participation Law was focused on the guarantee that - provided that equality was realized - men and women would be able to develop fully their abilities on an individual basis. They said that the participatory society (*kyōdō sankaku shakai*) was a 'dynamic concept' (*dōtaitekina gainen*), whose aim was equality on a high-quality level and which should be supported by men and women alike. The law not only aimed at the realization of equality of the sexes according to Paragraph 14 of the Constitution, but also the realization of individual dignity according to Paragraph 13.[10] Furthermore, it was essential for establishing actual equality that women should participate in all areas of society, both public and private (Furuhashi 2002:101). It was considered equally important that men should also be involved in the gender-equality movement (ibid. 103). For that reason, the law should be called (the) 'Gender-equal Participation Law'.

Whereas for women the Participation Law represented an important step towards the realization of a civil society, for others it meant Japan's certain downfall, as already intimated above. The critics' position could be paraphrased as follows: It is only through the maintenance of the existing gender order that Japanese society and culture can be rescued from its decline. In other words, the present gender order provides the foundation for the existence of the Japanese nation and culture.

It is my contention that this line of argument in particular makes obvious the major influence of modern gender order as a fundamental basis of the modern nation and culture since the Meiji Era in Japan. For the conservatives, the introduction of the Participation Law entails the gender-free concept, which for them equals the denial and destruction of this foundation, as I have already pointed out. According to Ōsawa, these critics have understood the intention of the Participation Law quite well in a certain way, even though the text of the law does not contain the term gender-free. Whereas these critics have a superficial understanding of gender-free which they caricature in a grotesque manner, the true meaning of gender-free is 'liberation from the gender' (*gender kara no kaihō*), as Ōsawa maintains (Ōsawa 2002b:13-15).[11] In this sense, the concept of gender-free is a radical consequence of gender studies. The controversy triggered by the gender-free concept contains a twofold gender problem: while on the one hand the gender order of the first phase of modernisation refers to a society which defines itself in terms of nationality and its own culturality, the gender-free concept, on the other hand, is linked to a society based on individualization and transculturality, i.e. a civil society which has stopped defining itself through nationality and its own culturality.

The criticism attracted by the gender-free concept with regard to its dissolution of traditional family structures and destruction of the 'normal' personality is justifiable to a certain extent. The question that still remains to be answered is why the disintegration of the existing gender order should lead to the destruction of a sense of belonging and of national community. For a better understanding of this issue, one has to return to the first phase of the modernisation process in which the sense of belonging and of community, i.e. national identity, still had to be created.

In the context of a twofold crisis situation in which Japan was exposed to the external threat of the West and confronted with the dissolution of its own traditional social order through modernisation, Japan was forced to create a unified national and cultural consciousness. This task was rendered difficult by Japan's variety of local, regional, religious and social traditions and developments. It was to be attained by the 'homogeneity ideology', the purpose of which was to reshape Japan's heterogeneous traditions into an homogeneous nation-state ideology. This transformation took place not only through so-called 'invented traditions', but also, and mainly, with the help of Western notions and concepts which were translated and incorporated into the Japanese language. The most influential of these terms were the modern concepts of culture and gender order.

5   Culture and Culturality

In the first phase of modernisation, Japan took over the western notion of civilization and translated and used it as *bunmei*. This term was not used with a clear differentiation between civilization (*bunmei*) and culture (*bunka*). It was not until the end of the 1880s that the term '*bunka*' began to be used specifically in the sense of 'culture'. The first proof of a clear awareness of a term designating the concept of culture in the modern western sense is the following text passage by the journalist Kuga Katsunan (1857-1907) from the year 1888 (cf. Nishikawa 2001):

Because nationality stems from the root of culture, which is typical of each nation, one has to unify and unite culture if one wants to unify and unite the nation (Kuga 1968: 1,399).

Kuga, who was familiar with Herder's concept of the interdependence of nation and culture, understood that there was a deep connection between nation building, on the one hand, and the cultural standardization and unification of society, on the other. Social standardization and unification are not only a prerequisite for nation building, they also represent the most important function of a nation in the process of modernisation.

Kuga's cultural theory underscores the tendency towards homogenization of the individual culture as well as its idiosyncrasies. Although he acknowledges Japan's actual cultural diversity and heterogeneity in his analysis, as in the above-mentioned quotation, he only sees the necessity to homogenize Japanese culture and to underscore its specific nature. Kuga's mistake was to fail to see the strength of his culture in its diversity and heterogeneity, and to aim at its homogenization. This way of thinking forms the basis of the narrow-minded modern concept of culture which sees culture in connection with a specific nation.

Japanese culture was declared unified and homogeneous according to the modern concept of culture which the imperial system justified and legitimized. In this way, culture became an instrument in the service of nation building. It was appropriated for the purpose of building collective identity because of its homogenizing potential and its usefulness as a source of national uniqueness embodied by the Empire.

Culture, therefore, fulfils two fundamental functions in the process of modernisation: it forms the basis of the ideology of homogeneity and of the dynamics of homogenization, while at the same time providing the basis of collective identity formation. The core of this concept of identity is a nation's or ethnic group's awareness of being special, in Japan's case even unique and incomparable. This includes the perception that these idiosyncrasies originate in and are determined by one's particular culture. I designate this self-centred concept of culture as culturality.

6   Gender Order in the First Phase of Modernisation

Historical gender research has demonstrated certain structural parallels between the conceptualization of nation and gender difference. These parallels are rooted in the fact that both concepts, nation and gender order, became integrative keywords in the process of modernisation. They were supposed to provide a sense of belonging and identity in the highly differenciated modern society.

The debate among the Japanese reformists of the early phase of modernisation about the status of women concentrated on the re-structuring of gender order for the building of a modern nation. Fukuzawa Yukichi (1835-1901) took an exceptional lifelong interest in the status of women and the relationship between genders. He acknowledged the basic equality between men and women (Fukuzawa 1959). However, a critical perusal of his works reveals the limitations of his recognition of women's rights, freedom and responsibility. These limits are identical with the line separating the public and the private spheres corresponding to the structures of the modern gender roles (cf. Mae 2002). Due to their identity as mothers, isolated in the private sphere of life, women were used for and integrated into the process of nation building. Because of their role and function, the Meiji reforming scholars and modernizers assigned them the central task as 'providers' and 'protectors' of a new national and cultural identity. Their important symbolical meaning and their high moral responsibilities resulted from the fact that they reproduced the nation and its cultural identity. They represented the collective unity of the national community and were constructed as *'symbolic border guards'* (Yuval-Davis 1997) of national and cultural distinction.

It is not only nation and gender which are interconnected with each other, but also gender relationships and culture. Each individual culture assigns certain meanings, roles and characteristics to gender differentiation, i.e. one can speak of a *culturalized* construction of gender identity just as one can also speak of a *nationalized* construction of gender. Thus, the symbolic function of women as representatives and carriers of national and cultural identity was linked to their role as mothers.

Since the 1970s, the new women's movement concentrates precisely on this point and critically reflects on the mother role and the structural division between the private and the public spheres, which is based on the gender roles. In this manner, the women's movement also questions the validity of the traditionally posited function of women in forming a national and cultural identity.

Originally, the new women's movement criticised the central role-model of women before the Second World War, namely the mother and her role and responsibility in the Second World War. They contended that women were accomplices in the terrible crimes of the Second World War in their role as 'mothers of the military state' (*gunkoku no haha*). They also held Japanese women co-responsible for the forced prostitution of Korean and other Asian women because of their support to the military state as mothers, even though they were not directly aware of such war crimes (Suzuki 1993, Ueno 1998, Mae 2000).

They argued that the roles of women in the patriarchal society of the nation-state were divided into those of mothers and prostitutes (see also Wöhr in this volume). Accordingly, this racist and sexist social structure led to the classification of Japanese women as mothers, and Korean and other Asian women as prostitutes. The two roles were seen in a complementary relationship within the patriarchal social system while at the same time they were separated by national and ethnic segregation. Women not only regarded themselves as victims of these structures, but also as accomplices in and responsible for these crimes. This consciousness of co-responsibility transformed them from mere victims into subjects of history.

Some features of the women's movement pointed in a transnational direction even before the Second World War. Yet, through their mother role, women were subject to the limitations of Japanese culture and thus unable to either subvert the structures of the Empire or see through the true character of the Asian invasion. They were not to succeed in this until the 1990s. Nonetheless, women first had to distance themselves from the culturally and nationally imposed mother role in order to be able to surmount national borders in the 1970s.

7   Transculturality and the Gender-free Concept

I maintain that the cross-border transnational and transcultural way of thinking and acting, on the one hand, and the individualization movement, on the other, are mutually complementary. They both emerge from the criticism of the nationally and culturally constructed gender order. The women's movement can be understood as a movement towards becoming the subject, the purpose of which was to live a full and unfettered life as an individual and not to be tied down by social roles and functions.

The liberation from culturally and socially predetermined roles and norms in order to allow for the free choice of individual life styles, partnerships and values, is a basic human right. This is also what defines the core of the gender-free concept. The authors of the already mentioned booklet of the Tokyo Women's Foundation, for instance, explain that they wish to replace the term 'equality of the sexes' (*danjo byōdō*), which mainly refers to the inequality between men and women, with gender-free. The latter term underscores the fact that the issue at stake is not solely a social and structural problem but also one which influences public perception of the problem of equality. The authors saw the differences between the sexes as a matter of public consciousness and of culture.

If, on the one hand, gender difference and gender order are influenced by culturality, then, on the other hand, the gender-free concept points in the direction of cross-border transculturality. Pertaining to transculturality are the recognition and overcoming of cultural constructs which create new ways of thinking and acting for the individual. A reflexive, open and de-centred culture can free the individual and lead to a new kind of solidarity.

In order to achieve this state, hegemonic national and cultural discourses and borders have to be overcome. No one should be forced into a certain gender identity pattern based on national and cultural affiliation. This would represent a violation of human rights. Therefore the gender-free concept and the Participation Law are based on human rights as stipulated in Paragraphs 1 and 3 of the Participation Law.

The different and the heterogeneous must not be reduced to the identical and similar but at the same time they must not be excluded because they represent 'the Other'. This fundamental principle of transculturality also forms the core of the gender-free concept. Critics see the gender-free concept as a threat to their own national culture. They fear that culture will lose its identifying potential which makes it possible for one culture to distinguish itself from other cultures. In other words, they have recognized the subversive possibilities for change embodied in the gender-free concept.

A culture and society founded on difference rather than identity has managed to overcome one-dimensional differences defined by dichotomies and social hierarchies such as identity vs. otherness, or manliness vs. womanliness. The reactionary behaviour of many conservatives who fear this new society can be understood as a gesture of defiance. They wish to re-establish and maintain the old nexus of the nation-state, national culture and gender order by *re-gendering*, i.e. recovering the old gender order. On the other hand, this reaction testifies to the increasing power of the women's movement and other civil movements which have led to the irreversible development of transcultural civil societies worldwide.

Michiko Mae

Notes

1   Although the official English title of this law is 'The Basic Law for a Gender-equal Society", the intention is the equal participation. Therefore it is abbreviated below as the 'Participation Law'.

2   These are the first three paragraphs of the preamble of: 'Danjo kyōdō sankaku shakai kihonhō' (The Basic Law for a Gender-equal Society; Law number 78, from 23 June 1999).

3   A series of laws have been passed since the ratification of the UN Anti-Sex Discrimination Law in 1985, such as the Equal Employment Opportunity Law (*danjo koyō kikai kintōhō*) in 1986 and its amendment in 1999, the Child-Care Leave Law (*ikuji kaigo kyūkahō*) in 1992 (amended in 2001 and 2005); and the Domestic Violence Prevention Law (*Domestic Violence bōshihō*) in 2001.

4   For more detailed information on this backlash-movement cf. Kanai; Hosoya 2003, Hosoya 2005.

5   The term *byōdō* mentioned in the Constitution refers rather to equal rights, whereas its newer meaning (from the 1970s on) has acquired the significance of a more active equal status. However, the Japanese term for this newer meaning should then be *byōdōka*. For reasons of a better understanding I translate the term *byōdō* as 'equality' and 'equal status' respectively, depending on the context.

6   Even though *gender* has been used by Japanese scholars for a long time, the term gender-free has been much disputed and criticized by the conservatives. Meanwhile there are some prefectures such as Tokyo, whose governor is the right-wing conservative Ishihara Shintarō, which have forbidden the use of gender-free in public documents. The Tokyo Women's Foundation was dissolved in 2003.

7   The following remarks are based on the internet articles: Nakagawa Yatsuhiro: *Kore ga jendā furī no shōtai da* [This is the true face of the gender-free concept]. http://nksagami.s25.xrea.com/katsudou/0501genderfree-eno-taioh.htm (14 November 2004). This website can no longer be found; a similar version can be found on a Wikipedia webpage with the Japanese term 'jendā furii': http://www5e.biglobe.ne.jp/tokutake/koregajendafuri.htm; http://animalkato.fc2web. com/kanrinin-001/001.htm (November 14, 2004). The article is no longer on the website.

8   Several books by critics of the gender-free concept have appeared in the meantime: Nishio, Kanji; Yagi, Shūji (2005): *Shin Kokumin no yudan*. Tokyo: PHP; Hayashi, Michiyoshi (2005): *Kazoku o sagesumu hitobito*. Tokyo: PHP; Nomura, Hataru (ed.) (2006): *Danjo byōdō baka*. Bessatsu Takarajima Real 069, and others.

9   3611 propositions and instances of reconsidered positions were registered between June 16 and July 31, 1998. Even more, a total of six meetings for exchanging ideas with a turnout of over 1900 participants was organized in Tokyo, Aomori, Fukui, Nagoya and Kitakyūshū (Ōsawa 2002c: 97).

10   Furuhashi describes the Participation Law and the building of the gender-equal society, whose focus is the respect of individuality and which aims at creating new values, as a flame which sends forth its light from the dark Japan of the end of the 20th century into the 21st century (Furuhashi 2002:101).

11   Ōsawa remarks not without pride that similar laws in western industrialized countries do not go as far as the Participation Law whose aim is liberation from gender (Ōsawa 2002c:75).

References

Fukuzawa, Yukichi (1959): *Fukuzawa Yukichi zenshū.* [Fukuzawa Yukichi. Collected Works]. Tōkyō: Iwanami Shoten.

Furuhashi, Genrokurō (2002): Danjo kyōdō sankaku shakai kihonhō seiteijō no keii to omona ronten. [The Main Arguments in the Drafting Process of the Participation Law]. In: Ōsawa 2002a, pp. 93–145.

Hosoya, Makoto (2005): *Danjo byōdōka ni taisuru kinnen no handō wa naze okirunoka?* [Why is there a Backlash Movement against Equality?] In: *Sekai,* April 2005, pp. 96–105.

Kanai, Yoshiko; Hosoya, Makoto (2003): *Danjo kyōdō sankaku seisaku e no bakku rasshu.* [Backlash against the Participation Politics]. In: People's Plan. Nr. 24, pp. 66–77. (Discussion article)

Kuga, Katsunan (1968): *Kuga Katsunan zenshū.* [Kuga Katsunan. Collected Works]. Tokyo: Misuzu Shobō, Vol. 1.

Mae, Michiko (2000): Wege zu einer neuen Subjektivität: Die neue japanische Frauenbewegung als Suche nach einer anderen Moderne. In: Lenz, Ilse; Michiko Mae; Karin Klose (eds.): *Frauenbewegungen weltweit: Aufbrüche, Kontinuitäten, Veränderungen.* Opladen: Leske + Budrich, pp. 21–50.

Mae, Michiko (2002): Öffentlichkeit und Privatheit im japanischen Modernisierungsprozess. In: *Japanstudien. Jahrbuch des Deutschen Instituts für Japanstudien,* 14, pp. 237–266.

Nishikawa, Nagao (2001): *Kokkyō no koekata.* [Overcoming National Borders]. Tokyo: Heibonsha.

Ōsawa, Mari (ed.) (2002a): *21 seiki no josei seisaku to danjo kyōdō sankaku shakai kihonhō.* [Women's Politics in the 21st Century and the Participation Law]. Tokyo: Gyōsei.

Ōsawa, Mari (2002b): Josei seisaku o dō toraeruka. [How Should We Understand the Women's Politics?] In: Ōsawa 2002a, pp. 2–26.

Ōsawa, Mari (2002c): Naze Danjo kyōdō sankaku shakai kihonhō ga hitsuyō nano ka. [Why is the Basic Law for a Gender-equal Society Necessary?] In: Ōsawa 2002a, pp. 62–92.

Suzuki, Yūko (1993), *„Jūgun ianfu' mondai to sei bōryoku.* [The 'Comfort Women' Problem and Sexual Violence]. Tokyo: Miraisha.

Tachi, Kaoru (1999): Jendā furī kyōiku no konseputo. [The Concept of the Gender-free Education]. In: Fujita, Hidenori et. al. (eds.): *Jendā to kyōiku.* [Gender and Education]. Tokyo: Seori Shobō, pp. 109–141.

Ueno, Chizuko (1998): *Nashonarizumu to jendā.* [Nationalism and Gender]. Tokyo: Seidosha.

Yuval-Davis, Nira (1997): *Gender & Nation.* London; Thousand Oaks; New Delhi: Sage Publications.

Dynamics of Masculinities in Japan –
Comparative Perspectives on Men's Studies

Annette Schad-Seifert

1   Introduction

Japan is usually regarded as a male-dominated or male-centred society. The structure of male dominance in modern Japan is described by some as being the result of traditional gender roles and the historical relict of Confucian ethics in which a gender hierarchy was defined as "the preference of men and the belittlement of women (*danson johi*)". The long-lasting character of Confucian-minded gender distinctions in modern society was the result of political and judicial reforms in the Meiji era (1868–1912), by which the moral values of the samurai status culture of pre-modern times permeated nearly all other strata of society.

With the beginning of modernisation, the distinction of gender roles became further established due to the emergence of a modern industrial society. A modern definition of male dominance is explained as a result of a gendered division of labour in modern Japanese middle class society, according to which full-time housework and the education and care of children is assigned to family women, whereas full-time professional employment is the responsibility of family men. In Japanese women's and gender studies the gendered division of labour of the modern family was named "modern patriarchy" because the structure of Japanese employment practices commonly prohibited family women from remaining in full-time professional employment and recruited almost exclusively men for the company career path (Ueno 1996: 213).

However, the situation has changed significantly over the last decades. Opportunities for women to work and to pursue professional careers have increased while men have come under pressure due to the so called restructuring process of the Japanese economy. For many decades since the era of high economic growth it was regarded as an important qualification for adult males to get married and to fulfil the breadwinner role. A male school graduate could expect to join a company, rise through the corporate ladder and receive a continuously growing salary. Due to the practice of lifetime employment and the principle of a seniority based reward system, the future outlook for male employees was rather secure and predictable although many male individuals felt increasingly chained to the corporation they were employed by. In the late 1980s when the economic bubble came to collapse, a very different category of male employee appeared on the job market namely that of the temporary worker whose conditions for getting contracted have significantly changed from those of permanent employees. The neologism "*furītā*" has been deployed not only in order to designate a different type of work force but also to identify a changed individual attitude towards work (Japanese term created by mixing the English word "free" and the German word "Arbeiter"). Newly established job patterns within the new economy seemed to be appreciated by young job seekers who were eager to find a career path different from that of their elders. The male breadwinner role that men had been expected to fill seems to be more and more questioned by men of the younger generation. When asked about their future professional career, their answers reveal that the corporate life-style is regarded as being extremely limited and narrowly defined, leading to a highly standardized one-dimensional life pattern (Mathews 2004: 124-25). By the late 1990s the somewhat trendy term "*furītā*" even came to be acknowledged by Japan's Institute of Labour as the official category for a permanent worker employed as part-time worker on a fixed-term contract (JIL 2000). In December 2002 the Institute published a survey, which indicated that business organisations are seeking more flexibility in labour adjustment by employing part-time workers instead of permanent employees. By then, already 40.7 percent of the surveyed business establishments had part-time workers engaged in duties equivalent to those of regular permanent employees. The trend clearly goes in the direction of replacing permanent regular employees by part-timers who also work permanently but with a different status (JIL 2002: 2-3). The ongoing changes within the Japanese job market are indeed notably affecting the structural traits of the Japanese employment system such as "lifetime employment" and "seniority principle". Since the institution of "lifetime employment" explicitly privileged men and discriminated against women, the erosion of the system has triggered a social dynamic that has brought many male individuals to the point of critically reflecting on their male gender identity.

Globalisation and economic restructuring are not the only forces which have had an influence on the establishment of the post-war gender system. Japanese society is now facing a radical demographic change with an age pyramid that has begun to reverse; the largest portion of elder persons in the age-group of 50 to 60 years moving up towards retirement.

The Japanese government has implemented measures to deal with the situation of an ageing society caused by continued decrease in the number of children and increase in the percentage of elderly persons in the population. One of the primary policies to respond to the rapid changes occurring in Japan's socioeconomic setting is to realise a gender-equal society. The realisation of this objective includes, among other measures, encouragement of men to take childcare or elderly care leave. The main argument of this article is that socioeconomic structural changes clearly have an impact on how the critical review of masculinity and traditional male gender roles has recently been discussed in various fields of gender studies, including sociology, social politics as well as labour and family related research. The multi-disciplined critique of a male oriented corporate culture, gender division of workplace and traditional gender roles at home has been brought together under the title of "men's studies".

In my article I will focus on the main features of Japanese men's studies and the dynamics of male gender identity reflected in this discussion.

2 The Definition of Gender in Japanese Politics

Since the World Congress on Women in Beijing in 1995, the term gender has found its way into political agendas in Japan and has become increasingly conspicuous in the media (Ōsawa 2000: 4).

During the same period the Japanese government started to design a reform program which aimed at building 'a gender-equal society'. Ōsawa Mari, in a paper on "Government

Approaches to Gender Equality", has pointed out that the governing Liberal Democratic Party under then Prime Minister Hashimoto for the first time ever in Japanese politics referred to the international gender discourse. Since the early 1990s the English language term 'gender' has become generally accepted and popular in different languages including Japanese with its peculiar pronunciation as "jendaa". The Japanese mainstream encyclopaedia *Kōjien* has since 1991 included the following definition for the term: "Gender means the socially and culturally constructed difference between men and women as opposed to sex, which refers to the biological difference".

However, it is important to keep in mind that "gender" in the Japanese understanding of the term has been established in the sense of discrimination, division or disadvantage based on differences between men and women. The French feminist and sociologist Christine Delphy who understands gender as a category of difference which divides human society and therefore has to be abolished became very influential in Japan (Delphy 1984). According to her usage of the term gender in the sense of 'stratified and asymmetric power relations' (Ōsawa 2000: 7, Ueno 1990, 1995), gender politics in Japanese society has been designed with the aim of establishing a gender free (*jendā furī*) society, which has been explained by Ōsawa in the following words: 'By "gender-free", I mean a society where the fact of being a man or woman has no effect on the options available to people as they make their way through life.' (2000: 6)

This definition of gender significantly differs from the use of the term which became established in Germany, where 'gender' does not necessarily refer to a reality which should be overcome or suppressed, but is rather used as an epistemological category which helps to understand how cultural and social differences between the sexes come into being and how they become reproduced or multiplied. In order to establish a public understanding and a political sense of how these differences have an effect on individual lives, the German government has established the politics of "gender mainstreaming". Gender mainstreaming is a kind of political agenda "such that in every project of society the different situation and different interests of women and men have to be taken into consideration from the outset and regularly since a gender free reality does not exist." The German original text reads as follows: „Bei allen gesellschaftlichen Vorhaben sind die unterschiedlichen Lebenssituationen und Interessen von Frauen und Männern von vornherein und regelmäßig zu berücksichtigen, da es keine geschlechtsneutrale Wirklichkeit gibt." (Homepage of the German Ministry of Family and Welfare which refers to the topic of "Gender Mainstreaming", URL: http://www.gender-mainstreaming.net; July 20, 2004).

Although differences in definition are obvious, German gender mainstreaming politics in effect does not stand in opposition to the Japanese politics of realizing a gender free society. Both programs pursue equal opportunities for women and men as well as the implementation of gender equality. But the politics of gender equality in recent years has definitely come to mean more than demanding better opportunities merely for women to participate more fully in society or that female professional employment should be improved by the implementation of quotas, positive discrimination and so forth. Gender politics ultimately has come to agree upon the conviction that not only women's lives and female living conditions have to be altered, but that men's lives and masculine lifestyles also have to be radically changed in order to solve the vital problems of society such as the need to raise the declining birth rate and to revive the economy.

In 1994 the Japanese Government created a Council for Gender Equality (official English title) which had the Japanese denotation *Danjo Kyōdō Sankaku Shingikai* meaning literally: Council for the Joint Participation of Men and Women. According to Ōsawa there are two issues reflected in the Japanese title of the council. On the one hand the Japanese Government in an obviously conservative manner intended to avoid the more radical definition of "gender equality" by promoting the more ambiguous Japanese term "joint participation". On the other hand, however, the title clearly reflects the aim of some of the councillors, to whom Ōsawa also belonged, that politics should be seeking to abolish gender as a paradigm dividing Japanese society in order to become a jointly managed project. Consequently, gender equality will only be realized when men as well as women become the objective of gender politics. In 1999 the Basic Law for a Gender-equal Society (*danjo kyōdō sankaku shakai kihonhō*) has been established by the Japanese government in order to define the basic principles that form a gender-equal society and to look for the factors that inhibit its realisation. The definition of a formation of a gender-equal society in chapter 1 of the Basic Law for a Gender-Equal Society reads: "Formation of a society where both women and men shall be given equal opportunities to participate voluntarily in activities in all fields as equal partners in the society, and shall be able to enjoy political, economic, social and cultural benefits equally as well as to share responsibilities." (http://www.gender.go.jp/english/basic_law/chapter1.html). Nevertheless, not only the State but many local authorities and citizens all over Japan have also since the mid-1990s begun to actively contribute to setting a course to end gender inequality. Community services are for example offering learning groups and introductory courses in gender studies and gender sensitivity training.

3   Men's Studies and Men's Liberation Movement in Japan

The demand for "joint participation of men and women" is also clearly reflected in the activities organized by local volunteer projects with the intention that men should be given equal opportunity "to participate in any field of society" and that both men and women should share the responsibilities for the benefit as well as the burden of society. Voluntary services which target men are in many cases offered by members of the so-called pro-feminist men's liberation movement in Japan. Nakamura Akira formed the first Men's Liberation Group in Osaka in 1991 together with a very small group of associates (Nakamura 1995). The group developed into a centre in 1995 and became the model for other men's centres founded thereafter in some of Japan's bigger cities as well as towns and villages. These centres engage in different kinds of activities such as counselling, information gathering and organising meetings for men. In 2005 the 10th Men's Festival was held in Osaka where the members of different kinds of men's organizations came together to celebrate, exchange information and give support to those who are still not able to "shake off one's shell of masculinity".

The formation of men's liberation movements is closely connected with stimulating academic research in the field of men's studies. Feminist researchers and female scholars active in gender studies have opened the field for men's studies in their publications and encouraged male colleagues to participate (Ehara/Inoue/Ueno 1995, Nishikawa/Ogino 1999). The Japanese sociologist Itō Kimio has become the most representative male figure in the field of research, both as a scholar in Japan's men's studies and as an activist in the men's liberation movement in Japan. Itō is also a very popular figure in the public media since having assigned himself with the mission of open education in men's studies. He is one of the first university professors who started to teach courses in men's studies at the universities of Osaka and Kyoto which he has been offering since 1992, and continuously publishes popular scientific works on the subject (Itō 1993, 1996, 2002, 2003a, 2003b, Itō/Fujitani 1997, Itō/Muta 1998, Itō/Kimura/Kuninobu 2002).

According to Itō the Japanese men's lib is not a political mass movement but rather comprises different kinds of small groups which are eager to raise awareness of gender related issues among men and to establish therapeutically oriented self help groups for men in distress, either through the internet or by offering hotline telephone services. The booklets published by men's centers of local communities in Japan regularly include personal statements of men confessing their experiences which have brought them to the point of changing their gender consciousness (Makino 2001, Menzu Sentā 1996, Menzu Sentā 1997, Menzu Ribu Tōkyō 1997). What triggered their awareness of gender varies from person to person. For one it was the burden of the traditional expectations of a first-born son which led him to question what masculinity is; another mentioned a poster he saw at a train station of a woman in a swimming suit which made him suddenly aware of the sexually biased images of females in order to attract men. Other members mentioned their experiences raising children, caring for elderly parents, and the violence that is inherently expected in men's behavior (Yokohama Women's Association 1998).

Itō is both trying to introduce the pro-feminist theoretical approach to masculinity from famous US-scholars in men's studies such as Michael Kaufman or Harry Brod, and to create a specific Japan-related theory in the field. Kaufman's critical review of masculinity holds the view that the traditional male gender role works like an emotional straitjacket, shell or masquerade which makes men continuously suppress their feelings (Brod/Kaufman 1994: 148-49). Masculinity as a masquerade is translated by Itō as *otokorashisa no yoroi*, literally meaning "the armor of masculinity". According to this view the traditional male gender norm requires the adequate suppression of feelings such as fear and feebleness in order to appear strong and virile. Male strength in the traditional definition of the term is commonly understood in the sense of "man as a fighter, warrior and protector". In Kaufman's critical review of masculinity the prestige of being a man lies in the demonstration of dominance, authority and power for which men have to pay a price and which causes emotional damage not only to themselves but also to those who are suppressed by them (Itō 1996: 150). According to Itō the display of male dominance in Japanese society is most conspicuously and dramatically operative in the working environment in the form of sexual harassment which is not only directed against women but also against hierarchically subordinated younger men. In recent years the public debate on sexual harassment has somewhat waned while particularly large companies in Japan have been implementing training schemes for their employees to prevent sexual harassment (*sekuhara kenshū*). This is done in order to minimize the damaging economic effects which this kind of provocation obviously has in teams comprising both sexes. Occasionally the rather embarrassing title *sekuhara kenshuu* (sexual harassment training) is exchanged for the more neutral label "training in business manners" (*bijinesu manā kenshū*) (Ueno/Shin 2002).

4   Men's Studies in the Japanese Mass Media

Public education in the field of men's studies has also in recent years become very popular in the Japanese mass media. For example, the broadcasting federation NHK in one of its popular television lectures bearing the title "human lectures" (*ningen kōza*) produced a series on the subject of men's studies called "The myth of 'masculinity' " (*'Otokorashisa' to iu shinwa*), held by the ever present Itō Kimio in eight courses and broadcast during the daytime from August until October, 2003. The seminar has also been published in a printed version (Itō 2003a). In the TV-courses Itō has lectured firstly on the cultural history of masculinity in Japan such as the feminized male hero or the men who cooked and cared for their children in pre-modern Tokugawa society. Secondly he has tried to clarify the social causes of contemporary men's domestic violence and the dramatically increased suicide rate amongst middle-aged and older Japanese men. Thirdly he made reference to the autonomy of men that is required to solve contemporary society's problems as shown through examples of house-husbands and by illustrating popular figures in private life, such as John Lennon and he himself being active in child-care. And finally he has tried to raise awareness for the international and Japanese local men's liberation movement.

In the very last course, which covers the title "Men's lifestyles in the 21st century – An encouragement of men's autonomy", Itō introduces a checklist by which men themselves – or women vicariously for the man with whom they cohabit – can check if they master the 20 basic techniques of being "able to care for oneself" (Table 1).

Table 1: **Basic techniques of being able to care for oneself**

1.	Knowing how to use a vacuum cleaner
2.	Knowing how to prepare 8 different kinds of meals without referring to a cookbook
3.	Knowing how to cook rice
4.	Cleaning up after meals at least 5 times per week
5.	Knowing how to set the controls at household electrical appliances
6.	Frequently cleaning the toilet and bathroom
7.	Having several close friends outside the work place
8.	Regularly hanging the washing on the line
9.	Knowing how to fill in documents for the authorities
10.	Ironing your (white) shirts by yourself
11.	Usually preparing tea you drink by yourself
12.	As a rule buying your clothes by yourself
13.	Being able to prepare the ingredients for a meal when eating alone
14.	Having knowledge of least one problem in your neighborhood
15.	Frequently going shopping at the supermarket by yourself
16.	Reading the circulars of the community council etc.
17.	Frequently taking the garbage to the collection point
18.	Having a personal hobby
19.	Knowing where to find your suits, ties, shoes and socks
20.	There being at least 10 persons in your neighborhood with whom you are acquainted

Source: Itō Kimio 2003a

The somewhat amusing side of the checklist with regard to managing everyday affairs has a serious background in so far as in recent years many men of the older generation who usually have no experience at all in household affairs have fallen into great distress after their wives divorced them or became bedridden or died. The traditional family role model generally assured the elderly husband would be the first to become ill or bedridden and therefore would be nursed by his wife. Nowadays the number of elderly husbands who have become nurses to their sick wives or their geriatric parents is continuously growing – which has shown that men too cannot avoid to bear the burden of non-paid social work.

Itō, as an active member of the men's liberation movement, further argues that it is important for men to study themselves in a self-reflexive way and it is in particular the lack of autonomy for which he criticizes Japanese men. In one of his recent academic publications Itō has accused Japanese men of "being unable" to manage social affairs and being dependent on their wives. He explains different ways for men to become independent and able to care for themselves. Itō holds the view that the dependency of Japanese men – which is not defined as a financial or economic dependency, but as a psychological one – originates both from the Japanese welfare system and Japanese employment practices (Itō 2002).

5   Dynamics of Masculinities and the "Company Man" Discourse

The growing quest for male autonomy has recently also been discussed in the context of economic restructuring and has led to a body of literature that can be called the "company man" discourse (Asahi Shinbun Shakaibu 1998, Fukuhara 2001, Miyata 2000, Miyata 2001, Mainichi Shinbun Tokubetsu Shuzaihan 2003, Tao 1996).

Due to the social imperative of the male breadwinner role, being responsible for oneself usually meant for men being responsible for the family income. Male self-responsibility was, so to speak, synonymous with family responsibility. But the main condition for becoming a male wage earner was life-long employment by one single company to which male employees had to fully commit themselves "with all their strength". The core of male identity consisted of a long-lasting personal bond to the corporation and its employees and managers as a community of common destiny. This is furthermore the reason why company men have been called "company warriors". The intense personal identification with the goals of one's company has been regarded as being typical of Japanese corporate men and already in the 1970s came under critical review. The then coined Japanese term *mōretsu shain*, literally meaning the "fiercely (working) company employee", was the description of workaholic habits and a disposition among men to radically sacrifice their individual interests for the company's benefit (Amano 2001: 47). Criticism of male extreme overworking in these times included disapproval of the lack of men's personal autonomy. The reason why this discussion had no impact on the reorganization of employment structures is to be seen in the then occurring oil embargo which forced most large Japanese corporations to downsize and to cut costs by encouraging the reduced number of male core employees to work overtime. Economic restructuring in the 1970s was well suited in encouraging the idea of assuming a male psychological habit which prescribed that men naturally think that "work is primary" (*shigoto daiichi*) and that "the company is paramount (*kaisha daiji*)" for them.

The phenomenon of male overworking originated secondly from a growing consumer society in Japan in the 1970s which led many individuals to direct their energies at enhancing their standard of living by buying durable consumer goods and taking out loans for real estate properties. Thirdly the period of high economic growth in the 1960s had created the widespread "system of the male wage earner (*dansei kasegigata*)", according to which the family man is entirely responsible for the family income, a family model which additionally put male wage earners under severe pressure to focus their lives primarily on work (Amano 2001: 48). These social processes obviously inhibited a differentiated political debate on the after-effects of the phenomenon of male overworking.

However, in discussing the gender identity of Japanese men and their tendency of almost naturally turning into company men, as usually ascribed to them, masculinity has to be understood as being the effect of a reciprocal relationship which renders the housewife entirely on housework, education, care and consumption and the husband-breadwinner on excessive work performance on the job.

In more recent discussions on corporate restructuring a recurrence of the company man discourse can be observed. Interestingly, it is now not only the men's lib movement or the surviving family members of those who have died from overwork (*karōshi*) who disapprove of the working habits of male employees, but rather the managements of corporations have begun to proclaim that male employees should become more independent from their company or that men should free themselves from being company men (*datsu kaisha ningen*). The hitherto existing patterns of Japanese employment practices such as life-long employment and payment by seniority with its specific all-round utilization of the male workforce (which historically emerged already in the 1920s) in order to protect male employees by a kind of company welfare system are now becoming disestablished. Due to shrinking financial budgets and persisting economic recession many corporations are reconsidering their company owned pension schemes and advising their male workforce to consider in good time an "alternative leg to stand on" or to become economically independent well before retirement. Financial advice to become independent and individually provide for one's old age is of course of a very different character from the men's lib's encouragement for male autonomy. But somehow ironically the men's lib's objectives of freeing men from their company's bonds appear to be in accordance with the necessary downsizing of economic corporations. The Japanese sociologist Amano Masako has pointed out that these different kinds of incentives should not be mistaken with one another since the corporations do not seem to consider very seriously the personal situation of individuals or their individual needs (Amano 2001: 41). We are facing the paradox of a development in which corporations in the past put extraordinarily great effort into turning their male employees into company men whereas nowadays company managements more or less overnight are declaring that the company man is no longer qualified to fit into the newly built structures of the Japanese economy. Many middle-aged and older male employees experience the negative evaluation of traditional employment structures as a grave personal rejection. The significantly increased rate of suicides in this age group needs to be explained in terms of the ongoing individualization and de-collectivization of economic organizations. Corporate collectivity in the past supported male gender identity by referring to males as being the sole wage earner of the family, whereas now the restructured corporations increasingly refer to them as individuals or single persons.

Behind this, there is obviously the trend that working conditions for new employees are worsening. Many companies keep their older workforce in regular employment because these employees usually have families to support, whereas young people who live alone or with their parents can afford to receive low incomes in temporary jobs. In addition to this trend of low regular employment among young graduates, organizations apparently tend to pay reduced wages even for the newly employed salary men who in the past have been expected to become the sole supporters of their families. To illustrate this argument, the Japanese publishing house *Jiyū Kokuminsha,* for example, presents a so-called "Grand Prix of new words" every year (see http://www.jiyu.co.jp/gendai/shingo/shingo.html). The 2003 edition has chosen the heading "three Million yen annual income" (*nenshū sanbya-kuman en*) as the new "word" of the year. The expression "three Million yen annual in-come" (equivalent to a yearly income of 22,000 Euro or a monthly income of 1,850 Euro) was coined by the economist and chairman of the Japanese economic research institute UFJ, Morinaga Takurō, in his bestseller "Economics for surviving in a period with three million yen annual income" (*Nenshū sanbyakuman en jidai o ikinuku keizaigaku*) (Morina-ga 2003). In this book, which sold 180,000 copies soon after being published, Morinaga analyzes the polarizing income difference in the Japanese labor market which is the result of implementing the US-style efficiency/competence system in Japanese employment struc-tures. The principle of efficiency is based on a guideline bearing the title "Japanese Manage-ment of a New Era" (*shinjidai no nihonteki keiei*) which was proposed in 1995 by the Japan Federation of Employers (*Nikkeiren*). The new management guidelines classify three differ-ent types of employees: (1) persons who accumulate and use abilities over the long term (with a single employer); (2) persons who hold knowledge and professional skills but are hired for short-term jobs on a contract basis; (3) persons who are employed temporarily (Morinaga 2003:136). The head of *Nikkeiren's* labor law division claimed that "the transformation Japan must make in its industrial structure requires the flexibilization of people (*hito ga ryōdōka*)." (Gordon 2002: 126).

Former prime minister Koizumi Junichirō heralded the realization of the principle of the merit based system (*seikashugi*) under the slogan 'structural reform' (*kōzō kaikaku*). Morinaga criticizes the reform for producing unfavorable conditions according to which only 10 percent of the workforce is in fact capable of receiving better pay than before, whe-reas the income of the other 90 percent is decreasing dramatically (Morinaga 2003: 87). "The traditional guideline of employing all persons permanently for a career path has been suspended." (Morinaga 2003:136). Morinaga forecasts in his book the decline of average annual incomes for male wage earners from 6.5 m Yen (2001) down to 3 to 4 m Yen (Mo-rinaga, 2003:134), a dramatic fall that is continuously being featured in the media.

The polarization of incomes has already produced a significantly growing rate of sin-gle males in Japanese society since the economic qualification for men to marry is still regarded measured terms of being able to support a family entirely with the income of the husband/father. Ōsawa Mari has pointed out that shrinking male incomes will definitely have an impact on the question of gender, since the traditional middle class gender role model of male breadwinner and female homemaker cannot any longer be upheld. The joint and equal participation of men and women in the labor market will become indispensable and will possibly lead to a new family model of double income working couples (Ōsawa, 2002: 200).

6 Conclusion

The fundamental process of economic restructuring and the demise of employment practices which supported male full employment and the male wage earner model have ongoing consequences on the paradigm of gender in Japanese society. The dissolution of the "company man" both as a work habit and a labor utilization system has an impact on male individual lives. Men of the so-called Japanese baby-boomer generation, namely those men born in the late 1940s, focused their lives primarily on the one-dimensional life pattern of the company man model and feel continuously deprived of the social and economic status which formed the core of their male gender identity. For men of the younger generation the ongoing changes in employment structures have at least potentially led to the possibility of alternative life-styles and a growing diversity of gender identity patterns. But many commentators of the employment system and the impact structural changes will have on the future of Japanese society have perceived a growing gap between winners and losers of the system. The changes are now challenging the middle class consciousness which has been so dominant in post war Japan and are producing a class society of "new rich" and 'new poor" (Miyamoto 2002, Satō 2000, Yamada 2004). The critique of Japanese society as a new class society is in some ways convincing but still bound to the traditional conception that young men as the potential breadwinners of their families should be guaranteed secure jobs and steady income, since without economic stability marriages and therefore the birth of children will be in decline. This negative interpretation overlooks the fact that the Japanese employment system has since the beginning of its implementation excluded women from regular employment and thereby has already for a long time produced a gendered division of society. Many of the negative interpretations of the "new misfits" in Japanese society do not take into consideration the individual opinion of the younger generation (Yamada 2004, 2005, Saitō/Genda 2005). The anthropologist Mathews has interviewed young *furītā* of both sexes who feel satisfied with their situation because part-time work enables them to avoid the social expectations they feel imposed upon them to live a more flexible and liberated life-style. There is a certain irony in the situation that the more a young male individual wants to liberate himself from traditional gender roles the more insecure his future outlook will become.

References

Amano Masako (2001): *Dankai sedai – shinron: ‚Kankeiteki jiritsu' o hiraku* [New Theories on the Babyboom Generation: Expanding the ‚relational' independence]. Tokyo: Yūshindō Kōbunsha.

Asahi Shinbun Shakaibu (ed.) (1998): *‚Kaisha ningen' tachi no matsuro – Tsugi wa sararīman ni naritakunai* [The End of the ‚company men' – The new generation says no to the salary man]. Tokyo: Daiyamondosha

Berfield, Susan; Murakami Mutsuko (1997): "A New Sexual Revolution – Some Japanese want to shed the salaryman image", http://www.asiaweek.com/97/1003/nat6.html. (September 3, 2002).

Brod, Harry; Michael Kaufman (eds.) (1994): *Theorizing Masculinities*. (Research on men and masculinities series, vol. 5). Thousand Oaks: Sage Publications.

Delphy, Christine (1984): *Close to Home: a Materialist Analysis of Women's Oppression*. London: Hutchinson.

Ehara Yumiko; Inoue Teruko; Ueno Chizuko (eds.) (1995): *Danseigaku* [Men's studies]. (Nihon no feminizumu, bessatsu). Tokyo: Iwanami Shoten.

Fukuhara Yoshiharu (2001): *Kaisha ningen, shakai ni ikiru* [The company men, living in society]. Tokyo: Chūō Kōronsha.

Itō Kimio (1993): *'Otokorashisa' no yukue – danseibunka no bunkashakaigaku* [The future of 'masculinity' – A cultural sociology of men's culture]. Tōkyō: Shinyōsha.

Itō Kimio (1996): *Danseigaku nyūmon* [Introduction to men's studies]. Tōkyō: Sakuhinsha, 1996.

Itō Kimio; Fujitani Atsuko (eds.) (1997): *Onna ga kawaru otoko ga kawaru 100 satsu no hon* [100 books on how women are changing and men are changing]. Kyoto: Kamogawa Shuppan.

Itō Kimio; Muta Kazue (eds.) (1998): *Jendā de manabu shakaigaku* [Learning sociology with gender]. Tōkyō: Sekai Shisōsha.

Itō Kimio, Kimura Minori, Kuninobu Junko (eds.) (2002): *Joseigaku, danseigaku – jendāron nyūmon* [Women's studies, men's studies – Introduction to gender studies]. Tokyo: Yūhikaku.

Itō Kimio (2002): *'Dekinai otoko' kara 'dekiru otoko'* [How 'unable men' become 'able']. Tokyo: Shōgakkan.

Itō Kimio (2003a): *'Otoko to iu shinwa' – Gendai dansei no kiki o yomitoku* [The myth of masculinity – Explaining today's men in crisis]: Tokyo: Nippon Hōsō Shuppankai.

Itō Kimio (2003b): *'Danjo kyōdō sankaku' ga toikakeru mono* [What 'Gender equality' is calling into question]. Tokyo: Inpakuto Shuppansha.

Japan Institute of Labor (ed.) (2002): "Working Conditions and the Labor Market." In: *Japan Labor, Bulletin*. Vol. 41, No. 12, pp. 2-3. (http://www.jil.go.jp/bulletin/index.htm)

Mainichi Shinbun Tokubetsu Shuzaihan (ed.) (2003): *sararīman to yobanaide – Gyakkyō o ikinuku ‚kaisha ningen' tachi wa, ima* [Don't call me a salary man – 'Company men' surviving in today's adverse circumstances]. Tokyo: Kōbunsha.

Makino, Catherine (2001): "Iron Takeshi. The men's liberation movement arrives." In: *The East*, Vol.37 No.3 (http://www.theeast.co.jp/2001/373/trend373.htm)

Menzu Sentā (ed.) (1996): *Otoko-rashisa kara jibun-rashisa e* [From 'manliness' to being oneself]. Kyoto: Kamogawa Shuppan.

Menzu Sentā (ed.) (1997): *Otokotachi no watashi sagashi – jendā toshite no otoko ni kizuku* [Men search for themselves – Becoming aware of gender in men]. Kyoto: Kamogawa Shuppan.

Menzu Ribu Tōkyō (ed.) (1997): *Otoko ga otoko-rashisa o suteru toki* [When men discard their masculinity]. Tokyo: Asuka-Shinsha.

Mathews, Gordon (2004): "Seeking a career, finding a job: how young people enter and resist the Japanese world of work." In: Mathews, Gordon; Bruce White (eds.) *Japan's Changing Generations – Are young people creating a new society?* London: RoutledgeCurzon, pp. 121-135.

Miyata Yasuhito (2000): *'Kaisha ningen' ga miushinatta mono – 21 seiki ni okeru nihonjin no ikikata o saguru* [What company men have lost sight of – In search for the life style of the Japanese in the 21. century]. Tokyo: Fujita Mirai Keiei Kenkyūsho.

Miyata Yasuhito (2001): *'Kaisha no hito' kara ,shakai no hito' e – 21 seiki, atarashii ikikata no susume* [The 'man of the company' is becoming a 'man of society' – An encouragement for a new life style in the 21. century]. Tokyo: Fujita Mirai Keiei Kenkyūsho.

Morinaga Takurō (2003): *Nenshū sanbyakuman en jidai o ikinuku keizaigaku* [Economics for surviving in a period with three million yen annual income]. Tokyo: Kōbunsha.

Nakamura Akira (1995): Menzu ribu, danseigaku, jendāron. (http://homepage2.nifty.com/akira-na/)

Nishikawa Yūko, Ogino Miho (eds.) (1999): *Kyōdō kenkyū danseiron* [Team research in men's studies]. Tokyo: Jimbun Shoin.

Ōsawa Mari (2000): "Government approaches to gender equality in the mid-1990s". In: *Social Science Japan Journal.* Vol. 3, No. 1, pp. 3-19.

Ōsawa Mari (2002): *Danjo kyōdō sankaku shakai o tsukuru* [Building a gender equal society]. (NHK bukkusu). Tokyo: Nihon Hōsō Shuppan Kyōkai.

Satō Toshiki (2000): *Fubyōdō shakai Nihon – Sayōnara sōchūryū* [Japan's unequal society – Farewell great middle class]. Tokyo: Chūō Kōron Shinsha.

Saitō Tamaki; Genda Yūji (2005): "NEETs: Young People who fear Society's Gaze". In: *Japan Echo*, Vol. 32, No. 1, pp. 14-17.

Tao Masao (1996): *Datsu kaisha ningen – Bijinesuman no tame no ningen kankeigaku* [Freeing oneself from being a company man – Learning in human relations for salary man]. Tokyo: Fukumura Shuppan.

Ueno Chizuko (1996): "Modern patriarchy and the formation of the Japanese nation state". In: Denoon, Donald; Hudson, Mark; McCormack, Gavan; Morris-Suzuki, Tessa (eds.): *Multicultural Japan. Palaeolithic to postmodern.* Cambridge: Cambridge University Press, pp. 213-23.

Ueno Cizuko; Shin Sugo (eds.) 2002: *Jendā furī wa tomaranai! – Femi basshingu o koete* [Gender free cannot be halted! Stop the bashing of feminism]. Kyoto: Uimenzu bukku sutoa Shōkadō.

Yamada Masahiro (2004): *Kibō kakusa shakai – 'Makegumi' no kibōkan ga Nihon o hikisaku* [Expectation-gap society – The despair of the 'losers' is dividing Japan]. Tokyo: Chikuma Shobō.

Yamada Masahiro (2005): 'The expectation Gap: Winners and Losers in the New Economy." In: *Japan Echo*, Vol. 32, Nr. 1, pp. 9-13.

Yokohama Women's Association (ed.) (1998): Men Thinking and Talking about Gender. Men's Studies Resources in Japan. http://www.women.city.yokohama.jp/english/tsushin/12/news-cont5.html, (September 1, 2001).

Actors

Within Gendered Spaces of Society

Dynamics of Global Gender Politics:
A Comparative Analysis of the Implementation of the
Convention on the Elimination of All Forms of Discrimination Against Women (CEDAW) in Japan and South Korea

Hiromi Tanaka and Mihee Hong

1   Introduction

The past decades have witnessed the global proliferation of gender equality norms. One of the most important contributors to this is a series of UN campaigns for the betterment of women's status around the world. The proliferation, however, does not mean that the norms are automatically applied to the locals. They tend to be interpreted by the local actors in the local context, thus variously from region to region, from country to country. This paper investigates how the global norms can be implemented in the different national contexts – similarly or differently – by analyzing the implementation process of the UN Convention on the Elimination of All Forms of Discrimination Against Women (CEDAW) in two East Asian countries: Japan and South Korea.

The CEDAW was adopted in December 1979 in the UN General Assembly and became effective in September 1981, when the twentieth country entered the convention. As of October 20, 2004, 179 countries entered the convention.[1] In the past three decades, it has become a powerful legal instrument containing internationally recognized norms on gender equality and has tremendous impact on promoting gender equality in many countries.[2] Our analysis underlines the importance of the local actors and contexts in the implementation of global norms such as the CEDAW and the existence of interaction between the two national units (Japan and South Korea) as well as between the global (UN) and the national (Japan/South Korea) in the implementation process.

We have selected the two cases, since East Asia represents a unique sub-region characterized by both regional commonalities and diversities in terms of histories, economies, political systems and cultures. Among the countries of East Asia, Japan and South Korea represent most similar cases with some differences (Brinton 2001). This dynamic character of the region tends to be overlooked in discussions on global gender politics, of which development is marked strongly by the dichotomy between the North and the South.[3] Japan as one of the earliest industrialized democracies and South Korea as one of the shooting stars of the East Asian NIEs do not fit the dichotomy well and therefore can offer a good illustration of dynamics of global gender politics that may develop crosscutting the dichotomy. We conduct a systematic comparative analysis of the two cases. In so doing, we seek to contribute to the research on the CEDAW, which still remains under-researched (Zwingel 2004:1) and on global gender politics in general, which tends to concentrate either on the Western industrialized democracies (Meyer/Prügl 1999), sometimes including Latin America (Lycklama à Nijeholt et al. 1998) or on local women's activism in the so-called 'Third-World' nations in the context of globalization (e.g. Basu 1995).

To study the implementation process of the CEDAW comparatively, we will first develop an analytical framework that can be useful for a detailed description of the implementation process in each country and for a comparison between the two countries. After displaying the two country cases respectively, we deliver a comparative analysis based on the framework. We will conclude with an evaluation of the findings and formulation of future research agenda.

2   Analytical Framework

In this paper, we focus on the national context, one of the four contexts relevant for the analysis of the CEDAW.[4] The key question that we seek to answer is: In which mechanism is the CEDAW implemented in national contexts?

Our analytical framework for tracing and comparing the implementation process of the CEDAW in both countries contains the following five dimensions:

- actors and constellation of actors;
- interaction between these actors;
- national context;
- policy-outcomes, and
- process over time.

2.1 Actors and constellation of actors

The central dimension of the framework refers to actors involved in the process and the constellation of these actors. We hypothesize that CEDAW can be implemented by various sets of actors who appropriate and interpret the Convention in their national context. We look at the following sets of actors in particular: a national government, a Women's Policy Machinery (WPM), and a women's movement. The CEDAW obliges national governments to be engaged in the advancement of women. Each government reacts to this obligation differently. We intend to examine varying reactions of the governments of Japan and South Korea in terms of their motives for action and political measures. The WPM refers to 'any structure established by government with its main purpose being the betterment of women's social status' (Stetson/Mazur 1995:3) and feminist[5] bureaucrats working there are called femocrats. Established under the direct influence of UN politics, the WPM developed into a central actor in gender politics in both countries. We investigate the emergence and development of the WPM in both countries as a key dimension to characterize and compare the implementation process of the CEDAW.[6] A women's movement represents another crucial set of actors. We conceptualize a women's movement as a set of collective actors who are not state-based in their struggle for change of unequal gender relations (Lenz 2001). A women's movement consists of various forms of organization and a wide range of strategies and discourses. We investigate how the women's movement participates in the CEDAW-related policy process and in which way it contributes to transform a global norm such as the CEDAW into a national norm on gender equality. Besides these sets of actors, the policy process can be thought to involve individual feminist actors such as female politicians and female experts such as legal experts and feminist scholars (Woodward 2001). Each (set of) actor(s) has its own set of preference for policy outcomes and of options for strategies. By constellation of actors, we mean the relationship between these actors each of whom has his/her strategy options and policy-preferences.[7] We study what kind of options and strategies each set of actors has in the implementation process of the CEDAW.

2.2 Interaction between actors

The implementation process of the CEDAW as a global norm in the national context can be seen as a continuous process of negotiation between various sets of actors who have varying strategies and interests. The forms of interaction between them vary according to issues and contexts. We investigate how they interact with each other and what forms of interaction can be identified.

2.3 National contexts

National contexts influence the implementation process of CEDAW, since they affect the orientation of actors in their actions and interactions between the actors. Drawing on Banszak et al. (2004:17), we regard the national contexts as constituting a set of political and socio-cultural factors. These can be relatively stable conditions or more variable or temporary settings in which interactions between the actors occur. We shall compare two different national contexts.

2.4 Policy outcomes

The impact of the CEDAW is likely to be most evident in the policy debates and their outcomes that occur due to the CEDAW. These policy debates and the process of negotiation over the policy outcomes can be analyzed in terms of the interplay between the aforementioned dimensions of the analytical framework – actors, interaction, and context.

We have thus developed a descriptive model on the interrelation of the dimensions for the comparative study of the implementation process (see Figure 1).

Figure 1: **Actors and context**

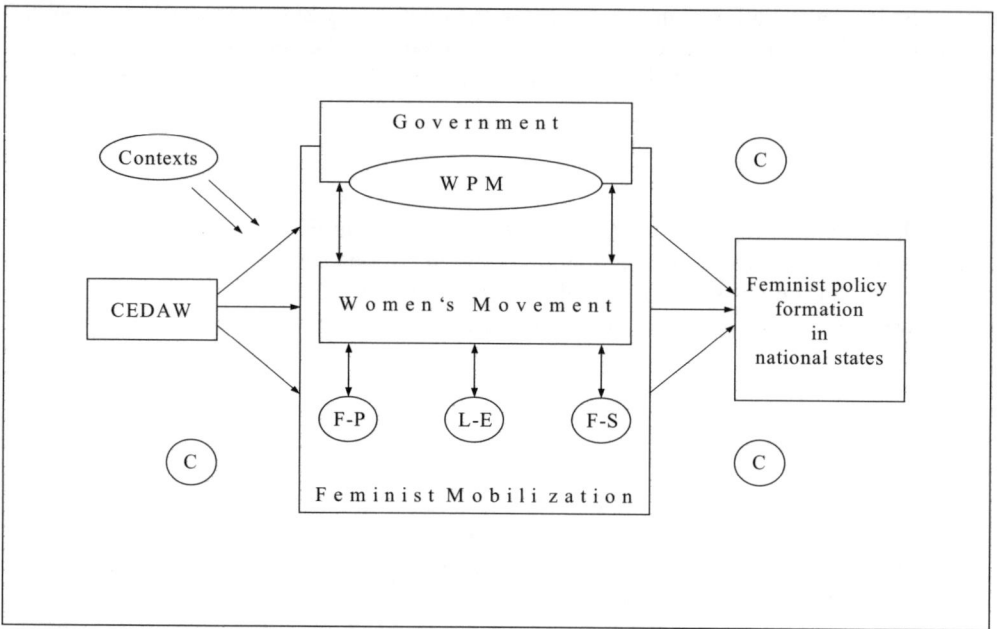

F-P: Female Politicians, L-E: Legal-Experts, F-S: Feminist Scholars, C: Context

2.5 *Process over time*

This model does not reflect any longitudinal process. Our analysis should, however, take the process over time into account, since the implementation is not a one-step action but a long-term process. Our analysis differentiates the implementation process in three stages: the stage of pre-ratification, the stage of signing and ratification, and the stage of post-ratification. Strictly speaking, the first stage does not belong to the implementation process of the CEDAW, because a 'constructive dialog' between the Committee on the Elimination of Discrimination Against Women (CEDAW Committee) and the state governments starts with the signing. But the CEDAW is a direct result of long-term efforts of feminist actors in the UN such as CSW before the International Women's Year (1975) and a series of UN feminist policies after the Year. Furthermore, a number of state parties participated in the drafting process of the CEDAW and many governments knew about the Convention before its adoption in 1979. The stage of pre-ratification is also critical to understand what constitutes pre-existing conditions that may affect the stage of signing and ratification and in which way they affect the stage.

Accordingly, we added the time dimension to our framework in order to investigate four dimensions in each stage of the CEDAW process for our comparative study: Actors and Constellations of these Actors; various national contexts; interaction between the actors; and policy debates and policy outcomes (see Table 1).

Table 1: **Emergence and the development of the Women's Policy Machinery**

Stage	Japan	South Korea
Pre-Ratification	Bureau for Women and Young Workers (1947) Headquarters (HQ) for Planning and Promoting Policies Relating To Women, the Prime Minister's Office; Office for Policies Relating To Women, the Prime Minister's Office; Council for the Planning and the Promotion Regarding Women's Issues (Private Advisory Body to the Prime Minister) (1975) National Women's Education Center (1977)	Division of the Welfare for Women
Signing and Ratification		Korean Women's Development Institute (1983) Committee for Women's Affairs (1983)
Post-Ratification	Reestablishment of the Council as Council of Intellectuals for the Planning and the Promotion Regarding Women's Issues (1986) Increased number of Special Advisors to the HQ (1987) Reestablishment (1994): HQ for the Promotion of Gender Equality; Office for Gender Equality and Council for Gender Equality in the Prime Minister's Office Reestablishment (1997): Council for Gender Equality; Appointment of Minister for Gender Equality Reestablishment (2001): Council for Gender Equality and Gender Equality Bureau in the Cabinet Office	Increase in focal points Upgrading: Ministry for the Second Political Affairs (1988-1998): Establishment of Special Committee for Women (1998-2000) under President and Ministry for Gender Equality (since 2000)

3   Case of Japan

Japan signed the CEDAW at the Second World Women's Conference in 1980 and ratified it in 1985 at the Third World Women's Conference without any reservation. In the case of Japan, most policy debates that emerged in the ratification process did not emerge due to the CEDAW. All the policy debates in the process referred to pre-existing political issues. Here, the CEDAW, together with the International Women's Year (1975) and the World Women's Conferences since 1975, offered an unprecedented political opportunity for feminist actors.

3.1   Pre-ratification phase (before 1979)

The decades before ratification of the CEDAW were characterized by a variety of women's policies and activities of the women's movement. We can distinguish two stages: before and after the International Women's Year (IWY) in 1975.

Before the International Women's Year

The years or the decades before 1975 witnessed the formation of several important pre-conditions for understanding of the CEDAW process in Japan. These pre-conditions also include the following four aspects.

First, Japan's democratization after World War II and the subsequent economic, political and social re-vitalization of Japan including its return to an international community constitute important environments in which the first pre-CEDAW phase developed. Japan experienced a transition from an agricultural and light-industry based economy to a heavy-industry based economy, whose astonishing development became known as the 'Japanese miracle.' During the few decades, a relatively short period of time, Japan achieved remarkable development, Japanese style of management and employment, characterized by 'life-long' employment, seniority principles and in-company unionism (Demes 1998), was established. More and more women entered the labor market to meet the strong demand for a labor force. Women's entry into the labor market also meant women's penetration of the male-dominated operating system of Japanese companies. Consequently, problems relating to women's employment, especially various ways of treating women differently from men at the workplace were recognized, as an increasing number of women were engaged with labor activity.

Second, the women's movement, women leaders in society such as politicians, and the Bureau for Women and Young Workers had emerged as important feminist actors by the 1970s and these actors had initiated the process of feminist policy formation by participating in the international as well as the national/local political arena.

The women's movement had (re-)developed into a full-fledged organized interest by 1975. The history of the Japanese women's movement can be traced back to the Meiji-era (1868-1912) and the following years before World War II. Most women's movement organizations in this period were forced to disband by 1940, though being integrated in the war system of the imperial state of Japan. After the War, several women's movement organizations were re-established. In the 1950s and 1960s, women's activism continued to be active in struggles to improve working conditions, to secure peace by rejecting nuclear weapons and criticizing the US-Japan security treaty, and so on. Several female legislators[8] supported the resurged and redeveloping women's movement in these years. In the early 1970s, the picture of the women's movement changed dramatically again. A new type of the women's movement had emerged. While the women's collective actions before is usually referred to as *fujin undō* (a movement of adult women or ladies), the newly emerged women's movement called itself *onna no undō* (movement of women) and *ūman ribu* (women's liberation) (see Mizoguchi et al. 1992). Sometimes clashing with, sometimes cooperating with one another, these different kinds of women's movement came to constitute an important set of actors in politics concerning women's status and gender relations by the time of the IWY.

There were also a number of women leaders in Japanese society. These women, mostly highly educated, had already been involved in gender politics in some way, for instance, as activists in the prewar and/or postwar women's movement, as politicians, as bureaucrats, or as journalist. They had already constituted feminist actors before 1975.

Third, Japan had implemented several women's policies. For example, after the war, many women who lost their husbands in the war were forced to become breadwinners in order to make a living for their children. To support these women, the state established a number of nursery schools. The Bureau for Women and Young Workers in the Ministry of Labour also conducted extensive administrative guidance and measures to protect women workers. The Bureau can be seen as the first WPM in Japan. Based on the American model, it was established under the support of GHQ in 1947.

Fourth, Japan became a UN member in 1956. This not only symbolized Japan's return to the international community, but also heralded the beginning of the intertwinement between domestic and international levels of gender politics involving Japan, which has intensified dramatically after 1975.

After the International Women's Year

In the first half of the 1970s, women's activism had developed around many political issues, including discrimination against women in the workplace, security and peace, sexuality and reproduction including abortion and contraception, sex tours of Japanese men in neighboring countries, and discriminatory practices in school education including the issue of home economics. Amid the contested political process over these issues in Japan, the UN decided the designation of the IWY and the First World Women's Conference (June 19 – July 2, 1975). This had tremendous impact on feminist policy formation in Japan, both on the Japanese government and on the Japanese women's movement. The government promptly established a national machinery for the advancement of women. On September 23, 1975, the Office for Policies Relating to Women (OPRW) was established within the Prime Minister's Office as an institution that should play a central coordination role in national women's policy. The Office soon reacted to the decision in the First Women's Conference by drafting the National Plan of Action, published on 1 February 1977. The government also established the National Women's Education Center (NWEC) as an organization attached to the Ministry of Education in 1977. The Center, equipped with accommodation and recreation facilities and an extensive library, soon became a place where women gathered nationwide.

The reaction of the women's movement was probably most signified in the emergence of networking between women from various backgrounds, in which several women politicians were largely involved, and the establishment of new women's movement organizations and their activities. The women's movement started to urge the government to appoint an NGO woman to a position in the official delegation to the Conference. Though only a handful, some women attended the Women's Conference in Mexico City. Many women who did not attend the Conference also heard about it from them and newspaper reports. The Conference motivated women in Japan to establish several new Women's movement organizations (WMOs).[9] The women's movement responded to each step of the government's implementation of decisions on the UN level such as the formulation of the National Plan of Action by analyzing government measures critically, framing problems, conducting dialogues continuously with the related government parties through lobbying, courtesy calls, invitation to NGO meetings, etc.

In terms of policymaking, however, the IWY and the Mexico Conference did not directly lead to substantive outputs. The National Plan of Action was a 'plan' without any binding authority. In the process concerning equal employment, the struggles in the judicial area, where many cases of discrimination in the workplace had been dealt with, were apparently blocked, when the Supreme Court decided in 1977 that the dismissal of female employees on the basis of their marital status should not be illegal. Several developments positive for feminist actors, nevertheless, occurred by the late 1970s. For instance, in the process regarding equal employment, the Ministry of Labor announced its resolution to counter the discriminatory retirement system for women in 1977. In the Diet, the Socialist Party also submitted a bill for an equal employment law in 1978. Although the bill was scrapped,[10] the momentum for feminist policy formation continued to gather strength, as can be seen in the establishment of a non-partisan organization, the Federation of Legislators to promote the UN Decade for Women by 169 legislators, of which twenty-two were women, in 1978. Concerning the issue of home economics, the Ministry of Education in 1978 started to work on its high school education policies including a measure on home economics classes, so that the classes would be available to male as well as female students.

3.2 CEDAW ratification phase: 1979-1985

It was due to CEDAW that concrete policy outputs were brought about in several equality-related issues. The process toward the outputs overlaps with what we call the ratification phase in this paper. The phase consists of two sub-stages before and after Japan's signing of CEDAW. The first sub-stage is characterized by contests over the signing. The second sub-stage concerns policy debates that intensified particularly after the signing.

Towards signing the CEDAW

Directly after the adoption, the process of implementing the CEDAW began in Japan.[11] In the UN General Assembly, Japan voted for the adoption of the CEDAW in December 1979. However, the existing Japanese laws contradicted the convention in many ways, and the government was, in fact, not eager to sign the convention (Nuita et al. 1994:403). For the public, this intention of the government was 'sugarcoated' due to several factors. First,

Japan voted for adoption in 1979. Second, on January 21, 1980, Japan appointed Nobuko Takahashi, a former labor bureaucrat as the Ambassador to Denmark. She became the first female ambassador in Japanese history. The internal decision of the government not to sign the convention became public rather abruptly through a newspaper article (see Asahi Shinbun 1980a).

This article, printed on the front page, angered feminist actors who had lobbied the government for years. The resonance created by this news promptly led to various activities to reverse the government decision. The women's movement put pressure on the government by holding conferences and gatherings, formulating declarations and resolutions to demand the signing of the CEDAW. The mobilization did not lead to change in the government's decision immediately. But the women's movement continued its actions such as lobbying and nationwide letter action and more and more letters objecting to the government's position arrived at governmental agencies. Other pro-CEDAW actors such as female politicians, members of the Council for the Promotion of Women's Issues, and staff members of the OPRW also worked, partly in cooperation with each other, to change the government decision. The reaction of the women's movement and the advice of the Council, which was delivered to the Prime Minister and the Foreign Minister as a written proposal, helped change the government position. After investigating the legal changes the CEDAW required, the Japanese government signed the convention at the Women's Conference. Various feminist actors contributed much to the reversal of the government decision. This contribution was also possible, because the national machinery was established in the Prime Minister's Office, at the center of the government structure, close to the Prime Minister, and all the important information centered around the OPRW (Nuita 2002:63-64).

Towards ratification

The second sub-stage toward ratification involved the same actors as could be seen in the first sub-stage: the women's movement, female politicians, the OPRW, ministries related to the CEDAW and the Prime Minister. One difference from the first sub-stage is, however, that the second sub-stage is characterized by the emergence of concrete policy debates and policy outcomes. Here, it became clear what kind of interests had to be negotiated for which parties with regard to the ratification. Feminist mobilization thus became even more contested than in the first sub-stage.

The difficult process towards ratification began directly after the signing. On the one hand, each ministry concerned started to work on the convention-related modifications of the existing measures. On the other hand, the women's movement was strongly concerned that the signing and possibly the following ratification might become only symbolic without a substantive policy impact (Asahi Shinbun 1980c; Nuita et al. 1994; Kōdōsurukai kirokushū henshū iinkai 1999:68). Within the government, there were, in fact, opinions that Japan should ratify with reservations so as to avoid or delay the actual implementation of the convention (Kōdōsurukai kirokushū henshū iinkai 1999:253-254). So, the process toward ratification was characterized particularly by negotiation between feminist actors outside the government such as the women's movement and actors inside the government.

The strategy of the women's movement concentrated on appealing to the public through the organization of conferences, demonstrations and petitions and on lobbying relevant state parties such as ministries and bureaus and politicians. The main purpose of the movement's action was to achieve the ratification of the convention. Female politicians also negotiated with important sections of the government. In May 1981, under the pressure of the women's movement and women legislators, the Headquarters for the Promotion of Policies related to Women specified three main areas of reform for the ratification: the patrilineal nationality system, home economics (including cooking, dietetics, sewing, etc.) compulsory only for women students at the high school, and equal employment that was not guaranteed by the existing laws. These three constitute the relevant policy debates in the ratification phase in Japan.

3.3 Revision of the patrilinear nationality system

The Japanese Nationality Law was discriminatory in its patrilinear character. Based on *jus sanguinis*, the Law stipulated that the children of a Japanese mother could have Japanese nationality, either if the nationality of their father was unknown or if the father had no nationality, while children whose father was Japanese had the right to claim Japanese nationality, regardless of their mothers' nationality. Before the IWY, many countries held to a principal of *jus sanguinis* through the father only.[12] This was blurred in a marriage between the same nationals, but became obvious due to the increasing number of international marriages and/or of children born between men and women whose nationalities were not identical (see below for South Korea).

This issue became contentious because of Article no. 9-2 of the CEDAW that clearly assures equal rights for women in terms of nationality of their children. This was a good political opportunity for two sets of actors who wished to change the existing Nationality Law: Japanese women married to non-Japanese men and their supporters; and Japanese women who had children with non-Japanese men without marrying them and whose children therefore became stateless, and their supporters. The first actor set includes women married to foreigners and living in or outside Japan.[13] The second actor set was concerned particularly with the issue of nationality-less children in Okinawa, which has the most US military facilities in Japan's territory. Stateless children were often born between Japanese women and American men in the military service. These two sets of pro-CEDAW actors also cooperated with each other.

On the side of the government, the Ministry of Justice was the main institution responsible for the Nationality Law. The Ministry entered the policy debate as an actor unwilling to adjust the existing law to the CEDAW, because for them no change was necessary.[14]

Additionally, the Tokyo Supreme Court ruled in March 1981 that *jus sanguinis* through only the father was not illegal. The ruling evoked protest. The Group to Consider International Marriage, a group of activists concerned about this issue, lobbied the Ministry of Justice and politicians and conducted media campaigns, often in cooperation with other groups. This was followed by a change of opinion in the Ministry: it decided to amend the Nationality Law in October 1981 and compiled an interim plan by February 1983. WMOs such as the International Women's Year Liaison Group (see endnote 9) continued their activities such as lobbying by May (Nuita et al. 1994: 405). Finally, in 1984, the revised Nationality and Registration Law passed the Diet, and became effective on January 1, 1985. Article no. 2-1 of the revised law guarantees that children whose mother or father is a Japanese national at the time of their birth can claim Japanese nationality. The conditions for naturalization became equal for all foreigners whose spouse was Japanese, regardless of sex.

3.4 Equality of boys and girls in education

The second policy debated is related to Article no. 10 of the CEDAW that declares equality of both sexes in education. For Japan, home economics, a subject compulsory only for female students, infringed the Article. This had already been a controversial issue by the mid-1970s. The subject was originally introduced as a subject for both sexes in the postwar period, but after the GHQ, which had promoted equal education for both sexes, left the country, traditional gender roles prevailing in society returned. A proposal for a new school curriculum for primary and junior high schools launched in July 1958 included the subjects, home economics and craft and engineering, the former for female, and the latter for male students. The clear separation between men and women in these subjects was introduced in April 1962, when the new curriculum started being applied in junior high schools. In high schools, the course was still for both sexes at that time. In the 1970s, however, the Ministry launched a plan to make the course compulsory for girls only in high schools, too.[15]

Under these circumstances, this issue evoked a movement primarily of women to make the subject compulsory for both sexes. In 1974, for example, a WMO called The Group to Promote Home Economics for Men and Women was established specifically for this issue. In the Diet too, the discussion on home economics began before the CEDAW process crystallized. The positions of political parties were not consistent at first. But, as the discussion proceeded, all parties including the ruling Liberal Democratic Party began supporting the idea of home economics for both sexes. This positive trend dominated by the end of the 1970s.

The debate on home economics began a second round, after Japan signed the CE-DAW. Despite the signature, the Ministry of Education was not willing to change the curriculum. In fact, the next revision of the school curricula was not planned in the near future. This caused feminist mobilization to realize the ratification including the reform of the school curriculum. In the 1980s, the discussion on home science intensified, because the countermovement became more active than before. A strong counter-mobilization came from the side of teachers, who were divided on this issue. In particular, the family section of the National Association of High School Principals rejected the introduction of home science for male students in high school. The issue was also raised in the Lower House of the Diet by several female and male legislators. The movement groups contributed much to the nonpartisan coalition of politicians by lobbying sympathetic politicians beyond the party lines. Besides, movement groups such as the Group to Promote Home Economics for Men and Women used the media to appeal to the public, lobbied the Prime Minister, the OPRW, the Minister of Foreign Affairs as well as the Ministry of Education by demanding direct negotiations. Additionally, they formulated policy suggestions, collected petitions and organized demonstrations (Kōdōsurukai kirokushū henshū iinkai 1999: 70; Kateika no danjo kyōshū o jitsugensuru kai 1997: 178-179). Finally in 1983, the Ministry of Education accepted a new 'era of co-education' in a training event for instructors of home economics. In 1984, the Education Minister agreed in the Diet to make the process in order 'not to hinder the ratification of the CEDAW' (Kateika no danjo kyōshū o susumeru kai 1997: 15).

3.5 Debate concerning equal employment opportunities

The third policy debate concerns equal employment. This turned out to be the longest, and probably the hardest process in the whole ratification process. One reason is that it involved strong actors against changing the existing employment system such as business interests. Another reason is that this policy debate involved the introduction of a new law, while the first two policy debates were concerned with the modification of existing measures. As in the two other policy debates, equal employment was already a quite contentious issue. There was already an active women's labor movement against discrimination in the workplace and the administrative work of the Bureau for Women and Young Workers to improve working conditions of women workers by cooperating with local offices for women workers and the women's labor movement. At this pre-CEDAW stage, it became clear to these actors that the existing legal system was too weak to protect women, let alone to achieve equality in the workplace. In this situation, the women's policy campaign of the UN began. The First Women's Conference, for instance, offered an opportunity to participants from Japan to learn that Western countries already had laws prohibiting sexual discrimination in employment. This led to their research on the existing equal employment law in other countries in order to draft their own equality law.

By this time, the following actors had emerged as feminist actors: the women's (labor) movement; feminist experts in an advisory council of the government and/or affiliated to the movement; feminist politicians; bureaucrats in the OPRW and Women's Bureau of the Ministry of Labour. This issue also involved a politically strong actor who is not necessarily 'women-friendly': the employers' or business interests. The central position of the employers was that the special protective provisions for women workers[16] should be abolished, if 'equality' was to be achieved.

After Japan had signed the CEDAW in 1980, the actors involved differed over the legislation of the law. The women's groups and women's organizations continued actions demanding an equal employment law. The Council of Specialists on Equality of Men and Women, a private advisory organ to the Labor Minister, however, defined equality as equal opportunity and denied equality of result. This shocked the women's movement, as it was demanding an equal employment law, not an equal employment opportunity law. The movement responded to this by intensifying its campaign. The counter-movement of strong employers' interests against the equal employment law also grew in the 1980s. Faced with the strong countermovement, the women's movement had difficulty in realizing its aim to achieve equality without losing the protective measures.[17]

Despite various actions and objection of the women' movement, the Equal Employment Opportunity Law (EEOL) bill passed both Houses in 1985, two months before the Third World Women's Conference, after almost seven years of debate (see Baier in this volume). It was a revision of the Working Women's Welfare Law of 1972. The demand of the women's movement for an equal employment law with penalties without revising the Labor Standard Law was not fully realized. Yet the EEOL, together with the revised Nationality Law and the planned school curriculum reforms on home economics, cleared the obstacles to Japan ratifying the CEDAW.

Several factors led to the signing and ratification of the convention by Japan. First, the action of feminist actors was effective in many senses. Second, UN events such as Women's Conferences gave important impulses. Third, the tendency of the Japanese government to be concerned about its image in the international community also affected positively. At the same time, the CEDAW process in Japan was strongly contested. One reason is that gender differentiation remains embedded in various social practices and institutions such as the family, school, firms, parliaments and bureaucracy. The fact that the case of equal employment was particularly tough for feminist actors shows the strength of business interests in a Japanese corporate society against social interests.

3.6 Post-ratification phase: after the ratification in 1985

After the ratification, 'everybody was exhausted. [...] Women's policy in Japan achieved a great deal by ratifying the CEDAW, but this also meant a loss of concrete aims for women's policy in the government and in the women's movement' (Kawahashi 1998). Yet feminist policy formation regained its momentum in Japan, when the holding of a Fourth World Women's Conference was decided and its preparation began.

The reactivation is related to several important changes in feminist policy formation in Japan. First, women's activism had developed further in the past ten years since the Third Women's Conference. Women's NGOs became professionalized in terms of tactics and strategies. Second, this process of professionalization involved a paradigm change in feminist policy formation from the emphasis on women as the same sex group as its target to the emphasis both on the diversity among women and on gender relations between men and women. This can be seen clearly in the introduction of the concept of gender equal society or 'danjo kyōdō sankaku shakai' (a society based on the joint-participation of men and women) into national women's policy or gender policy (see Ōsawa 2000).

Third, at the state level, the reactivation includes the expansion of Japan's national machinery. The national machinery has been improved several times since its establishment in 1975. In 1987, the number of Special Advisors to the HQ was increased. The other times involved more drastic reforms. In 1993, first, the OPRW, whose establishment or existence did not have any legal grounds, was re-established as the Office for Gender Equality (Danjo kyōdō sankakushitsu). The Council on Women's Issues, which was a private advisory body to the Prime Minister, was also upgraded to the Council for Gender Equality (Danjo kyōdō sankaku shingikai). And the Headquarters for the Promotion of Gender Equality, whose president was the Prime Minister and members were all cabinet ministers, was also established. In 1997, the Council for Gender Equality (Danjo kyōdō sankaku shingikai) was re-established by law (Danjo kyōdō sankaku shingikai setchihō; proclaimed on 3/26/1997, in effect on 4/1/1997). Finally, in 2001, the Council for Gender Equality and the Office for Gender Equality were upgraded to the Council for Gender Equality (Danjo kyōdō sankaku kaigi) and the Gender Equality Bureau in the newly created Cabinet Office. It is remarkable that the organization in charge of politically not necessarily strong, soft issues such as women's policy was expanded in an administrative restructuring, whose aim was largely to reduce the structure financially and organizationally.

Finally, under these circumstances, a number of new policy outputs occurred. These outputs include the legislation of the Basic Law for A Gender-Equal Society (1999) and the revision of EEOL (1999).

Overall, the post-ratification phase is characterized by the improvement of what was achieved due to the IWY and the First World Women's Conference in the 1970s and the signing and ratification of the CEDAW in the 1980s. In the case of Japan, the Convention continues to be significant for the feminist actors in Japan after the ratification and the full realization of the ideas of the CEDAW is still a difficult task. Yet considering the policy outputs in the 1990s, it can be said that the government was rather supportive of a feminist policy formation in this period. This was positively affected by the changed conditions of the Japanese economy after the end of the 'bubble economy' of the 1980s and the restructuring of government due to a structural change of Japanese society developing into an aging society with fewer children (Ōsawa 2000).

4 Case of South Korea

The South Korean government ratified the CEDAW in 1984 with reservations regarding several articles of the Convention. Nevertheless, the ratification marked a milestone in the development of feminist policy formation in South Korea. By entering the CEDAW, the 'advancement of women' or 'equality between men and women' became a legitimate political agenda. At the time of the signing and ratification, however, the CEDAW received little attention from feminists outside the government, who recognize the power of the CEDAW today.[18] This was mainly due to the political situation of the country at that time. The military regime constrained feminist mobilization and also cooperative interaction between government and the women's movement. In the post-ratification stage, the implementation process became more dynamic, involving more sets of actors and bringing about more substantial policy-outcomes. This was largely affected by the country's democratization since 1987.

4.1 Pre-condition: social context and the consciousness-raising of women

The pre-ratification stage is characterized by the uneven modernization of a society that lacked any formation of feminist policy and the emergence of new feminist activism. During the 1960s and 1970s, South Korean society underwent an unprecedented social change through modernization. The process of modernization included the rapid economic growth and a number of political crises that hindered democratization (see M. Suh 1993). Traditional cultural values prevailing in society influenced asymmetric gender relations between men and women. In this period, there was almost no substantive feminist policy. Women were either integrated in the industrialization policy as low-waged workers or became a target of the state population policy promoting birth control.

The lack of substantive feminist policy is related largely to the political conditions at that time. The authoritarian regime repressed and controlled political and social activities and manipulated the existing NGOs including women's organizations. The umbrella women's organization, the Korean National Council of Women (KNCW), founded in 1959, for example, even supported the dictatorial regime (M. S. Suh 1989). Therefore, there was hardly any feminist activism. One exception was the campaign by the KNCW for the revision of the Family Law (see below).

The situation has changed since the mid-1970s. The political consciousness of women such as women workers, female students, and female intellectuals has grown. These women not only formed a coalition to constitute a democracy movement, but also raised women's issues such as sex tourism by Japanese men and equal rights in the labor market. They were also encouraged by new developments of global women's activism such as the IWY to mobilize themselves (Sohn 1994: 440). Their efforts resulted in the introduction of women's studies in 1978 and a Master program in Women's Studies at the Ewha Women's University in 1982 as well as various educational programs for women outside of the college. Participants or students of these formed several women's movement organizations in the early 1980s to struggle for democratization and gender equality.

4.2 Ratification with reservation

The government signed the CEDAW in 1983 and ratified it in 1984. The ratification, however, involved a number of reservations.[19] The government might have ratified it to compensate its lack of legitimacy within the country so that it could acquire a reputation in the international community.[20] However, it does not mean that the CEDAW had no impact at all. This can be seen in the establishment of the WPM including the National Committee on Women's Policies in the Prime Minister's Office, which consisted of ministers and experts and the Korean Women's Development Institute (KWDI) soon after the signing (Initial Report submitted to CEDAW 1986). The KWDI was of particular importance. Established as a state-funded institute associated with the Ministry of Health and Social Welfare in 1983 with a staff of 164, the KWDI aimed at integrating women into the development process by enhancing women's social participation and promoting their welfare programs. Its main activities include survey and research on women, producing educational programs for the cultivation of women's potential, supporting women's activities, and participating in international exchange programs (KWDI 2003). It also drafted the Guideline for the Elimination of Discrimination against Women (1985). The KWDI began publishing gender-specific statistics and official reports such as the White Paper on Women.

These actions of the government marked an important step forward in feminist policy formation. But the reactions of the women's organizations to the ratification and its results varied according to their attitude toward the state. The Korean National Council of Women (KNCW) launched a campaign for Family Law reform again, petitioning and lobbying the government and the assembly for the reform, without achieving any success. On the contrary, women's movement organizations[21] established in the early 1980s reacted to the CEDAW and the government's reaction to it with distrust. They called for a radical political change including democratization instead of governmental policy on women without expecting the dictatorial government to do anything good for women.[22]

4.3 Post-ratification phase

The post-ratification phase saw a more dynamic process leading to substantial policy outcomes. A crucial factor that influenced the further implementation of the CEDAW in this phase is the country's political transformation from an authoritarian regime to a more liberal regime. Facing a number of protests by students and citizens in June 1987, the government promised to amend the Constitution including a revision of the Presidential Election

Law. Based on the new constitution, the sixth Republic of Korea was established and the president was elected through direct presidential election (see M. Suh 1993; see also H.Y Cho 2003). The political change created a new constellation of actors in the implementation of the CEDAW. The main actors in the post-ratification stage are the WPM, the women's movement and women assembly members. Women politicians, some of them former activists, have newly emerged as a crucial set of actors due to the country's transition to democracy, contributing to the legislation of the Equal Employment Law and the revision of the Family Law since the 1980s.

The most remarkable change in the constellation of actors is the relationship between the state and the women's movement. The government, particularly the WPM, which was the main actor in the implementation at the stage of the signing and ratification, sought more cooperation with NGOs, particularly with the women's movement organizations in Korean Women's Association United (KWAU). The WPM became eager to adopt their opinions and reflect these for their policy-making. The growth of a solid relationship between the WPM and the women's movement is related to the fact that former activists began working in the WPM, after the opposition leaders came to power in 1993. The country's democratization also changed the strategy and orientation of KWAU, which used to be against the state's women's policy. Now it pursues the 'politics of participation' in order to increase the number of women in local and national institutions, lobbying for bills that eliminate discrimination against women and promote gender equality (K.H. Kim 1998). The KWAU also started referring to the CEDAW when making claims and putting pressure on the government and the male national politicians. This marked a strategic change in the women's movement.

Another important development at this post-ratification stage is the expansion of the WPM. Before the signing, there were two important institutions for women's affairs in the state administration: the Women's Welfare Division of the Family Welfare Bureau and the Women and Youth Workers Division of the Labor Standards Division of the Labor Standards Bureau. The Women's Welfare Division of the Family Welfare Bureau, located in the Ministry of Health and Social Affairs (since 1948), is mainly responsible for women in need of protection such as single mothers, teenagers or prostitutes. The Division for Women and Youth Workers in the Ministry of Labor (since 1981) worked for the improvement of labor conditions and provided the guidelines for the protection of women workers at a minimal level. The signing of the CEDAW led to the establishment of the KWDI and the CWP (see above). In 1988, the first WPM at a ministerial level, the Ministry of Political Affairs (II) was established to coordinate activities related to women's policies. In 1994, women's focal points were established in all the Ministries and Offices, and the National Assembly established the Special Committee on Women to facilitate the legislation of gender-related law and their implementation. The Ministry of Political Affairs (II) was upgraded to the Special Committee on Women under the President in 1998, and then to the Ministry of Gender Equality in 2000.

The aforementioned three sets of actors – the WPM, women's movement and women politicians – are linked with each other and cooperate on many issues related to gender equality. However, in how far they involve themselves in the implementation process of CEDAW varies from issue to issue. In the following, we discuss three central policy-outcomes which were brought about in relation to CEDAW – the Equal Employment Law,

Family Law and Nationality Law – and show the specific roles of these sets of actors and varying attributes to the implementation.

Equal Employment Law

The Equal Employment Law (EEL) was introduced in 1987 and amended four times in 1989, 1995, 1999 and 2001. The government learned that many countries have an equal employment law and considered the legislation of the EEL as a way of meeting the requirements of the Convention (E. Kim 1999:6). The Equal Employment Opportunity Law (EEOL) of Japan in particular had a significant influence on the legislation in South Korea. Female bureaucrats in the Ministry of Labor and the KWDI prepared a bill quickly by taking Japan's EEOL as an example (ibid.). The female politicians of the ruling party had great influence on the legislature.[23] Furthermore, the ruling Democratic Justice Party made the legislation pledge in order to win the election in 1988 (ibid.). Under these circumstances, the EEL passed without any mobilization of the women's movement. After the law was passed, the women's movement found that the law could be useful for the improvement of the women's status in the labor market and that the law, passed without enough preparation, was deficient in many aspects. This recognition led to their mobilization for the revision of the law. Their actions included a publicity campaign with labor unionists, so that female workers, who did not know about the law, could use it in case of discrimination, support for legal disputes of women workers, etc. The KWAU, together with legal experts, femocrats and labor unionists, drafted a bill to revise the EEL. Female politicians proposed the bill in the assembly and lobbied for the legislation.

Reform of the Family Law

The debate on the Family Law of 1958 shows a different pattern of CEDAW's impact on national policy formation. Here, CEDAW, as a political opportunity for the national women's movement, becomes an effective instrument for exercising pressure on policy-makers and combating the counter mobilization against change. It also shows to what extent CEDAW as a global norm can be effective, if feminist policy formation is confronted with the existing cultural norms that are deeply rooted in the national society.

The Family Law was discriminatory in many ways, for example, in terms of the male family headship system, the prohibition of marriage between the parties whose surname and place of family origin were the same, the patrilinear definition of relatives, discrimination in parental custody rights, unequal inheritance regulations between sons and daughters, etc. The Law was revised in 1977 and again in 1990.

The mobilization for the revision of the Family Law has a long history. Several women leaders and women's organizations began to work on this matter in the late 1950s, as the Law was based not on the modern Constitution but on traditional Korean norms. Large-scale mobilization under the initiatives of the KNCW in the 1970s ended with little success, and the mobilization at the beginning of the 1980s ended without any success. The central reason for the limited success was a strong counter mobilization by various social groups protesting against the reform (H.J. Lee: 1996: 256). The women's movement organizations began to mobilize again in the late 1980s, forming a broad coalition. They could use CE-

DAW as an effective instrument to put pressure on the government and the assembly members. The women politicians even used their personal contacts in order to persuade the male assembly members to approve the revision (Yŏyŏn 1992).

In the revised Law of 1990, many discriminatory regulations were corrected, though two central discriminatory clauses – the family headship system and the prohibition of marriage between the parties whose surname and place of family origin are the same[24] remained untouched. The revision of 1990 withdrew the reservation of the subparagraphs (c) (d) and (f) of paragraph 1 of Article no. 16 of CEDAW. Now only the subparagraph (g) of paragraph 1 of Article no. 16 concerning the freedom to choose the family name remains reserved. In Korea, both women and men traditionally retain their pre-marital surnames after marriage. The discriminatory element of the principle of "surname unchangeability" lies in the fact that the children are given their fathers' surnames.

Currently, the women's movement therefore concentrates on correcting this practice, for example, by launching a campaign to promote the combination of the surnames of both parents. This campaign successfully attracted public attention, but problems that might occur from such combined names were also recognized: e.g. the possible creation of extended, unrecognizable names, the different surnames of the same parents etc (fourth report 1998, CEDAW/C/KOR/4). Today, there is not yet any consensus on this issue. Experts on gender policy including politicians, femocrats and activists think that it will take a long time before a new regulation on the freedom to choose the family name can be introduced, since many still preserve the opinion that the surname which the person is given at birth by his/her father is not changeable for a lifetime (N.S. Kang et al. 2000). This indicates that the full implementation of CEDAW can be restricted due to the existing cultural norms of the national society.

Nationality Law

The case of the Nationality Law shows that the implementation of the Convention or the withdrawal of the reservation can be delayed without the active participation of social actors. The Republic of Korea reserved Article no. 9 referring to gender equality in terms of nationality. The Nationality Law enacted in 1948 does not allow children of a foreign man and a Korean woman to claim Korean nationality. Under the law, foreigners married to Korean women cannot acquire Korean nationality either, while a foreign woman married to a Korean man is eligible for this.

Despite these discriminatory regulations and the reservation of the CEDAW by the Korean government, women's movement groups and other social groups did not take up this issue until the mid-1990s. The growth of migrant workers from South Asia involved a dramatic increase in the number of international marriages. Children having a Korean mother and a foreign father were treated as stateless, deprived of basic rights to education and health insurance. Under these circumstances, several organizations supporting the migrant workers started to work for the revision of the Nationality Law. The Ministry of Justice considered this situation and recognized both paternal and maternal lineages in terms of the nationality of children born in an international marriage.[25]

5   Comparative Analysis

The implementation process in both countries differs, first of all, in the formal procedures of the implementation and the related feminist mobilization. In the case of Japan, the government ratified CEDAW without any reservation by meeting all the legal requirements, although not all initial policy outcomes due to the CEDAW were strong enough to achieve a substantive improvement of women's status. To the ratification, the mobilization of various feminist actors including the women's movement, women leaders in society such as politicians, bureaucrats, and journalists contributed much. For the mobilization of the women's movement, the establishment of new women's movement organizations under the influence of the women's policy campaign of the UN was critical. In contrast, the South Korean government ratified the Convention with reservations. At that time several women's movement organizations had just been established and therefore there was hardly any feminist mobilization over CEDAW. The CEDAW-related process became more dynamic only after the country's democratization, when feminist actors were engaged for the substantial realization of the ideas of the CEDAW at the end of the 1980s.

Despite the differences, the two cases show that the CEDAW as a global norm can play a significant role in national feminist policy formation.

Actors and the implementation of the CEDAW

Actors participating in the implementation process of CEDAW help largely to architect the process. Simultaneously, CEDAW affects the lineup of the actors in various ways. In both cases, the Convention offered existing feminist actors new opportunities for mobilization, serving as a key reference to their formulating feminist goals. It also helped new feminist actors emerge.

National government and the CEDAW

The national governments as important actors ratified the Convention, first of all, for their own sake. The Japanese government was concerned about its image as a developed country comparable to western developed countries. The South Korean government sought to compensate the lack of its legitimacy by being integrated into the international community. Thus, the ratification of CEDAW did not depend on the character of the government, namely on the question to what extent the government could be pro-feminist. However, the subsequent political measures, implemented to fulfill the requirements of CEDAW in both countries, show that the government has been playing a role as a relevant feminist actor since the ratification. This is especially evident in the establishment of the Womens's Policy Machinery (WPM) both in South Korea and Japan.

WPM and the CEDAW

The emergence and/or the development of the WPM were deeply related to the CEDAW implementation process (see Table 1). In Japan, the Office for Policies Relating to Women (OPRW) was established under the direct influence of the IWY. Despite its weak legal status, it has become a crucial women's policy agency since the 1970s, while the older one, the Women's Bureau, also contributed to the ratification particularly in the legislation of the EEOL. In South Korea, the KWDI and the Committee for Women's Affairs (CWA) were established after the signing. The Korean national machinery, established at the stage of singing and ratification, was affected by Japan's machinery. Both the OPRW and the CWA were established organizationally close to the Prime Minister in the governmental structure. A similarity can be seen between the NWEC and the KWDI, too. But the programs and activities of these two institutions differ largely today: the KWDI developed into a kind of think tank and thus a political actor by conducting research and making policy proposals, while the NWEC retains the strong character of a women's center that offers space for further learning and communication to women and men (see also Bardsley 1999).

The national machinery developed further in both countries in the 1990s (see also True/Mintrom 2001). A common tendency is the increased number of focal points, the expanded scale of resources such as staff, and the changed or upgraded function of the machinery.

The WPM plays a significant role in the further implementation process. However, its role differs in terms of political issues and contexts of both countries. In the case of Japan, the Headquarters, consisting of politicians of a ruling party appointed as ministers and high-level officials of ministries, was not always eager to sign the CEDAW. This reluctance constrained the activity of the OPRM and the Women's Bureau a lot in the legislation of the EEOL. In South Korea, the WPM began to be engaged actively in the advancement of women's status after the democratization, which led to the appointment of several former activists of the women's movement to relevant posts in state bureaucracy. In Japan, though the government also promotes partnership between the government and NGOs as in South Korea, such appointments have been almost impossible. Instead, feminist intellectuals have been appointed as the members of the former private advisory body on women's issues to the Prime Minister or the Council for Gender Equality.

Women's movement and the CEDAW

In both countries, the women's movement constitutes an important set of feminist actors (Table 2). The Japanese women's movement contributed much to the ratification. For the movement, CEDAW has proven to be a powerful vehicle for organizing and achieving its goals. In its efforts to achieve the ratification, the women's movement was also empowered by networking between different sets of actors. In South Korea, the women's movement recognized the usefulness of CEDAW after democratization. The comparison between the two cases also shows that it is crucial for women's movements to have some international orientations in order to use global norms such as CEDAW for their mobilization (see Lenz 2004). Yet such orientation differs largely between the two cases in terms of the period of its emergence, which can be determined largely by the national (e.g. political) context of each country.

5.1 Interactions between actors

The implementation of CEDAW influences and is influenced by interactions between the actors involved. The forms of interaction differ from issue to issue. We identified four

Table 2: **Women's movement and the CEDAW**

	Japan	South Korea
IWY	Establishment of new women's movement organizations based on the networking among women with various backgrounds (incl. women politicians); interpersonal and inter-organizational networks Strong international orientation	Establishment of the Department of Women's Studies Ewha University Educational programs for women's political awareness
Ratification	Mobilization for signing and ratification: lobbying, nationwide petition and letter action, demonstration Strong international orientation	Women's movement for democracy and nation (strong national orientation) Confrontation with the state
Post-Ratification	Professionalization Paradigm change from 'women' to 'gender'	Differentiation Institutionalization International orientation (since the mid-1990s)

Table 3: **Forms of interaction between actors by issues**

Issues	Japan	South Korea
Signing of CEDAW	Cooperation: WM, WPM and female politicians	No-Concern of WM
Ratification of CEDAW	Cooperation: WM, WPM and female politicians	Initiative – Government; No-concern of WM
EEOL (Japan)/ EEL (South Korea)	Tension between WM and WPM (Different views on EEL and EEOL and protective measures) Conflict between WM and employers	Initiative: Ruling Party & WPM; No-Concern of WM (First Making) Co-operation: WM, Politicians and WPM (reform of EEL, Initiative – WM & female politicians; Support – WM, Labour Unions)
Nationality Law	Cooperation: WM, WPM and female politicians; Conflict with the Ministry of Justice	Co-operation (Initiative – WPM in the Ministry of Justice, Support – WM)
Home Economics	Cooperation: WM, FP and WPM (leading role of WM); Counter mobilization (conservative teachers)	
Family Law		Co-operation: WM and Female Politicians; Counter mobilization (Conservative Confucians)

Note: WM – Women's Movement, WPM – Women's Policy Machinery, EEOL – Equal Employment Opportunity Law, EEL – Equal Employment Law forms of interaction: Co-operation, tension, confrontation and no-concern (see Table 3). The form of 'no-concern' means that only one set of actors is involved in the implement-tion of CEDAW. This applies to the signing and ratification stage in South Korea, in which important actors in feminist mobilization such as the women's movement were not con-cerned about the actions of the government and the Convention. In South Korea, the coop-eration between the women's movement and female politicians plays a central role in bring-ing about substantial policy outcomes, while the WPM plays a supporting role (see debates on the EEL and the Family Law) or an initiating role (e.g. see the debate on the Nationality Law). Yet, the relationship between the women's movement and the WPM can become tense, as seen in the process concerning the EEOL in Japan. Conflicts can also arise, if strong counter mobilization emerges (see the cases of the Family Law in South Korea and the EEOL in Japan).

5.2 Policy outcomes and the CEDAW

Several policy outcomes were brought about in both countries due to CEDAW (see Table 4). In both countries, despite differences in details, similar issues concerning gender equali-ty developed into relevant policy debates for the ratification. These issues also tend to con-tinue to exist in both countries and in both cases we can apply the earlier introduced ideas about interactions of actors and context (Figure 1).

Table 4: **Policy debates and outcomes in relation to the CEDAW**

	Japan	South Korea
Pre-Ratification	Debate on Nationality Law Debate on home economics in school education Debate on Equal Employment Law	Debate on Family Law (1973-1977)
Signing and Ratification	Legislation of Equal Employment Opportunity Law (EEOL)(1985) Revision of Nationality Law (1984) Revision of school curriculum decided in 1984 (new curriculum published in 1989, implemented in 1994)	Mobilization for the Revision of Family Law (1984-1986)
Post-Ratification	Revision of EEOL (1999, etc.) Other debates specified in CEDAW (e.g. family names, violence against women) Legislation of several laws including Basic Law for a Gender-equal Society (1999)	Legislation of Family Law (1990) Legislation of Equal Employment Law and its revisions (1987, 1989, 1995, 1999, 2001) Revision of Nationality Law (1997)

Both cases show that CEDAW can bring about policy outcomes in two ways. First, the Convention, as a political opportunity for feminist actors, can help re-activate the already existing policy debates in which the actors may not have been successful in achieving their goals. Second, CEDAW can help a new debate emerge. In Japan, CEDAW-related policy debates did not necessarily emerge due to the Convention. In this case, the CEDAW gave momentum to the existing issues. This also applies to the case of the Family Law in South Korea in which the Law was revised despite strong counter mobilization owing to the CE-DAW. The second way can be seen in the revision of the Nationality Law in South Korea. Except for several court cases initiated by individuals, it had not been controversial before. The main reason for the revision of the Law was that the South Korean government recognized the importance of the full implementation of CEDAW and the necessity to withdraw the reservation on Article no. 9.

6 Conclusion

This paper has studied the effects of CEDAW by focusing on how differently the CEDAW as an instrument staffed with global gender equality norms can be embraced in the national context. To scrutinize different ways of the implementation of the Convention, we analyzed two cases, Japan and South Korea, comparatively. Our analysis attests the diffusion of feminist policy formation across borders, particularly transcending global gender politics developing around the UN and domestic politics of national or local societies. Both Japan and South Korea ratified CEDAW in the 1980s and this led to some policy outputs. In both countries, this occurred under a government, not necessarily led by a left-oriented party. Another common factor is an important role of the WPM in feminist policy formation during and after the CEDAW ratification process, although activities of the WPM, representing just a part of the government, can be constrained by other parts of the government. Other similarities between the two cases include that the CEDAW does not necessarily incite new policy debates and the CEDAW continues to be a powerful instrument even after the ratification.

By comparing the two cases, we also found that the process of the implementation of the Convention can vary largely in terms of political opportunity structures and social circumstances within each country. In Japan, gender politics had already been established as a contested political arena in which various sets of actors had emerged before the ratification stage. As pre-conditions useful for promoting gender equality, the existence of women's policies, the women's movement, and several women politicians before the 1970s had a positive effect on the ratification of CEDAW. In South Korea the development of feminist policy formation was constrained under the rule of the military regime. Under these circumstances, the CEDAW was, nevertheless, ratified without the involvement of feminist actors and it was not until the 1990s that a wide range of feminist actors recognized the usefulness of the CEDAW and the state institutions to achieve gender equality. This shows that local or national contexts can affect the implementation of global norms in national societies, even if the norms are internationally acknowledged.

In this paper we conducted a systematic comparative analysis of gender politics in East Asia. It is one of the first efforts to analyze the effects of the CEDAW comparatively and its efforts to work on the under-researched topic and area of study can be seen as a contribution the paper has made. Yet, due to its preliminary character, the analysis is limited in many regards. Further research on this topic needs the refinement of a research question and an analytical framework through more interaction with theoretical contributions of various types of research including those on comparative gender policy and state feminism. With regard to research on CEDAW, the Optional Protocol to CEDAW may be another interesting theme in future. An interesting result of the analysis also includes the impact of Japan's feminist policy formation on that of South Korea (see above for the legislation of the Equal Employment Law in South Korea). Future research should include this dimension of inter-national interaction between two national units as well as between the global and the national. Finally, the analysis of the effects of CEDAW should also include other important dimensions which this paper was not able to cover. A change in public consciousness and its effect on gender equality in the policy-making process would be increasingly significant amid the rise of anti-feminist forces in and across many national societies.

Notes

[1] See 'States Parties' on the Website of the Division for the Advancement of Women, Department of Economic and Social Affairs of the UN http://www.un.org/womanwatch/daw/cedaw/states.htm accessed on Nov. 15, 2004.

[2] It is important to note that global gender politics is not restricted to activities of and events related to the UN. Many local women's movements, for example, tackle problems caused by global capitalism and expand their linkages with actors outside their locality across borders (e.g. Basu 1995; Naples/Desai 2002). These movements may or may not use political opportunities offered by the UN, but may locate their activities outside the UN system.

[3] During the Cold War, the divisions between the West (democratic capitalist economies) and the East (Socialist or communist countries) were often seen in gender politics as well, for instance at the World Women's Conferences in the 1970s and the 1980s.

[4] Zwingel (2004: 5) notes that four contexts should be considered in order to understand fully how the CEDAW matters. These four contexts are international, global, national or local, and transnational contexts.

[5] Following Mazur (2002: 28), we use the term 'feminist' to pinpoint policies or actors that have the intention of promoting women's rights and equality between men and women.

[6] Instead of assuming that the WPM represents feminist interests, we investigate what kind of role the WPM can play in feminist policy formation and to what extent it can be considered as being feminist. It does not seem plausible to assume that the WPM would act as an independent feminist actor, although the main purpose of the establishment is the advancement of women, because the WPM, as a part of the government, is likely to need to negotiate with other parts of the government and thus be affected by the conditions and situations of the whole government structure.

[7] This relationship is shaped according to the resources or power each set of actors has (Scharpf 2000) and the constellation of actors can thus be characterized by highly unequal power relations. We assume that actors can negotiate despite unequal power relations and previous constellation changes through negotiations (Lenz 2001a).

[8] The first lower-house election, in which women could participate as both voters and candidates, was held on October 4, 1946. In this election, 39 women were elected. The next year, the first upper-house election was held on April 20, 1947. Ten women were elected. The same year, another lower-house election took place (April 25, 1947). Fifteen women were elected.

[9] In Tokyo, for example, the International Women's Year Liaison Group (Kokusai fujin-nen nihon taikai no ketsugi o jitsugensuru tameno renrakukai), one of the largest WMOs, and Women in Action (Kokusai fujinnen o kikkake toshite kōdō o okosu onnatachi no kai) were established. For the Kansai area, see Kanatani (1997).

[10] In Japan, legislation tends to result from bills submitted by the ruling party or the government. As the Liberal Democratic Party had dominated the position of the ruling party for some fifty years since1948 and still dominates in the ruling coalition (except the Hosokawa and the Hata governments in 1993 and 1994), the other parties as the opposition can submit a bill yet usually with little chance of having it passed in the Diet.

[11] In February, before the original text of the convention arrived at Japan, a legislator started posing a question on Japan's position on the CEDAW. See Nuita (2002), p. 59.

[12] In the 1970s, several countries including France (1973), West Germany (1974), Switzerland (1978) und Denmark (1979) changed the legal principle.

[13] Japanese women who married non-Japanese men and were living abroad, for instance, in Germany, protested against the Law in order to get their children Japanese nationality.

[14] The ministry replied to the socialist party, which pointed out in the Diet that the nationality law infringed the constitution and the human rights convention, by repeating that 'the law has no intention of discriminating women against men and therefore is not against the international human rights convention.' See *Fujin minshu shumbun*, June 27, 1980, p.1. Another reason for the reluctance was to prevent double nationality, which might affect national security.

[15] The revised curriculum for high school, implemented on April 1, 1973, included home economics as a compulsory subject only for female students.

[16] Overtime work, work on days off, menstrual leave, late night work, the handling of dangerous materials, and work in mines were limited for women by the law. Concerning the overtime, the Labor Basic Law (Article no. 62) prohibited women and workers under 18 from working from 10 pm to 5 am. See Nuita et al. (1994), pp.405-406.

[17] Conventionally, the women's movement in Japan made much of Motherhood and so the protective measures for women workers in the then Labour Basic Law too. For the women's movement, therefore, it was not easy to 'lose' the protective measures at that time.

[18] In a survey of 2000, activists in the women's movement, assembly members and governmental officials stated that the CEDAW had been playing a crucial role in feminist policy formation in South Korea (Kang et al. 2000). The activists in the women's movement regarded the CEDAW as an essential reference for the women's movement (Kang et al. 2000: 57).

[19] Reserved were Article no. 9 and the sub-paragraphs c, d, f, and g of paragraph 1 of Article no. 16. Article no. 9 referring to equal rights between women and men in acquiring, changing and retaining nationality and Article no. 16 concerning the equal rights in marriage and family were not in accordance with the Nationality Law and the Family Law.

[20] The South Korean government at the time of the ratification was led by Chun Doo Whan, an ex-general. Chun's regime lacked legitimacy, because he seized power in a military coup in 1980 and killed approximately 200 participants in a demonstration against the coup (Kwanju Massacre, May 1980). The military regime tried to compensate the lack of legitimacy in South Korea by acquiring a reputation in the international community. Under these circumstances, the government ratified the CEDAW, most likely in order to secure its international reputation. In its initial report submitted to the CEDAW Committee, the government emphasized the democratic character of the Constitution of the Republic of South Korea. See Ministry of Political Affairs (II) (1986).

[21] These organizations founded another umbrella organization, the Korean Women's Association United (KWAU), in 1987, which developed into the most influential women's organization in South Korea.

[22] For example, Minuhoe, one of these organizations expresses its distrust of the KWDI and women's policy of the government in its foundation declaration. See Minuhoe (1987).

23 Yet, male politicians supported the bill, '[...] only because the men thought that the legislation for women was insignificant and that the new law would have little impact' (Sohn 1994: 442).
24 The regulation on the prohibition of marriage between the parties whose surname and place of family origin are the same has not been in force since the Constitutional Court ruled that the regulation was unconstitutional in 1997.
25 In the proposal for the amendment, the government refers to the CEDAW and argues as follows: 'As the Korean government ratified the CEDAW in 1984, it reserved the article on the nationality. Now, it is necessary to withdraw the reservation by eliminating discrimination against women in order to follow the international tendency of the development.' (Agenda no. 838, 1997 http://www.assembly.go.kr, accessed on Oct. 20, 2004).

References

Asahi Shinbun. 1980a. Fujin sabetsu jōyaku shomei miokuri [Postponing the signing of the CE-DAW]. In *Asahi Shinbun* June 7, 1980.

Asahi Shinbun. 1980b. Fujin sabetsu teppai jōyaku shomei miokuri no haikei [Background of the postponing of the signing of the CEDAW]. In *Asahi Shinbun* June 8, 1980.

Asahi Shinbun. 1980c. Fujin sabetsu teppai jōyaku. Seifu shomei e ugoku [The Government signing the CEDAW]). In *Asahi Shinbun* June 28, 1980.

Bardsley, Jan. 1999. Spaces for Feminist Action: National Centers for Women in Japan and South Korea. *NWSA Journal* 11 (1): 136-149.

Banaszak, Lee Ann, Karen Bechwith, and Diether Rucht. 2003. When Power Relocates: Interactive Changes in Women's Movements and States. In *Women's Movement's Facing the Reconfigured State*, eds. L. A. Banaszak , K. Bechwith and D. Rucht. Cambridge University Press: Cambridge.

Basu, Amrita, ed. 1995. *The Challenge of Local Feminisms: Women's Movements in Global Perspective*. Boulder, CO: Westview.

Brinton, Mary C. 2001. Married Women's Labor in East Asian Economies. In *Women's Working Lives in East Asia,* ed. M.C. Brinton. Stanford: Stanford University Press.

Cho, Hee Yeon. 2003. Die zweite Phase der Demokratisierung Südkoreas [The Second Phase of the South Korean Democratization]. *Korea Forum* No. 1/03: 11-13.

Demes, Helmut. 1998. Arbeitsmarkt und Beschäftigung [Labour Market and Employment]. In *Wirtschaft Japans: Strukturen zwischen Kontinuität und Wandel* [Japanese Economy: Structures between Continuity and Change], ed. Deutsches Institut für Japanstudien. Berlin/Heidelberg: Springer.

Kanatani, Chieko. 1997. Atarashii shakai undō toshiteno gyōsei seisaku eno sankaku. 'Kokuren josei no 10 nen' to josei undō no hirogari o jōsei shita mono [Participation in Administrative Policies as a New Social Movement: 'UN Decade for Women' and What Cultivated the Stretch of the Women's Movement]. In *Kansai daigaku jinken kenkyūshitsu kiyō* 36: 1-18.

Kateika no danjo kyōshū o susumeru kai, ed. 1997. *Kateika, otoko mo onna mo! Kōshite hiraita kyōshū e no michi* [Home Economics for Men and Women! How We Have Paved the Way to Home Economics for Men and Women]. Tokyo: Domesu shuppan.

Kim, El-Lim. 1999. *Namnyŏkoyong pyŏngdŭngpup simnyŏn-ŭi sŏngkwa-wa kwaje* [Achievements of the Equal Employment Law in the Past Ten Years and Further Tasks], KWDI: Seoul.

Kim, Kyounghee. 1998. *Gender Politics in South Korea: The Contemporary Women's Movement and Gender Policies, 1980-1996.* Dissertation. University of Wisconsin – Madison.

Kōdōsurukai kirokushū henshū iinkai, ed. 1999. *Mekishiko kara nyūyōku e. Kōdō suru onnatachi ga hiraita michi* [From Mexico to New York. The Way paged by Women in Action]. Tokyo: Miraisha.

KWDI Koren Women's Development Institute. 2003. *KWDI isimnyŏn* [20 years of the KWDI]. Seoul: KWDI.

Lee, Hyo-Jae. 1996. Pundansidae-ŭi Yŏsŏngundong [Women's movement in the time of the division of the country]. In *Yŏsŏngundong-ŭi ŏje-wa onŭl* [Women's movement – the Past and the Present], Lee, Hyo-Jae. Seoul: Chŏngusa.

Lenz, Ilse. 2001. Bewegungen und Veränderungen. Frauenforschung und Neue Frauenbewegungen in Deutschland [Movements and Changes. Women's Studies and New Women's Movements in Germany]. In *Zwischen Emanzipationsvision und Gesellschaftskritik* [Between Vision for Emancipation and Social Critics], eds. U. Hornung, S. Gümen and S. Weilandt. Münster: Westfälisches Dampfboot.

Lenz, Ilse. 2004. Globalization, Varieties of Gender Regimes, and Regulations for Gender Equality at Work. Unpublished Paper. Bochum.

Lyclama à Nijeholt, G., V. Vargas and S. Wieriga, eds. 1998. *Women's Movements and Public Policy in Europe, Latin America, and the Caribbean.* New York: Garland.

McBride, Dorothy E. and Amy G. Mazur. Forthcoming. Measuring Feminist Mobilization: Cross-National Convergence and Transnational Networks in Western Europe. In *Transnational Feminism: Women's Global Activism and Human Rights*, eds. M.M. Ferree and A.M. Tripp. New York: New York University Press.

Mazur, Amy G. 2002. *Theorizing Feminist Policy.* Oxford: Oxford University Press.

Meyer, M. L. and E. Prügl, eds. 1999. *Gender Politics in Global Governance.* Lanham/Boulder: Rowman & Littlefield.

Ministry of Political Affairs (II), Government of Republic of Korea. 1986. Initial Report submitted to CEDAW. http://www.kwdi.re.or accessed on Oct. 1, 2004.

Minuhoe. 1987. Ch'angnipsŏnŏnmun [Foundation Declaration]. http: //www.women-link.or.kr accessed on Sept. 1, 2000.

Mizoguchi, Akiyo, Yoko Saeki and Soko Miki. 1992, 1994 and 1995. *Shiryō nihon ūman ribu shi* [Historical materials on women's lib]. Kyoto: Shōkadō shoten. Vol. 1 – 3.

Naples, N.A. and M. Desai, eds. 2002. *Women's Activism and Globalization: Linking Local Struggles and Transnational Politics.* New York: Routledge.

Nishi, Kyoko. 1989. *Senryōka no nihon fujin seisaku* [Japan's women's policy during the Occupation]. Tokyo: Domesu shuppan. 2nd edition.

Nuita, Yoko, Mitsuko Yamaguchi and Kimiko Kubo [translated by Elizabeth J. Clarke]. 1994. The U.N. Convention on Eliminating Discrimination Against Women and the Status of Women in Japan. In *Women and Politics Worldwide*, eds. B.J. Nelson and N. Chowdhury. New Haven, CT: Yale University Press.

Ōsawa, Mari. 2000. Government Approaches to Gender Equality in the mid-1990s. *Social Science Japan Journal* 3(1): 3-19.

Scharpf, Fritz W. 2000. *Interaktionsformen: Akteurzentrierter Institutionalismus in der Politikforschung.* [Forms of Interaction: Actor-centered Institutionalism in political science] Opladen: Leske + Budrich.

Sohn, Bong-Scuk (1994): Women's Political Engagement and Participation in the Republic of Korea. In *Women and Politics Worldwide*, eds. B.J. Nelson and N. Chowdury. New Haven/London: Yale University Press.

Stetson, D.M. and A.G. Mazur, eds. 1995. *Comparative State Feminism.* Newbury Park, CA: Sage.

Suh, Mark B.M. 1993. The long march toward democracy: Assessment of the Political Modernization in the Republic of Korea. *Internationales Asienforum* 24 (1/2): 57-74.

Suh, Myung-Sun. 1989. Yushinch'ejeha-ŭi Kukka-wa Yŏsŏngdanch'e [The State and Women's Organizations during Yu-Shin Period]. *Yŏsŏnghak-nonjip*, 79-97.

True, Jacqui and Michael Mintrom. 2001. Transnational Networks and Policy Diffusion: The Case of Gender Mainstreaming. *International Studies Quarterly* 45: 27-57.

Woodward, Alison. 2001. Die McDonaldisierung der internationalen Frauenbewegung: Negative Aspekte guter Praktiken [The McDonaldization of the International Women's Movement: Negative Aspects of Good Practices]. *Zeitschrift für Frauenforschung und Geschlechterstudien* 19(1/2): 29-44.

Hiromi Tanaka and Mihee Hong

Yŏyŏn. 1992. Minjuyŏsŏng [Women for Democracy], Nr. 12.

Zwingel, Susanne. 2004. From international regime to transnational implementation network: Effects of the *Convention on the Elimination of all Forms of Discrimination Against Women* (CEDAW) on women's lives. Paper submitted to the 45th Annual Convention of the International Studies Association Montreal, March 17-20, 2004.

Women's Labour Activism in the Context of Globalisation: The Working Women's International Network in Osaka

Maria Sachiko Baier

1 Discussing Globalisation and Gender – A Theoretical Approach

Until the end of the 1990s, mainstream debates on globalisation more or less ignored gender issues or were shaped by the sense that women were seen as victims of broader economic and socio-political forces (Frank 1999). The relatively recent feminist debate on the relationship between globalisation and gender in German speaking countries has concluded that globalisation can be seen as a thoroughly 'sex-specific process' (Young 1999:1). Therefore, political scientists such as Erna Appelt, Eva Kreisky, Birgit Sauer, and Brigitte Young use a gender-sensitive approach, which does not merely focus on the consequences of globalisation on women (or on men) but rather on the contradictions within globalisation in order to expose the 'hegemonial discourses' (e.g. Appelt/Sauer 2001:130). Globalisation does not happen in a gender-free vacuum, but is instead, in itself, an 'inherently gendered process' (Kreisky/Sauer 1998:31), which powerfully transforms the economic, social, political and symbolic spaces (in national, regional and local gender regimes) as a discourse, which in turn effects globalisation processes (Appelt/Sauer 2001:130).

Feminist theory has various distinct hypotheses concerning the effects of globalisation. One hypothesis suggests that globalisation is an antidemocratic process of 'masculinism'; i.e. a strengthening of the political, symbolic, ideological exaggeration of maleness (Kreisky/Sauer 1998:32). Central to this view is that not only the production but also the reproduction of maleness is installed in modern political regulation patterns, as the gender order of the political sphere may easily adjust itself to social conditions (remasculinisation) (Kreisky 2004:41). Another feminist hypothesis focuses on the chances and barriers of an intervention by the women's movements in 'global governance'.[1] Nevertheless, we can find a wide range of positions from highly positive expectations to substantially improve women's conditions across the world and hope for new non-hierarchical, cooperative politics to the most pessimistic estimations that global governance restructures nation states, including all unequal international power relations (e.g. Lenz 2001, Ruppert 1998a:249-252, 1998b). Perhaps because of the outstanding achievements during the 1990s of worldwide mobilisation and networking by women's organisations, optimists hope that globalisation would weaken local patriarchal cultures and could possibly bring some advantages to women (Young 1999).

In this article, I shall investigate the impacts of globalisation on female labour. The situation in Japan, where women's (labour) activism experienced tremendous transformations during the 1990s (e.g. Bishop 2002, Lenz 2000:101-104) is described as an example of globalisation's impact. Women's groups became gradually aware of the significance of human rights norms and they started to seek more rigorous legislation against sex discrimination (Bishop 2002, Gelb 1999, 2003, Moriya 2000a, Yoneda 2000). Women struggled for concrete policy reform by insisting on the implementation of the Beijing Platform for Action[2] (*kōdō kōryō*) and the UN-Convention on the Elimination of All Forms of Discrimination against Women (*Josei sabetsu teppai jōyaku*, hereafter referred to as CEDAW)[3] in new nation-wide networks, which gained increasing popularity especially after the Fourth World Conference on Women in Beijing 1995 (*Pekin Josei Sekai Kaigi*) (Yoneda 2000:63). An explanation for the rise of new women's networks not only in Japan, but also in other parts of the world is that globalisation creates the most favourable conditions for networks and that these networks form the 'skeleton of the international women's movement' (Wichterich 2000:266). At the same time, the sphere of social problems became more globalised, with a necessity to tackle common problems and to pursue common aims beyond borders and cultures (Ruf 2000:66-67).

The central research interest is to understand how globalisation and increased opportunities affect the organisation, networking, communication and activities of Japanese women's groups. This goal will be met through a detailed description of a case study of the Working Women's (International) Network [WW(I)N][4] (hereafter referred to as WWN), which has successfully organised women workers across the boundaries between distinct firms and full-time and part-time employees. Feminist struggle is not confined to the grassroots level, but the feminist strategy for political change includes global institutions. This raises the question as to whether it is easier for Japanese women's groups to incorporate women's local and national issues through the transnational rather than the national level – mechanisms that have already been described in the case of the European Union (Schöpp-Schilling, E-Mail, January 6, 2006).

This article introduces results from a case study in Japan[5] that used participant observation, literature collected at the library of the Osaka Prefectural University and at the Women's Information Library (Dawn Center) in Osaka and interviews with 15 activists and experts during fieldwork in 2001. The interview methodology included semi-structured 'expert interviews' (Meuser and Nagel 1991)[6] in Japanese or English, depending on the mother tongue of the interview partners: nine Japanese WWN activists, two Australian Women Helping Women (WHW) activists and one Japanese WHW activist. In addition to this, interviews were conducted with three Japanese experts in contact with WWN; Harano Sachiko, who appeared as a lawyer for the plaintiffs in the cases of Sumitomo Metal and Sumitomo Life insurance; Yoneda Masumi, an international human rights law and gender equality expert and Tsujimoto Yōkō, a journalist working for Yomiuri Shinbun. This paper uses pseudonyms instead of the real activist's names to preserve privacy. After interview transcription, Meuser's and Nagel's 'analysis strategy' was used to build categories of given topics by integrating them in theory (Meuser/Nagel 1991:457-465). The author translated all the interviews.

Before introducing WWN's work, I will look at the most recent developments within the broader Japanese women's movement after the Fourth World Conference on Women in Beijing 1995 (Section 2). Section 3 addresses the situation of working women still facing gender discrimination despite the amended Equal Employment Opportunity Law (implementation 1999, *Danjo kōyō kikai kintōhō*, hereafter referred to as EEOL). Discrimination against women working for various branches of Sumitomo Company is described as an example of gender disparities in Japanese companies. Supporting these female workers' claims in court became a central task of the Working Women's Network. Section 4 examines WWN as a new post-Beijing-group, whereby I highlight WWN's development from its foundation to its consolidation and to its professionalisation. In Section 4.1, a closer look is given to the "cocktail mix" of WWN's different activities ranging from those of passionate public protests to routine educational and advocacy activities (both seen as necessary for effective change). Another specific feature of WWN is alliances between feminists of different backgrounds (Gelb 2003:38), thus I focus on networking (Section 4.2), and also reveal the stratification within the network. Section 4.3 introduces the Sumitomo court cases (with a special focus on the Sumitomo Electronic court case) and examines how WWN can make "use" of the CEDAW. Section 4.4 explores *gaiatsu* (foreign pressure) as an important tool for WWN in and outside Japan. The conclusion (Section 5) summarizes and draws on the future perspectives of WWN.

2　The Post-Beijing Women's Movement in Japan – in the Light and Shadow of Globalisation

Some publications on gender relations in Japan argue that the Japanese women's movement in the 1990s is limited to the local sphere, fragmented and very loosely organised (e.g. Liddle/Nakajima 2000). This clearly distinguishes it from the US women's movement with its big national umbrella networks (Gelb 2003:31). Due to the fact that we can hardly find a common coordination after 1975, it almost seems that the movement lost its 'subject' (Mae 1997:240). At the beginning of the 1970s, women activists of many *uman ribu* (women's liberation) groups aimed at transforming cultural patriarchal norms by raising women's self-consciousness. In the later movement, women became more single-issue oriented and tried to change particular social conditions (Tanaka 1995:351). The Japanese women's movement in the 1990s may not appear as structured as the US women's movement. However, seemingly loosely connected groups cooperate to influence Japanese institutions as well as policies (Gelb 2003:31). Before 1995, the year of the Fourth World Conference on Women, women's networks organised various campaigns on the Equal Employment Opportunity Law, on computerization, on health and on reproductive rights (Lenz 2000:101; see also Tanaka/Hong in this volume).

Even if the Japanese women's movement seems calmer and more conservative now, there is continuity, the movement's impact has increased and the participation has noticeably expanded (Mae 1997:240). There are only 51 officially registered NGOs (Isis International Manila 2002:19), but the 600 page Japanese women's directory, *Onnatachi no Benrichō*, published in 2000, lists around 779 women's groups in different areas such as psyche and body, anti-discrimination, anti-war, anti-nuclear power, environmentalism, children and school, political participation, women's rights, women and work, lesbianism/sexuality, old age and human rights (Onnatachi no Benrichō San Henshū Shitsu 2000). From 1995 onwards, the women's networks emphasized political activities and influencing legislation (Lenz 2000:101). This, and other developments, need to be seen in the context of the Fourth World Conference on Women in September 1995 in Beijing, which is indeed a 'new turning point and expansion' (ibid., own translation) of the Japanese women's movement (Yoneda 2000), not only because of its high number of participants.

Maria Sachiko Baier

An estimated, 5,000 Japanese women (of the 30,000 total participants) are said to have participated in the NGO Forum in Huairou (Yokohama-shi Josei Kyōkai 1997:234).[7] In contrast to the World Conference on Women in Nairobi held a decade earlier, Japanese women have started to reflect on Japan in the Asian context (Moriki 1997:1) and human rights in relation to the issues of Japan's system of enforced military prostitution during the Second World War,[8] with Asian women migrant workers in Japan and, as well, as with militarism and sexual violence by US-soldiers in Okinawa prefecture (Mackie 2003:222-223). Moreover, during the conference, Japanese women's groups started lobbying the Japanese government's representatives to push the Platform for Action in national legislation (Inoue 1997:204, Saito 2000:254).

After the Fourth World Conference on Women in Beijing, there are four developments to be observed within (and around) the Japanese women's movement.

- The Fourth World Conference on Women encouraged the empowerment of Japanese women and the further development of gender-equality policies. Women who participated in the Beijing Conference or in the NGO Forums returned to Japan and founded groups (e.g. the Beijing Joint Accountability Committee, known as Peking JAC) for the implementation of the Beijing Platform for Action and strengthened those networks (Yoneda 2002:2). The newly built networks introduced international perspectives (*gurōbaru na shiten*) and proposed concrete measures to the local and central governments (Moriya 2000a:273). Another effect, probably connected to newly-organised schools for aspiring female politicians (Moriya 2000b), was that more women began to participate in regional and national governments, although female politicians are still marginalized compared with other developed countries. Following the Beijing World Conference on Women, 38 prefectural women's centres and 200 centres, built by local governments, have been set up. Policy changes that promoted gender equality included the amendment of the Equal Employment Opportunity Law and the introduction of the Basic Law for a Gender-equal Society (*Danjo kyōdō sankaku shakai kihonhō*, implementation 1999),[9] which also obliged local governments to create and implement gender-equality policies (Yoneda 2002:2).

- The Japanese women's movement also includes extensive use of modern information and communication technology. In particular, newly formed networks have access to and profit from the Internet (Isis International Manila 2002).

- Some in the Japanese women's movement welcome support by male activists – an indication of a reinterpretation and extension of *feminizumu* (feminist social and cultural criticism) and feminist struggle through gender (*jendā*). At the same time, a common female identity and a seemingly natural gender order is questioned and deconstructed by feminists (Lenz 2000:101).

- Furthermore, the Japanese women's movement is intensively discussing the issue of gender and ethnicity. This issue, which has already been discussed in the 1970s (ibid. 101–102), is present through topics such as migration, sex tourism and forced prostitution (Yunomae in Kitazawa/Matsui/Yunomae 1996:32) and indicates that Japan indeed has an 'imperial and colonial past' (Mackie 1998:599).

3   Women's Work in the Japanese Labour Market

In Japan, working women still face serious gender-based differences. Although women's enthusiasm to continue working has increased every year, women still suffer great problems to continue working after marriage, childbirth and child rearing. The typical M-shaped employment pattern based on age groups still shows the difficulty to arrange family responsibilities and job (Takenaka 2001:1). One of the laws, which should assure gender equality in the field of employment, is the EEOL introduced in 1985 (implementation 1986)[10] and amended in 1997 (implementation 1999) and again in June 2006. Japanese women's groups were actively fighting for the introduction of this law (Hayashi 1995:42) that was introduced to comply with the requirements of the CEDAW, which in turn was not ratified by the Japanese government until the end of the UN Women's Decade in 1985 (Weber 1998:54; Tanaka/Hong in this volume).

Although the 1985 EEOL was introduced to create more options for women to break the glass ceiling, this has not been the case for the majority of women workers. In reaction to the 1985 EEOL, 42.3 percent of companies with more than 5,000 or more employees and 11.3 percent of companies between 300 and 900 employees (Lam 1993:212) have introduced the so-called two career tracks for regular workers that is, in fact, based on gender segregation. Although regular women workers are formally allowed to enter the managerial track (*sōgō shoku)*, most women end up in the general track (*ippan shoku*), where career options for them are very limited. A survey conducted by the Ministry of Health, Labour and Welfare in 2004 found out that the ratio of women in managerial track positions is only five percent (The Asahi Shinbun, December 27, 2005). Karen Shire argues that there are two main reasons for companies to keep the two career tracks (or any other gender based personnel management practices). First, the company's personnel management system is strongly based on the belief that women workers by themselves give up their jobs upon marriage and child rearing. Second, companies assume that women workers in the *ippan shoku* lack qualifications to be promoted to the *sōgō shoku*. Both assumptions are not true. Besides the fact that the length of employment of women workers has increased during the 1990s, *ippan shoku* – a track that has been associated mainly with easy administrative duties – has also started to integrate qualified work (e.g. sales, customer service). The introduction of information technology and the demand for competent knowledge-intense services are two central reasons for this new trend. Thus, differences between those two tracks are less defined by the differences of tasks. *Ippan shoku* is rather a track that is characterized by low wages and almost no possibilities for promotions. In retrospect, the 1985 EEOL and its revision (1997) could not challenge the gender based recruitment- and personnel management practices (Shire 2003:248-250).

In spite of the revision of the EEOL (which *prohibits* discrimination towards women), gender equality is far from being achieved and discrimination continues. The number of working women in precarious employment situations has enormously increased: While 54.8 percent of the female workforce and 88,9 percent of male workforce are regular workers, 45.2 percent of female workers are employed as non-fulltime workers, such as part-time workers, time-fixed workers, and temporary workers in 1999 (compared to 11,1 percent for men) (Kumazawa 1999:56). Another serious problem is the disparity of wages. Women workers receive 66.5 percent of the male worker's wages (1992: 61.5 percent) (Kōsei Rōdōsho 2002). Also, the disparity in wages between female part-time workers and female fulltime workers has increased further. In 2000, a female part-time worker received only 66.9 percent of the female fulltime worker's income (Sakai referring to Ministry of Health, Labour and Welfare, Basic Statistical Survey on Wage Structure, 2001). According to Haken Rōdō Network (a network that supports the rights of temporary workers), the average wage for temporary workers dropped from about 1,704 Yen per hour (~12.23 Euro) in 1994 to 1,430 Yen per hour (~10.26 Euro) in 2004 (Weathers 2005:2).

However, another positive development can be seen along with the passage of EEOL. This new law may have helped to raise awareness and expectations for better chances in the workplace and led to political activities of frustrated women workers (Gelb 2003:35). A heterogeneous women's movement could point to the deficiencies of the 1985 EEOL and demand sanctions for discrimination during the consultation process in the Ministry of Health, Labour and Welfare. Some important factors that led to the 1997 government decision to revise the 1985 EEOL include: pressure from media and women's networks, "delegitimisation" of the EEOL, good internal negotiations, little organised opposition (Lenz 1998:166-167) and Japan's concern about its global image (Boyle/Liu 2001:10). An important international influence was the CEDAW Committee's Concluding Comments that evaluated Japan's compliance with the CEDAW (Schöpp-Schilling, E-Mail, January 6, 2006). In regard to the 1997 EEOL, a part of the Japanese women's movement criticizes the lack of understanding for the need to define indirect discrimination, the lack of a job evaluation system to create "equal pay for equal work" and the lack of independent administrative organisations, which can issue orders to eliminate gender discrimination in the workplace. In June 2006, yet again, the EEOL was amended, also because of criticism by the Japanese women's movement and the Concluding Comments by the CEDAW Committee. Although the new revisions of EEOL address indirect discrimination, women's groups such as WWN are sceptical and criticize the development that companies, especially in the construction industry, have started to abolish the two track system in favour of new discriminatory methods of personnel management (WWIN 2006b:1). These developments indicate that women workers are not yet perceived as long-term workers by Japanese companies (Shire 2003:249).

Another approach to building a gender-equal society is to file a complaint at court. Generally, court cases have helped to increase public awareness for gender discrimination and harassment (Gelb 2003:54). From 1995 on, we can see an increase of court cases against sexual discrimination in wages and promotions (Yoneda 2002:2). In 2000, there were 20 wage discrimination cases, mostly from women who had been working without a break for more than 20 years (Japan NGO Report 1999). A good example of the character of discrimination is the Sumitomo Company's policy towards women employees. Women who started working at the company in the 1960s and 1970s (thus before the implementation of the EEOL) have suffered severe discrimination in wage and promotion due to an extremely discriminatory personnel management. In the case of Sumitomo Electric, male high-school graduates were hired on a head-office basis as prospective management personnel and then promoted to management positions after 17 years, which is in sharp contrast to the situation of female employees with the same educational background and the same length of service in company who were hired on a branch basis for clerical work. They had no chances other than to stay in the clerical positions and they had to accept monthly wages as much as 250,000 Yen (~1,799.97 Euro) lower than their male colleagues (e.g. WWN 2004:13). The women employed at various branches of the Sumitomo Company who filed a suit identified this discrimination as resulting from the two track employment management system, which in their eyes is nothing else than the continuation of gender-segregation politics and has to be recognized as indirect discrimination (e.g. WWN 2004a). Aside from the fact, that they received low wages and no additional vocational training, they were burdened by monotonous routine work (Mori 2001: Interview), received no relevant information, were even denied access to meetings (Yamanaka 2001:Interview) and were discouraged by their superiors. At work, one plaintiff (Sumitomo Chemical) was told: 'Remain a cornerstone of the company until retirement age' (*Teinen made kaisha no ishizue ni natte kudasai*). Another plaintiff (Sumitomo Chemical) was told that 'women should be guarding the home front' (*Josei wa jūgo no mori ni tesshite kudasai*) (Ishida/Yatani 2004). To protest discrimination, the women first went to the Labour Union to ask for support, but the Labour Union denied its support and even refused to provide the Sumitomo women with data on wages (*Nihon kara no tegami gurūpu* 1995:20-21) because of 'data security reasons' (Yoneda 2001, interview). With the solidarity of some male colleagues (Mori 2001, interview), the women could collect wage data and through this could 'clarify the real discriminatory situation they face' (Nihon kara no tegami gurūpu 1995:21).

Then the Sumitomo women went for mediation at the Osaka Women's and Young Worker's Office (Ōsaka Fujin Shōnen Shitsu, regional office of the Ministry of Health, Labour, Welfare), an institution provided by the Equal Employment Opportunity Law.[11] However, the procedure could not be initiated because the company refused (Shirafuji 2000a:21, 24).[12] Finally, the women thought that there was no other way than to take the matter to court. In the Sumitomo cases, nine women employed at Sumitomo Electric, Sumitomo Metal and Sumitomo Chemical started to file a suit on the 8th of August 1995 at the Osaka district court to correct wage and promotion discrimination (Agora Ōsaka 2000:78). A few months later, in December 1995, twenty-two women employed at Sumitomo Life Insurance started their lawsuit against the company. It was the same time, when activists saw the need to found a new network. The basic spirit behind this network was the thought: 'If we cannot rely on our labour unions or the Japanese government, why not develop our own network and make our own organization?' (WWIN/HP 2003)

4   The Working Women's (International) Network in Osaka: The Way to Gender Equality Goes Beyond Borders

In October 1995, (e.g. WWN 2000a:93), immediately after the Fourth World Conference on Women in Beijing, 100 women (Yoneda 2000:64) decided to found the Working Women's (International) Network (Wākingu Uimenzu Nettowāku or Hataraku Josei no Nettowāku) in Osaka to support women who face discrimination in the workplace (WWN 2000a:93).[13] Since then, its membership has grown to 800 women (Yoneda 2000:64), including women workers, feminist lawyers, scholars, plaintiffs and would-be plaintiffs of sex discrimination suits (WWIN/HP 2002). Because of their concern for women's working conditions, WWN may show characteristics of a women's labour union. However, the activists would prefer to support the formation of independent women's unions; the WWN's main purpose is to support the Sumitomo plaintiffs, to work for a more rigorous EEOL and to improve the status of working women in general (WWIN 2006a:1).

WWN has a long history. Even though the network was founded in 1995, the roots go back to four different regional groups and some of its activities can even be traced back to the 1970s[14] (Koyama 2001, interview; Murano 2001, interview; Yamanaka 2001, interview). One of the groups active after the introduction of the Equal Employment Opportunity Law was the Network Course on the EEOL (founded in 1990) that grew out of a study group (WWN 2001a) to discuss the rights of working women (Murano 2001). By 2006, WWN has developed into a professional network, which has experienced large-scale changes concerning its contents, strategies, communication and structure. For example, the WWN has expanded into extensive international lobbying activities towards officers and committee members at the International Labour Organization (ILO), the European Union, the Committee on Economic, Social and Cultural Rights (CESCR) or the CEDAW Committee (Koedo 2005a:1, 2005b:5-6). One can see an individual and collective learning process from the very first international activities of some previous groups to the present network. In the following part, I trace WWN's development from the very beginning to the present, discussing four major events as examples of its international activism.

As early as 1985, some of the women from the previous groups of WWN attended the Third World Conference of Women in Nairobi. One woman from the Japanese group, Circle of Women Working for Trade Companies, noted the difficulties to simply communicate in English: 'At that time we were also engaged in peace and we brought photos from Hiroshima to the conference. We showed them the photos, because we could not speak [English]' (Koyama 2001, interview). Also, Japanese participants in general realised during their exchange with other Asian feminists that they had been unaware of other Asian women's problems (Moriki 1997:1). Such was the case of some of the women from the previous groups of WWN, when they were asked about Japan's economic invasion (*keizai shinryaku*) and about sex tourism of Japanese men in Asia. A representative of a group that merged into WWN noted that for Japanese women's groups it was painful not to be perceived as victims but as assailants by other Asian and African women (Shōji 1996:4). Nevertheless, this experience motivated the present WWN president to intensively engage with other Asian women by participating in a network dealing with issues such as Japanese aggression (Murano 2001, interview).

Almost a decade later, women activists could already make use of institutional mechanisms for monitoring women's working conditions. In January 1994, one and a half year before the establishment of WWN, women activists employed at Sumitomo Metal, Chemical and Electronic together with the International Year of Women Osaka North Ward Association went to New York (cf. Ikeda 1997:14) to explain their very first alternative report[15] entitled 'A Letter from Japan' (an alternative report from 10 Japanese women's NGOs) to the UN Committee on the Elimination of Discrimination against Women (hereafter referred to as CEDAW Committee) that was going to review Japan's Second and Third reports to the CEDAW (CEDAW/C/JPN/2, CEDAW/C/JPN/3) on national actions taken to implement its provisions. In the alternative report, activists called attention to the Japanese government's failure not to have fully implemented the CEDAW into the EEOL (Nihon kara no tegami gurūpu 1995). At that time it was helpful for the activists that the

CEDAW Committee not only accepted additional information from representatives of non-state organisations, but also allowed them to report orally in a non-formal meeting (cp. Schöpp-Schilling 2004:12-13). During such a non-formal meeting, Silvia Rose Cartwright, New Zealand member of the CEDAW Committee (1993-2000), praised the detailed report 'A letter from Japan' with its persuasive power (Shōji/Koedo 2005:127). Another woman recalled that experts from the CEDAW Committee encouraged them to take legal steps: 'The foreign women encouraged us and confirmed our opinion that the abolishment of discrimination is important and self-evident (...). Then we went to the Osaka Women's and Young Worker's Office. That was the basis. Then we went to court. If we had not travelled to New York, we would not have gone to court' (Kitano 2001, interview). In retrospect, New York 1994 could be seen as a cornerstone for all following international activities: 'We gained a lot of energy, because we had experienced something like this. Since then, it became a habit to go abroad' (Mori 2001, interview).

During WWN's consolidation process shortly before and after its formation (which was at the same time as the beginning of the Sumitomo court cases), WWN could further develop international orientation and gain a more global understanding for women's human rights. At the parallel forum of the Fourth World Conference on Women in Huairou 1995, WWN members (at that time the group was called 'Working Women in Japan') presented their own workshop (Shōji 1996:3) examining the question: 'Why do Japanese women only earn half of men's wages?' (Murano 2001, interview). Listeners, especially those from the so-called Third World countries, did not only bring a comparative view into discussion, but also made statements critical towards capitalism which attached a new meaning to gender discrimination in Japan. Some women feared that other Asian countries could take over Japanese employment practices, including the exploitation of women (Suzuki 2001, interview). The workshop was perceived as a fruitful exchange that could strengthen the understanding of each other (Koyama 2001, interview).

Five years later, WWN participated at Beijing+5, the Special Session of the UN General Assembly entitled 'Women 2000: Gender Equality, Development and Peace for the Twenty-first Century' (*Beijin+5 Kokuren Josei 2000nen Kaigi*) in New York (Koedo 2000:2), which reviewed the progress in the implementation of the Beijing Declaration and the Platform of Action. Beforehand, women's NGOs were invited to submit their own alternative reports (Yoneda 2000:64). This in turn propelled the development of a Japan-wide network, which was set up as a coalition of women's groups in Japan to write an alternative report in 1999. The network decided to compile sub-reports (including WWN's comment) along the 12 critical areas of the Platform for Action, around the topics of poverty, education and training, health, violence, conflict, economy, power and decision-making, advancement of women, human rights, communication systems (especially the media), and environment and girls (Japan NGO Report Preparatory Committee 2000). As many as 300 organisations and individuals sent their comments for the report which was finalized at a public meeting and then published as Japan NGO Alternative Report (Yoneda 2000:64). WWN did not only participate in this greater network of Japanese women NGOs; at the Special Session, WWN achieved the status of an accredited NGO for the first time in its history[16] (Koedo 2000:2) – another step towards professionalisation. Next to taking part in the Beijing+5 conference as observers, WWN members held their own workshop (The Sumitomo Trials and the Discrimination of Japanese Women), spoke to Japanese government's representatives, distributed flyers in front of the Sumitomo America building in New York and exchanged data with institutions such as the Union of Needle trades, Industrial and Textile Employees (UNITE), the Equal Employment Opportunity Commission (EEOC) and the Legal Defence Fund (LDF) (WWN 2000a).

The development of policy-oriented, temporary Japan-wide networks continues. In 2002, Japanese women's groups, including WWN, formed another coalition of 42 NGOs [Nihon Josei Sabetsu Teppai Jōyaku NGO Nettowāku, Japan NGO Network for CEDAW (JNNC)] to submit their summary shadow report to the CEDAW Committee, before it reviewed Japan's report on the implementation of the CEDAW in Japan (Wijers-Hasegawa 2003). Such a development shows the highly organised elements of the Japanese women's movement that participates in this kind of monitoring process. WWN also continues its own international activities: In 2003, members went to the CEDAW Working Group and to the CEDAW Session examining the Japanese report in New York. In February 2005, members participated at the Beijing+10 Session and in June 2005 at the Women's Worlds Conference 2005 in Seoul (WWIN 2006a:1).

4.1 Communication, actions and places of networking

As '[t]he women's movement is more a process than an organisation, more a river than a riverbed' (Milz 1991:57), WWN's international activities and its success cannot be understood without considering its base, its roots in the local sphere and its various communication forms and its networking. The WWN's grassroots meet in diverse places for diverse reasons. Along with regular plena, English lessons or (when needed) specific project groups in the living rooms of activists (Kitano 2001, interview; Mori 2001, interview) or small talks during lunch break in the canteen of the Sumitomo building (Mori 2001, interview), women can meet at the Osaka Dawn Center, a women's centre established by the Osaka prefectural government in 1994. The Dawn Center is opened 12 hours a day from 9:30 a.m. to 9:30 p.m. and has already attracted more than 4 million visitors during the first nine years. It is equipped with a big event hall, an editing room and audiovisual room, diverse meeting rooms, a child play room, a counselling room, a women's library and a performance space used for special events, concerts or gallery exhibitions (Dawn Center 2006). Since many of the WWN activities (seminars, workshops, press conferences…) are taking place in the Dawn Center, it became a kind of "communication hub" for WWN members. Since 2001, WWN's office is opposite the Dawn Center close to the feminist lawyer's office (Tanaka 2001, interview), thus a little bit closer to the "centre". WWN women do not only come to the Dawn Center to exchange information with other women, they also rent the performance space for big symposia (e.g. WWN 2001b), often with international guest speakers. For example, in July 1998, Beate Schöpp-Schilling (CEDAW Committee member of Germany and CEDAW Vice-chairperson) and Ursula Rust (jurist teaching at Bremen university) were invited by WWN to the symposium 'The International Level of Gender Equality – Learning from the EU and the CEDAW' (Agora Osaka 2000:78). Schöpp-Schilling regularly gives lectures to WWN (WWIN/HP 2005). In 2003, 550 people came to listen to her lecture on indirect discrimination and the Optional Protocol to the CEDAW in Fukuoka, Tokyo and Osaka (WWIN 2003).

Other activities also include street actions. WWN members distribute flyers in front of train stations, discuss with other workers, or they demonstrate in front of the court to protest unjust court decisions. For example, on the 31st of August 2000, some 330 people formed a "human chain" (*ningen no kusari*) around the Osaka District Court to protest the rejection of the suit filed against Sumitomo Electric (Agora Osaka 2000:79) and called for a judicial reform (*shihō kaikaku*) (The Asahi Shinbun, August 31, 2000). The action attracted a big response from the major Japanese newspapers (see The Asahi Shinbun, August 31, 2000; The Daily Yomiuri, September 1, 2000; Izumi, Manichi Shinbun, August 31, 2000; The Japan Times, September 1, 2000, Nihon Keizai Shinbun, August 31, 2000). The newspaper Asahi Shinbun had headlines, 'To surround the Osaka District Court with women's anger. Resistance through a "human chain"' (The Asahi Shinbun, 31.8.2000). On the same day, the judge had received 41 protest E-mails (Agora Ōsaka 2000:79). WWN's actions are not restricted to the local scenery. Even in New York, activists spread flyers in front of the Sumitomo Life America Incorporated building to protest against unfavourable working conditions for female workers in Japanese companies (Yamamoto 2000:42).

In contrast to street actions are WWN's domestic lobbying activities at the Ministry of Health, Labour and Welfare, at the Ministry of Foreign Affairs, at the Ministry of Justice, at the Cabinet Secretary, with some Diet members, at the Supreme Court, at the Japanese Trade Union Confederation Rengō or at the local ILO Office in Tokyo (WWIN 2002a:4-5, WWN 2002b:2-3) as well as WWN's international lobby activities, mainly in Europe and the United States (WWN 2005). At the international level, activists who can travel abroad (Toda 2001, interview) seek to establish contacts with other women's organisations, legal or other experts, or functionaries of international organisations or even with Committee members (Mori 2001, interview). For example, by submitting their alternative reports they can give their opinions in non-formal meetings with the Committees. Often the handing in of shadow reports for instance at the CEDAW Committee (in 1992 and 2002) or the participation at an international conference on women's issues are a good reason for WWN to subsequently lobby domestic institutions (e.g. WWIN 2002a:4-5, 2002b:2-3). Furthermore, WWN is participating in campaigns such as the Equality Action 21 (Kintō Taigū Akushon 21)[17], which is also supported by researchers, lawyers, parliamentarians and other women's groups. Originally initiated by 30 people, the campaign's supporters increased to 800 people after a year (Sakai 2001:2). The Equality Action 21 campaign has three main objectives: First, the campaign demands government actions against indirect discrimination in employment; second, the government adopt the ILO and UN conventions for equal remuneration and to amend the Part-time Work Law (enacted 1993); and, third, to achieve "real" gender equality (Kintōhō Nissennen Kyanpēn 2000).

In times of globalisation, WWN cultivates cyber connections. WWN's website[18] was already set up in 1996 (WWN 2001a). It contains regularly updated information on the court cases including the final judgements on the Sumitomo cases, newspaper articles, a calendar of court meetings and lectures, a list of WWN's publications, a news section and other general information on WWN's work in Japanese. A comprehensive overview is also given on the English sub-pages (WWIN/HP 2005). E-Mail communication simplifies international as well as local and national exchange and brings activists to see things from a different point of view. Furthermore, activists appreciate the informality of the Internet: 'It is important that Internet exists. I just send the e-mail, although my English is not that good. It's only important to write and to send it'. The Internet is not only perceived as a chance to communicate with people. The same activist also points to the necessity for the network: 'If you want to become global, you need the Internet and English'. Since 2001,

WWN also built its own mailing list, which was used by 180-200 members in 2001 throughout Japan (Koyama 2001, interview). In addition to English-Japanese booklets (WWN 1997, 2000a, 2000b, 2004) which include research data and reports on discrimination, WWN produces a monthly newsletter in Japanese with a circulation of 1000 copies (Murano, E-Mail, December 16, 2003) and sporadically English newsletters to inform international sympathizers on the latest developments of the court cases. Often those English newsletters are produced in advance of international conferences and are then distributed on the spot (Koedo 2000:3). What Ilse Lenz has stated for the women's movement in general is also true for WWN: information on WWN's activities can reach the semi-public space through the Japanese newsletter and other publications available for all interested people at the women's library in the Dawn Center (Lenz 2000:128).

4.2 Networking towards gender equality

One of the most active woman, Ms. Koyama, noted, '*Interpersonal relationships are the most important*' (Koyama 2001). A great part of WWN's power comes through networking with heterogeneous actors. WWN successfully joins efforts of women directly suffering discrimination and concerned people such as experts (e.g. university professors, lawyers), lobbyists from international women's organisations, individuals from the CEDAW Committee, students and male activists, journalists and also other women's groups both in Japan and abroad. An important advantage for WWN in their actions is their high acceptance by the mass media. Despite mass media generally reporting on Japanese women's movement's activities only when there are 'spectacular actions or demonstrations' (Lenz 2000:129, own translation), WWN continually receives coverage. Between 1994 and 2004, local and international newspapers and journals reported 228 times on WWN and the Sumitomo court cases; TV stations broadcasted reports on their activities 31 times (WWN 2005:514-528). How can the positive media coverage be explained? There are a few reasons for this: Women activists did establish and keep in close touch with mass media even before the foundation of WWN. Also, the women journalists themselves are motivated to report on discrimination, because they 'see it as their own problem' and ask themselves 'What happens if they themselves get children?' (Koyama 2001, interview) Another activist, Ms. Mori, said that mass media presents the Sumitomo women as 'pioneers' and added: 'We were supported by the mass media, because we are not the only ones with this problem. This problem exists in entire Japan' (Mori 2001, interview). Women's and men's solidarity and the common goal to achieve a gender-equal society are the bases of networking. Networking allows women to gain more power and knowledge; however, the network can also cause further stratification, as illustrated by the following three examples.

One example is men's involvement. A new development within the general Japanese women's movement is support through gender-sensitive emancipated men who developed a critical attitude towards traditional gender role models in Japanese society. As Lenz has observed: 'Parts of the women's movement pose the "men's question within the women's question", that means, they seek for an alliance with the (small) men's movement and call on men to support the women's or men's liberation' (Lenz 1998:157, 2000:101; see Hashimoto 2001:3). Ten per cent of the WWN-members are men (Koyama 2001). The international members of the WWN-subsidiary group Women Helping Women (WHW), located in Kyoto had different opinions about male participation. Non-Japanese members argued against the regular participation of men and allowed men a very restricted access to its own WHW meetings (Tanaka 2001). One activist explained this with the wish to have a 'feminist grassroots group', in which 'women's issues could be discussed freely' (Roberts 2001). While at first glance, it appeared that Japanese women in WHW supported and non-Japanese women were against men's participation, a closer look revealed that Japanese members of WWN had different opinions, too. Whereas one woman emphasized, 'If men were denied the opportunity to participate, the WWN movement could not have been successful' (Tanaka 2001); another woman said: 'Most men think they are feminists, but when we discuss intensively, we have different opinions. It is strange that they think they are feminists' (Toda 2001). An article in a WWN booklet quoted a male WWN-member pointing out that the future of men's equal participation is an important task for the movement (Takahara 2000:44). Despite various opinions about men's participation, male supporters are seen as important allies. Another point of stratification can be seen in the past cooperation of WWN and its international support group Women Helping Women (WHW). WHW-members from English-speaking countries and Japanese women discussed feminism, violence, pornography, sexual harassment and sexism in mass media. Regional activities included an anti-pink-flyers-campaign (flyers often found in telephone boxes or in post-boxes advertising sex services) (Tanaka 2001, interview), and they participated with an information desk at international festivals, where they also distributed information on the Sumitomo court cases (Roberts 2001, interview) and collected donations for WWN (Flowers 2001, interview; Roberts 2001, interview). Furthermore, WHW supported WWN by helping with translations into English (Koedo/Shōji 2005:134,141), collecting signatures from abroad for a petition supporting the Sumitomo court cases (Roberts 2001) and by going to demonstrations and to several court meetings (Flowers 2001; Kitano 2001, interview; Koyama 2001, interview; Roberts 2001, interview; Suzuki 2001, interview). WWN-members also see this kind of support of foreign women as *gaiatsu* (Suzuki 2001, interview), while non-Japanese WHW members saw this pragmatically, as one Australian woman told me: 'If my non-Japaneseness can help, it is ok' (Flowers 2001, interview). Although there are different expectations and aims, WHW members showed their solidarity by joining the court meetings, distributing flyers and participating in demonstrations. This cooperation was seen as a great support by WWN.

Within WWN, a well-established team of a few activists and experts can travel internationally (Sumida 2001, interview; Toda 2001, interview). Although in theory, all interested women could participate in international activities, only women who can take time to go abroad and who can independently pay the travel expenses actually attend the international meetings. Ms. Toda said: 'Everyone who wants to go can go, but I have a small child. Even so, I would love to go' (Toda 2001, interview). She also mentioned another problem: 'I think they are great [WWN's activities abroad]. I cannot go, because I cannot speak [English]' (Toda 2001, interview). Members who are experienced international travellers act as agents and help to assert interests of women with less international experiences. Ms. Nonaka noted that this international group also helps groups with much less international orientation: 'One woman employed by Sumitomo Life Insurance went to a conference at the European Union in Brussels. She could not speak English. Because there were also other women from WWN it was okay, but it would have been hard for her alone' (Nonaka 2001, interview). None of the interviewed women saw the existence of such a group as a problem; they rather see this as a form of work sharing. This aligns with Lenz's observations: Although formal representatives or leaders exist in 70 percent of Japanese women's groups; 'group processes and communication in turn [contain] flattening and horizontal mechanisms', so that possible power differences are evened out (Lenz 2000:125).

4.3 Tackling the problem of indirect discrimination: using the CEDAW during the Sumitomo court cases

Local, national and international activities were done to attract attention to discriminatory employment practices in Japan. However, one of WWN's core activities has been to support plaintiffs at court. Media paid special attention to the Sumitomo Electric court case and to WWN ongoing analyses of discrimination. Because this case was the first that used the CEDAW, as a result, the court had to present its own interpretation on the CEDAW (Yoneda 2000:69).

In the Sumitomo Electric case, the plaintiffs argued that the Japanese government was in violation of the CEDAW's Article 2, which demands state parties to find 'appropriate means' to end discrimination 'without delay'. The plaintiffs argued that the gender segregated track model should have been abolished with the introduction of the Equal Employment Opportunity Law, claiming that gender-based hiring, in times before the CEDAW came into effect, led to negative consequences even after its ratification. The Japanese government held the view that discrimination does not necessarily have to be eliminated immediately, that the equality between men and women should be achieved progressively and that the CEDAW does not indicate that it should be applied retroactively. In addition, the Japanese government argued (and the court agreed) that according to Article 8 of the 1985 EEOL, women and men enjoy the same rights in recruitment, hiring, assignment, promotion, vocational training, fringe benefits, compulsory retirement age, and retirement only under the same conditions. Also, the Osaka District Court dismissed their claim by stating that the hiring track model was not illegal before the enactment and that neither the CEDAW nor the EEOL were retroactive. This view, the plaintiffs responded, would violate the Vienna Convention on the Law of Treaties (Article 28 = non-retroactivity of treaties) and the CEDAW (Article 1, 2 and 11)[19] (WWN 2004a, 2004b).

The ruling was handed down on the 31st of July 2000. The Osaka district court stated that the Sumitomo Electric's personnel management had practiced gender discrimination and thus had violated article 14 of the Japanese Constitution (women's equal rights in civil affairs), but it also held the view that gender-based division of work was widely accepted in Japanese society between 1965 and 1975 and that the practice of gender-based hiring at that time was not against 'public order and good morals' (kōjo ryōzoku) (Osaka District Court 2000:6,8). After having appealed against this ruling to the Osaka Appeals Court, an amicable settlement was achieved in December 2003. Judge Igaki Toshio of the Osaka Appeals Court sharply criticized the ruling of the Osaka district court stating: 'Allowing vestiges of discrimination to remain unchanged because of the social consciousness of an earlier age ignores the way society has evolved.' Finally, Sumitomo Electric agreed to pay the two plaintiffs a compensation of 10,000,000 Yen (~71,755 Euro) and to promote one plaintiff to a rank equivalent to division chief and the other plaintiff to a position equivalent to section head (The Japan Times, January 6, 2004).

WWN referred to the Sumitomo cases[20] and to the discrimination plaintiffs faced in the workplace in its counter reports to the Japanese Government's Second (Nihon Kara no Tegami Gurūpu 1995) as well as Fourth and Fifth Periodic Report on the implementation of CEDAW. In the 2002 counter report, WWN demanded several changes in legislation for gender equality. One of WWN's main objectives is to integrate an explicit prohibition of indirect discrimination into the EEOL and in the Basic Law for a Gender Equal Society. An important step would be to revise the EEOL guidelines, which permits comparison only within the same employment categories, to integrate a provision for the principle of equal pay for work of equal value in the Labour Standards Law and to fully implement the CEDAW and the ILO Convention No. 100 (equal remuneration for men and women workers for work of equal value). A second WWN objective is ratification of the ILO Convention No. 111 (concerning discrimination in respect of employment and occupation) and the ratification of the Optional Protocol to CEDAW (WWN 2004b:26). Once a state has ratified the Optional Protocol (implementation 22 December 2000), individuals or groups of women can submit claims to the CEDAW Committee in the scope of the 'communication procedure' (Art. 2/ Optional Protocol) when all national remedies have been exhausted (Art. 4/ Optional Protocol). To make complaints against discrimination in the name of victims is a new option and a progress for women and human rights organisations (Schöpp-Schilling 2004:5).[21] If the Japanese government should ratify the Optional Protocol, another effective tool will be given to correct the discrimination against women workers. A third WWN objective is special gender-sensitive education programs for members of the judiciary, because the decisions in the Sumitomo Electric and Chemical cases both showed an extreme gender-bias (*jendā baiasu*) in the judiciary. WWN criticized a judge who supported the prejudicial view that women were unenthusiastic short-term workers. In the 2002 counter report to the CEDAW Committee, WWN called the gender neutrality of the judicial system a 'myth' and noticed: 'But it is clear from the court reasoning that the judicial system is not gender neutral and holds the same socially accepted ideas as the general and corporate society' (WWIN 2004b:25).

The CEDAW Committee which considered the Fourth and Fifth reports of Japan (CEDAW/C/JPN/4 and CEDAW/C/JPN/5) in June/July 2003 expressed similar concerns as WWN in the Concluding Comment.[22] The CEDAW Concluding Comments noted that the Japanese government did not have a "specific" definition of discrimination and recommended a legislative definition of direct and indirect discrimination (corresponds to art. 1/CEDAW). Another recommendation was for campaigns on the CEDAW, especially the concept of indirect discrimination, aimed for, among others, the parliamentarians, the judiciary and the legal profession in general. Another criticism concerned the gender wage gap which the Committee attributed to three factors: first, the different type of work; second, employment segregation such as the two-track employment management system; and, thirdly, the Japanese government did not understand indirect discrimination – e.g. the guidelines to the Equal Employment Opportunity Law. In another crucial point, the Committee "urged" Japan to amend the guidelines to the Equal Employment Opportunity Law and to increase de facto equal working opportunities for women and men also through taking temporary special measures (corresponds to art 4, paragraph 1/ CEDAW). It also asked the Japanese government to take steps against horizontal and vertical occupational segregation (CEDAW Committee 2003). Because these CEDAW Committee comments raised similar concerns and recommendations as WWN, the WWN interprets this as a full success. The interest in and focus on CEDAW is important for WWN. In December 2004, the Japanese Association of International Women's Rights (JAIWR) honoured WWN's efforts to promote the CEDAW within Japan by awarding WWN the 8th Akamatsu Ryōko Award (Kokusai Josei no Chii Kyōkai 2005).[23]

4.4 Gaiatsu - a significant tool for WWN

WWN could also use the international discourses on indirect discrimination[24] or on the principle of equal pay for equal work,[25] but this alone is not sufficient to change government policy. Yoneda Masumi, who wrote on Japan in the first CEDAW Impact Study, says that it is crucial to remind the government of its responsibilities (Yoneda 2001, interview), which seems to be WWN's great strength. The following section deals with how WWN gains attention locally, nationally and internationally and how WWN promotes the CEDAW through international pressure (gaiatsu). The political scientist Joyce Gelb, who has compared women's movements and gender-based policies in Japan and the United States, declares that 'emerging international norms on gender equity and transnational feminist mobilisation have been used by Japanese women's groups as an additional resource for rights-based claims, creating kansetsu gaiatsu [thus indirect pressure from outside] in an era of greater internationalisation (kokusaika) with which to embarrass and challenge a reluctant Japanese government' (Gelb 2003:4). Domestic women's groups and networks, which have difficulties to convince the government on the national level, might have more chances to – metaphorically speaking – put pressure on their governments from an international level. Margaret Keck and Kathryn Sikkink (1998) who examined the emergence and effectiveness of transnational advocacy networks assume that the emergence of transnational networks correlates to the exclusion of repressed groups from domestic political process. This would lead to a boomerang-effect: Repressed domestic groups appeal to supportive groups abroad who engage in bringing international pressure on certain regimes, whereas governing elites experience that increasing repression gives rise to international criticism and pressure (Keck/Sikkink 1998). WWN's international activism can be interpreted as a variation of this kind of boomerang-effect, which is called gaiatsu by the activists, thus a consciously-exerted, much-needed strategy to set things in motion. When asked about gaiatsu, an activist called it 'one of the great powers' (Tanaka 2001, interview); a journalist called it 'an effective strategy' (Tsujimoto 2001, interview). When speaking about gaiatsu, two interviewees called attention to Japan's wish to be a 'leading nation' (Mori 2001, interview; Suzuki 2001, interview). In this context, Japan would only accept changes when its good international reputation is in danger, and further: 'When criticism is coming from Japan, the Japanese government is not acting. In this case, there are no new laws' (Mori 2001).

Gaiatsu is not only used at the international level (such as writing alternative reports for international monitoring efforts), but is also an activity deeply rooted in the region, thus it is both a global and local tool. During the court cases, lawyers appearing for the plaintiffs in the Sumitomo cases referred to the CEDAW to show that the Equal Employment Opportunity Law was not fully implemented in line with the CEDAW. In this context, the CEDAW can be also seen as an important 'mobilization resource' (Boyle/Liu 2001:9) and as establishing standards that can be monitored. Although those court cases are limited to the local sphere, WWN used opinions of international experts (e.g. reference to the

Concluding Comments of the CEDAW Committee). By referring to international conventions, it was also possible to include international opinions in the political activities around the local court cases. Such was the case when Marsha Freeman, the director of the International Women's Rights Action Watch (IWRAW), wrote an analysis during the Sumitomo Electric case in 1999 in which she harshly criticized the culturally-based, gradualist view of the Japanese government that Japanese tradition was an obstacle to the immediate implementation of CEDAW. (Freeman 1999:57). Freeman's comments as well as a press conference organised by WWN attracted enormous media attention (Ogura 1999, Moguchi 1999).

WWN used shadow reports and indirectly court cases to point out the weakness of the Equal Employment Opportunity Law. The Sumitomo court cases are extended to local fields of political activism. There are four main reasons to use the court sessions politically. First: The plaintiffs try to show that it is not only about compensation. They are eager to point out that their case is not a particular case, but an example for wage discrimination all over Japan (WWIN 2001c:1). Second: WWN mobilises sympathisers and mass media to court sessions (Shirafuji 2000b:54). In this connection, the members try to bring international supporters to attend court sessions to put pressure on the judges' decision – as one of the women told me: 'They [foreign women] also come to the court sessions as listeners, and the judges probably make more efforts than usually. This is very good. It is good that the foreign women support us. It appears as if we were international.' (Suzuki 2001; Kitano 2001) WWN also gathers support petitions from Japan and abroad, which are then announced in its own publications or in other women's newsletters (WWN 2001b:18). Third: WWN (and national and international feminist experts and representatives of supporting international NGOs) continuously comment on the court cases at WWN's own conferences in Japan or at conferences abroad (e.g. WWN 2000a, 2001b). And fourth: WWN's critical view on discrimination is not limited to problems in the Japanese private sector. The WWN also criticizes gender bias at certain public institutions such as the Osaka Women's and Young Worker's Office (which belongs to the Ministry of Health, Labour and Welfare) and the courts (members of judiciary). Calling for 'gender education' in the court is one example of how WWN uses alternative reports and its events (WWN 2001b) to highlight lack of sensitivity to gender issues.

5   Take the Global, Make It Local!

In her analysis of feminist engagement in an unequal global governance structure, Sauer points out that the 'feminist perspective allows for the paradoxical intervention of anti-state politics with state actors' (Sauer 2004:125, own translation) – which WWN tries to live by creating an emancipatory niche. WWN urged the Japanese courts and the government to implement the CEDAW in Japan and to catch up with global gender norms by embedding specific, gender-discrimination cases in a greater context by arguing that, for example, the CEDAW is not fully implemented in Japanese laws. Important in accomplishing this was to reach out to the media and thus the public and policy-makers. The WWN work is greatly supported by the existence of the 'global governance instrument CEDAW' (Pansieri 2000:106) with which they have more options to insist on women's human rights, equality and empowerment in Japan. To gain attention locally, nationally and internationally, WWN uses various strategies. Crossing borders (trans-national level) apparently opens up new options, when women are well informed, active and continue to stay connected with each other (networking) in Japan and abroad. One of the wonderful tools for WWN is *gaiatsu*, which can be used in and outside Japan in different configurations. Going global also led to a structural change in WWN: further professionalisation, specialization (work sharing), integration of allies and strategic cooperation on common topics with groups having different aims.

To translate international agreements – e.g. CEDAW – into local action, WWN must be well informed and able to intervene constantly.

If WWN wants to endure, it needs to address some new developments too. While the number of larger companies using the dual career track system fell slightly, especially in the financial sector, more mid-size companies have started to introduce this system. However, Suganuma Tomoko, a lawyer in anti-discrimination court cases, stated that 1998 was the 'divide' when more women who were employed as non-regular instead of regular workers went to court than women who were assigned to the general track (Weathers 2005:2-3). Rather than more gender equality, we can see in globalised times an 'institutional embedding of a gender-segmented labour market, with men continuing in relatively protected and regulated standard employment and women relegated to flexible and deregulated employment' (Shire/Imai 2000:abstract). WWN keeps up with the new developments and is engaged in criticizing the restriction of women to unstable employment and bad pay, not only the two career tracks, but indirect discrimination in general. In June 2005, WWN supported the foundation of a Kansai-based national network of fix-term contract women workers in their 20s and 30s (Koedo 2005b:7) and is engaged in creating more alliances.

All in all, the new Japanese women's networks are pushing for reforms from a marginalized position (Lenz 1998:168). Although there is certainly a positive sign with the introduction or amendments to gender equality policies (e.g. Basic Law for a Gender Equal Society; EEOL), a neo-conservative backlash is an unsettling development, as some Japanese still believe that gender-based division of labour is an essential part of Japanese culture and tradition (Kogure 2005). The political scientist Brigitte Young noted 'gender regimes represent a symbolic gender order on one hand. On the other hand, they embody an arena of power in which the definition of gender relations has to be eked over and over' (Young 1998:177, own translation). In the context of globalisation, there are both setbacks and small steps forward on the way to gender equality in Japan.

Notes

[1] Global governance was first formulated by the Commission on Global Governance as a new vision of an interactive decision process by governmental and non-governmental participants of all levels (local-national-global) in the sense of a 'neighbourhood democracy" (Commission on Global Governance 1995). One example for the result of a collective decision process is the development of the social and UN-World Conferences on Women during the 1990s leading to important results (Lenz 2001:17). However, the action platforms adopted by the UN World

Conferences are not legally obligatory. This is in contrast to human rights conventions, which are legally binding obligations when ratified by a state (Schöpp-Schilling, E-Mail, January 6, 2006).

[2] The Platform for Action was adopted at the September 1995 Fourth World Conference on Women and is 'an agenda for women's empowerment'. It aims at improving the advancement of women and 'at removing all the obstacles to women's active participation in all spheres of public and private life through a full and equal share in economic, social, cultural and political decision-making' (UN 2005).

[3] The CEDAW was adopted in 1979 by the UN General Assembly.

[4] In international contexts the network's name is Working Women's International Network (Suzuki 2001, interview).

[5] This paper is based on my master's thesis (Baier 2004). In September 2000, I had the opportunity to participate in several meetings of WWN's international support group Women Helping Women (WHW), where I met two WWN activists. After some preliminary research, I conducted fieldwork in Osaka from June to August 2001 with the financial support of the University of Vienna. Many great thanks to all activists of WWN and WHW, to Ass. Prof. Dr. Wolfram Manzenreiter, supervising and commenting my master thesis, to Prof. Dr. Sepp Linhart for supervising my master thesis, to Prof. Dr. Ilse Lenz for advising me right at the beginning of my master thesis, to Dr. Susanne Kreitz-Sandberg for her comments on this paper, to Dr. Hanna Beate Schöpp-Schilling for her comments on my master thesis and to Harold Otto, M.A. for his help in proofreading this article. Last, but not least I would like to thank the editors of this book, Susanne Kreitz-Sandberg and Claudia Derichs a lot for their invaluable work on this publication project.

[6] Experts, in my understanding, are not only experts commenting from the outside, but also people who are part of the research area. I also take a different stance towards Meuser and Nagel's definition of expert knowledge to see only organisational and institutional contents as relevant expert knowledge (Bock 2002:79) and to neglect the 'whole person […], i.e. the person with its orientations and attitudes in the context to individual and collective life contexts' (Meuser/Nagel 1991:442, own translation).

[7] Some estimate that as many as 6,000 Japanese participated in the Beijing conference (e.g. Bishop 2002:9, Yoneda 2000:63). This number might include those who only went to the official conference.

[8] Between 1938 and 1945, the Japanese Imperial Army mainly forced Asian women (for the most part Korean women) to enter prostitution. The so-called "comfort women" (*jūgun ianfu*) were forced to work in "comfort stations" for the war machine (Mae 2000:33). "Comfort stations" could be found in China, in Hong Kong, in the Philippines, in Malaysia, in Singapore, in Borneo, in Indonesia, in Thailand, in Burma (Myanmar), in Papua Neuguinea, and in Okinawa prefecture. It is assumed that "comfort stations" could be found wherever the Japanese Imperial army had been based (Yamazaki 1996:91, see also Wöhr in this volume).

[9] See also Mae and Tanaka/Hong in this volume.

[10] The 1985 EEOL 'granted women very few new rights and imposed only limited legal obligations on employers'. It made a difference between 'prohibition' (*kinshi kitei*) and 'exhortation' (*dōryoku gimu kitei*). The 1985 EEOL prohibited discrimination in areas such as vocational training, fringe benefits retirement and dismissal, but only morally obliged employers not to discriminate in recruitment, job assignment and promotion (Lam 1993:207).

[11] Articles 13-19 of the EEOL provide for settlement of complaints. When the director of the Prefectural Labour Bureau (regional office of the Ministry of Health, Labour and Welfare) receives the request to assist in the settling of a labour dispute from one or both parties, the director gives advice, guidance or recommendations. The Director of the Prefectural Labour Bureau can then refer to the Disputes Adjustment Commission for mediation (EEOL).

12   In February 1995 (Agora Ōsaka 2000:78) a mediation could have been initiated for the first time (10 years after the introduction of the EEOL). One of the applicants held the view that the proposal of the Commission was not only vague and 'insulting', but would have been to their disadvantage, so that they dismissed the mediation (Kitakawa 2000:68).

13   In Osaka, WWN supported plaintiffs employed at Sumitomo Electric, Sumitomo Chemical, Sumitomo Life Insurance, Shōko Chūkin, Sharp Life Electronic and, Shionogi Pharmacy (WWN 2000b:24-25).

14   Those four groups were: Kokusai Fujinen Ōsaka Kitaku no Kai (International Year of Women Osaka North Ward Association), Ōsaka Danjo Sabetsu Chingin o Nakusu Renraku Kai (Osaka Contact Group against Wage Discrimination of Women), Kintōhō Jissen Nettowāku (Network Course on the Equal Employment Opportunity Law), Shōsha ni Hataraku Josei no Kai (Circle of Women Working for Trade Companies) (WWN 2001a).

15   'The development of an alternative, or shadow report provides an effective means for NGOs to critique or supplement information in the official state report' (INSTRAW 2005).

16   In March 2000, the General Assembly decided that interested NGOs can apply for accreditation to the special session, if they were neither in a consultative status with the Economic and Social Council nor were accredited to the Fourth World Conference on Women (Divison for the Advancement of Women 2004).

17   This succeeded the Equality Action 2000 campaign (2000-2001) and the Equality Action 2003 (Kintō Taigū Akushon 21 2005).

18   On the 27[h] of September 2006 the website counted 99.842 visitors (WWIN/HP 2006).

19   Article 1 contains a definition of discrimination, article 2 demands measures to be taken to eliminate discrimination and article 11 demands measures against discrimination in the field of employment.

20   'Along with the Sumitomo Electric Case ruling, rulings in other Sumitomo Cases were handed down. At first the plaintiffs working for Sumitomo Life Insurance – who had suffered double-discrimination as married women – won the suit on the 17th June of 2001. In the case of Sumitomo Chemical the first negative ruling was handed down by the Osaka district court on the 28th of March 2001, and an amicable settlement could be achieved in favour of the plaintiffs in 2004. And in March 2005, the last ruling on the case of Sumitomo Metal was handed down in the plaintiffs' favour.'

21   Under the Optional Protocol to the CEDAW, there are two different procedures: a 'communication procedure' and an 'inquiry procedure'. There are some criteria to be admitted for the consideration by the Committee, which includes that all national remedies have to be exhausted (art 4/ Optional Protocol). In the case of 'inquiry procedures', which do not require the exhaustion of all national remedies in contrast to the 'communication pocedures' (Schöpp-Schilling 2004:5), the Committee can initiate 'confidental investigations' in cases of 'grave or systematic violations by a State Party of rights established in the Convention" (art. 8/ Optional Protocol), whereas states have the choice to decide on an 'opt-out clause' after ratification or accession, which allows them not to accept the inquiry procedure (art.10/ Optional Protocol).

22   Schöpp-Schilling adds that WWN's alternative reports were influenced by the comments made by the
experts of the CEDAW Committee and by specific CEDAW trainings provided by the International Women's Rights Action Watch (IWRAW) Asia Pacific (Schöpp-Schilling, E-Mail, February 01, 2006).

23   One of the early women's NGOs active for the advancement of women through research on one hand and distribution of information about the CEDAW on the other is the Japanese Association of International Women's Rights (JAIWR, Kokusai Josei no Chii Kyōkai) with its president Akamatsu Ryōko, former education minister and CEDAW Committee member. In 1997 an

Akamatsu Ryōko Award (Akamatsu Ryōko Shō) was sponsored to honor people for their considerable efforts to contribute to women's advancement by promoting the CEDAW. President Akamatsu herself funded the award by a personal contribution (Kokusai Josei no Chii Kyōkai 2005).

[24] WWN refers to the ILO Convention No. 111 (concerning discrimination in employment and occupation) which is not yet ratified by Japan. WWN's definition of indirect discrimination is based on court rulings and definitions of the European court of justice, whereas WWN was informed about this by the CEDAW expert Beate Schöpp-Schilling and the German jurist Ursula Rust who held speeches on indirect discrimination (Schöpp-Schilling, E-Mail, January 6, 2006).

[25] WWN refers to the ILO Covention No. 100 (equal remuneration), to the International Convenant on Economic, Social and Cultural Rights, art. 7 (equal remuneration) and to the CEDAW, art. 11 paragraph 1b (equal remuneration) (Appendix) (WWN 2004b:21-22).

References

Agora Ōsaka (ed.) 2000, WWN Gonen no keika to kongo no tenkai [WWN's Five Last Years and Its Future Development]: Kono saiban o yurusemasu ka? Sumitomo Denkō saiban ni ikaru! [Is such a Court Acceptable? Anger about the Sumitomo Electric Court Case!], *Agora* No. 263, pp. 78-79.

Appelt, Erna and Birgit Sauer 2001, Globalisierung aus feministischer Perspektive: Globalisierungsmythen. *Feministische Perspektiven, Österreichische Zeitschrift für Politikwissenschaft* 2001/2, pp. 127-135.

Asahi Shinbun, Osaka-edition 2000, Josei no okori chisai kakomu [Court Building Surrounded by Women's Anger], August 31, 2000, (evening edition).

The Asahi Shinbun 2005, Editorial. Equal Opportunity Law, December 27, 2005. http://www.asahi.com/english/Herald-asahi/TKY200512270124.html (Access January 06, 2006).

Baier, Maria Sachiko 2004, Japanische Frauennetzwerke im Zeitalter der Globalisierung. Das Working Women's Network in Ōsaka [Japanese Women's Networks in the Age of Globalisation. The Working Women's Network in Osaka], unpublished Master Thesis, Wien: Universität Wien.

Bishop, Beverley 2002, Globalization and Women's Lab Activism in Japan, *electronic journal of contemporary japanese studies* (ejcjs). http://www.japanesestudies.org.uk/articles/Bishop.html (Access January 05, 2006).

Bock, Stephanie 2002, *Regionale Frauennetzwerke. Frauenpolitische Bündnisse zwischen beruflichen Interessen und geschlechterpolitischen Zielen.* Opladen: Leske und Budrich (=Politik und Geschlecht 10).

Boyle, Elisabeth Heger and Liu Dongxiao 2001, The Global Dynamics of Women's Rights: Sovereignty, Accountability, and the International Reform Strategies of States, IGOs, and NGOs. http://www.soc.umn.edu/~schofer/2001soc8311/pub/BOYLE%20Social%20Politics%20manuscript.rtf (January 5, 2005).

CEDAW Committee 2003, http://www.un.org/womenwatch/daw/cedaw/cedaw29/ConComm/JapanE.pdf (December 7, 2005).

Commission on Global Governance 1995, *Our Global Neighbourhood. The Report of the Commission on Global Governance.* Oxford: Oxford University Press.

The Daily Yomiuri 2000, Women Protest Sexual Discrimination Ruling, September 01, 2000.

Dawn Center 2006, About the Dawn Center http://www.dawncenter.or.jp/english/introduction.html (January 05, 2006).

Division for the Advancement of Women 2004, Civil Society and NGO Participation http://www.un.org/womenwatch/daw/followup/ngo.htm (January 03, 2005).

Frank, Susanne 1999, Globalisierung und Gender. Die Geschlechterverhältnisse in der Globalisierungsdebatte, Jungle World, June 16, 1999. http://www.nadir.org/nadir/periodika/jungle_world/_99/25/15a.htm (Access January 5, 2006).

Freeman, Marsha 1999, Eiko Shirafuji and Katsumi Nishimura v. Sumitomo Electric and the Government of Japan. Statement of Dr. Marsha A. Freeman, Working Women's Network (ed.): *Josei sabetsu teppai jōyaku wa Nihon de ikasarete iru ka. Māsha ga Nihon no saibansho ni tsutaeta koto* [Is the CEDAW Realized in Japan? Marsha Freeman's Commentary to the Japanese Courts] (2000). Osaka, pp. 55-70, (booklet).

Gelb, Joyce 1999, Globalization and Feminism: The Impact of the New Transnationalism. http://www.csun. edu/~iggd00/IPSA_Quebec_papers/IPSAGelb.doc (Access June 30, 2002, January 05, 2006).

Gelb, Joyce 2003, *Gender Policies in Japan and the United States: Comparing Women's Movements, Rights and Politics*. New York: Palgrave Macmillan.

Hashimoto, Hiroko 2001, Men's Involvement in Gender Equality Movements in Japan, Women in Action 2001/1. http://www.isiswomen.org/pub/wia/wia101/japan.html (Access January 05, 2005).

Hayashi, Yoko 1995, Legal Issues in Employment, *AMPO: Japan-Asia Quarterly Review* 25/4-26/1 (=98-99), pp. 42-45.

Ikeda, Naoki 1997, Kaisha ga chōtei o kotowatta – Sumitomo Kagaku no baai [The Company Dismissed a Mediation – The Case Sumitomo Chemical], Working Women's Network (ed.): *Hanbun no chingin demo danjobyōdō?* [Women Receive Only Half of Men's Wages. Is this really Gender Equality?]. Osaka, pp. 14-19, (booklet).

Inoue, Teruko 1997, *Joseigaku e no shōtai. Kawaru/ kawaranai onna no isshō* [Introduction to Women's Studies. Women's Whole Lives Change/ Do Not Change]. New edition. Tokyo: Yūhikaku ['1992].

INSTRAW 2005, NGO Alternative Reports, http://www.un-instraw.org/en/index.php (December 15, 2005).

Ishida, Kinuko and Yatani, Yasuko 2004, Wakai kaiketsu ni atatte no genkoku seimei [The Plaintiff's Commentary upon the Settlement], Working Women's Network Homepage: http://www.ne.jp/asahi/wwn/wwin/ (Link: Sumitomo kagaku saiban) (September 19, 2004).

Isis International-Manila (ed.) 2002, *NGO_Women@Asia.Net. The Use of Information and Communication Technologies by Women's Organisations in Seven Asian Countries. A Regional Study*. Manila: Isis International-Manila.

Izumi, Kayoko 2000, 'Ningen no kusari' de kōgi. Ōsaka chisai torikomu [Resistance by Forming a 'Human Chain'. Surrounding the Osaka District Court Building], *Mainichi Shinbun*, August 31, 2000, Osaka-edition, (evening edition).

Japan NGO Report Preparatory Committee 1999, Women 2000. Japan NGO Alternative Report. http://www.jca.apc.org/fem/bpfa/NGOreport/0_en_Overview.html (Access January 2, 2006).

Japan NGO Report Preparatory Committee 2000, http://www.jca.apc.org/fem/bpfa/index_en.html (Access January 2, 2006).

The Japan Times 2000, Bias Suit Ruling Draws Protest, September 01, 2000, p. 3.

The Japan Times 2001, Sumitomo Women Lose Wage Bias Suit, March 03, 2001. http://www.japantimes.co.jp/cgi-bin/getarticle.pl5?nn20010330a8.htm (Access January 5, 2006).

The Japan Times 2004, Sumitomo Unit Settles Sex Bias Suit, January 6, 2004. http://search.japantimes.co.jp/member/member.html?appURL=nn20040106a3.html (Access January 11, 2004, January 5, 2005).

Keck, Margaret E. and Kathryn Sikkink 1998, *Activists Beyond Borders: Advocacy Networks in International Politics*. Ithaca: Cornell University Press.

Kintōhō Nisennen Kyanpēn 2000, Mienai josei sabetsu [Invisible Discrimination against Women], back: Igirisu ni manabu 'Kansetsu sabetsu' [Learning from Great Britain: ‚Indirect Discrimination'], (flyer).

Kintō Taigū Akushon 2005, www.ne.jp/asahi/kinto/2000/ (Access January 5, 2006).

Kitakawa, Kiyoko et al. 2000, Sumitomo Kinzoku jinjutsusho [Comment to the Sumitomo Metal Company], 'Sumitomo' ni tai shite watashitachi wa tatakau [We Fight against 'Sumitomo']: Kono saiban o yurusemasu ka? Sumitomo Denkō saiban ni ikaru! [Is such a Court Acceptable? Anger about the Sumitomo Electric Court Case!], *Agora* 263, pp. 66-71 (Kitakawa pp. 66-68).

Kitazawa, Yoko, Matsui Yayori and Yunomae Tomoko 1996, The Women's Movement: Progress and Obstacles, AMPO-Japan Asia Quarterly Review (ed*.): Voices from the Japanese Women's Movement*. Armonk/New York/London (et al.): ME Sharpe, pp. 23-37.

Koedo, Shizuko 2000, Hajime ni. Wākushoppu no junbi, Kokuren e no tōroku nado [Introduction. Workshop Preparations, the Registration at the United Nations etc.], Working Women's Network (ed.): Kokuren josei 2000nen kaigi to WWN [The UN Women's Conference 2000 and WWN]. Osaka, pp. 2-5, (booklet).

Koedo, Shizuko 2005a, Using the UN, Working Women in Japan, Working Women's International Network (ed.): Using the UN, Working Women in Japan (English Newsletter), Osaka, pp. 1-2.

Koedo, Shizuko 2005b, WW05 Session. Situation of Working Women in Japan, Working Women's International Network (ed.): *Using the UN, Working Women in Japan* (English Newsletter), Osaka, pp. 5-7.

Kogure, Satoko 2005, Turning Back Clock on Gender Equality, The Japan Times, May 3, 2005. http://search.japantimes.co.jp/print/features/life2005/fl20050503zg.htm (Access November 23, 2005).

Kokusai, Josei no Chii, Kyōkai 2005, Kokukusai Josei no Chii Kyōkai ni Tsuite, http://www.jaiwr.org/index.html (December 1, 2005).

Kōsei Rōdōsho (ed.) 2002, *Hataraku josei no jitsujō* [The Situation of Working Women]. Tokyo.

Kumazawa, Makoto 2000, *Josei rōdō to kigyō shakai* [Women's Work and the Corporate Society]. Tokyo: Iwanami shinsho.

Kreisky, Eva 2004, Geschlecht als politische und politikwissenschaftliche Kategorie, Sieglinde K. Rosenberger and Birgit Sauer (eds.): *Politikwissenschaft und Geschlecht. Konzepte – Verknüpfungen – Perspektiven*. Wien: WUV, pp. 23-43.

Kreisky, Eva; Birgit Sauer 1998, Geschlechterverhältnisse im Kontext politischer Transformation, Eva Kreisky and Birgit Sauer (eds.): *Geschlechterverhältnisse im Kontext politischer Transformation*, Sonderheft der Politischen Vierteljahreszeitschrift 28. Opladen und Wiesbaden: Westdeutscher Verlag, pp. 9-49.

Lam, Alice 1993, Equal Employment Opportunities for Japanese Women: Changing Company Practice, Janet Hunter (ed.): *Japanese Women Working*. New York: Routledge, pp. 197-223.

Lenz, Ilse 1998, Zum Verhältnis von neuer Frauenbewegung und Frauenpolitik in Japan, Claudia Derichs and Anja Osiander (eds.): *Soziale Bewegungen in Japan*. Hamburg: Gesellschaft für Natur- und Völkerkunde Ostasiens (=Mitteilungen der Gesellschaft für Natur- und Völkerkunde Ostasiens 128), pp. 139-172.

Lenz, Ilse 2000, What does the women's movement do, when it moves? Kommunikation und Organisation in der neuen japanischen Frauenbewegung, Ilse Lenz, Michiko Mae and Karin Klose (eds.): *Frauenbewegungen weltweit. Aufbrüche, Kontinuitäten, Veränderungen*. Opladen: Leske and Budrich (= Geschlecht und Gesellschaft 18), pp. 95-132.

Maria Sachiko Baier

Lenz, Ilse 2001, Globalisierung, Frauenbewegungen und internationale Regulierung: Themenschwerpunkt: Lokal, national, global? Frauenbewegungen, Geschlechterpolitik und Globalisierung, *Zeitschrift für Frauenforschung und Geschlechterstudien* 19/1+2, pp. 8-28.

Liddle, Joanna; Nakajima, Sachiko 2000, *Rising Suns, Rising Daughters. Gender, Class and Power in Japan*. London/New York: Zed Books (Bangkok: White Lotus).

Mackie, Vera 1998, Dialogue, Distance and Difference: Feminism in Contemporary Japan, *Women's Studies International Forum* 21/6, pp. 599-615.

Mackie, Vera 2003, *Feminism in Modern Japan. Citizenship. Embodiment and Sexuality*. Cambridge: Cambridge University Press.

Mae, Michiko 1997, Die Frauenbewegungen im japanischen Modernisierungsprozess, Ilse Lenz and Michiko Mae (eds.): Getrennte Welten, gemeinsame Moderne. Opladen: Hembsbach (=Geschlecht und Gesellschaft 4), pp. 210-246.

Mae, Michiko 2000, Wege zu einer neuen Subjektivität. Die neue japanische Frauenbewegung als Suche nach einer anderen Moderne, Ilse Lenz, Michiko Mae and Karin Klose (eds.): *Frauenbewegungen weltweit. Aufbrüche, Kontinuitäten, Veränderungen*. Opladen: Leske und Budrich (= Geschlecht und Gesellschaft Band 18), pp. 21-50.

Meuser, Michael and Ulrike Nagel 1991, ExpertInneninterviews – vielfach erprobt, wenig bedacht. Ein Beitrag zur qualitativen Methodendiskussion, Detlef Garz and Klaus Kraimer (eds.): *Qualitativ-empirische Sozialforschung: Konzepte, Methoden, Analysen*. Opladen: Westdeutscher Verlag, pp. 441-471.

Milz, Helga 1991, How to become frauenbewegt: vom bewegten Leben in der Institution, Eva Koch-Klenske (ed.): *Die Töchter der Emanzen: Kommunikationsstrukturen in der Frauenbewegung*. Frauenoffensive: München, pp.53-84.

Miyachi, Mitsuko 2000, On the Unjust Court Ruling over the Sumitomo Electric Gender-based Wage Discrimination Case, Working Women's Network (ed.): *Kokuren josei 2000nen kaigi to WWN* [The UN Women's Conference 2000 and WWN]. Osaka, pp. 30-31. (=Sumitomo Denkō danjo chingin sabetsu jiken. Futō hanketsu ni tsuite, pp. 28-29), (booklet).

Moriguchi, Kenzo 1999, State not Fighting Gender Bias: Activist, The Japan Times, October 21, 1999.
http://search.japantimes.co.jp/cgi-bin/nn19991021a9.html (Access January 5, 2005).

Moriki, Kazumi 1997, Japanese Women Seek Solidarity with Asian Women, DAWN, November 1997. http://www.dawncenter.or.jp/english/publication/edawn/9711/asian.html (Access January 5, 2005).

Moriya, Yuko 2000a, Kansai chiku no NGO [NGOs in the Kansai area], NGO no kanōsei to kadai [The Possibilities for and Issues of NGOs], Ōsawa Mari (ed.): *21 seiki no josei seisaku to danjo kyōdō sankaku shakai kihonhō* [Women's Policies in the 21st Century and the Basic Law for a Gender Equal Society]. Tokyo: Gyōsei, pp. 264-280.

Moriya, Yuko 2000b, Gender-free Perspective in the Legislature. Report on the Activities of 'More Women to Assemblies Backup Schools', DAWN, Newsletter of the Dawn Center (Osaka Prefectural Women's Center), December 2000, pp. 8-9.

Nihon, Kara no Tegami Gurūpu [A Letter from Japanese Women Circle] (ed.) 1995, Nihon kara no tegami [A Letter from Japan] *Counter-Report to the Japanese Government's Second Periodic Report as a State Party to the Convention on the Elimination of All Forms of Discriminination against Women* (July 09, 1992). Osaka (booklet).

Nihon Keizai Shinbun 2000, Osaka chisai kakomu 'ningen no kusari' ['Human Chain' around the Osaka District Court Building], August 31, 2000, Osaka-edition, (evening edition).

Ogura, Izumi 1999, Danjo no chingin sabetsu soshō ni Nihon de ikensho o dashita hito Māsha Furīman [Marsha Freeman's Commentary on a Wage Discrimination Court Process in Japan], *Asahi Shinbun*, 23.12.1999, Osaka-edition.

Onnatachi no Benrichō San Hen Shū Shitsu (ed.) 2000, *Onnatachi no benrichō 3* [Practical Women's Directory No.3]. Chiba: Jōjō.

Osaka District Court 2000, Hanketsu riyū no yōshi [Main Points of the Reasons Given for the Judgement]. Osaka, (court document).

Pansieri, Flavia 2000, Global Governance for the Promotion of Local Governance. The Case of CEDAW, Barbara Holland-Cunz and Uta Ruppert (eds.): *Frauenpolitische Chancen globaler Politik. Verhandlungsverfahren im internationalen Kontext.* Opladen: Leske und Budrich, pp. 105-115.

Ruf, Anja 2000, Frauennetzwerke im Spannungsfeld von Globalisierung und Vielfalt, Ruth Klingebiel and Shalini Randera (eds.): *Globalisierung aus Frauensicht. Bilanzen und Visionen.* 2. ed. Bonn: Dietz (¹1998), pp. 66-84.

Ruppert, Uta 1998a, Perspektiven internationaler Frauen(bewegungs)politik, Uta Ruppert (ed.): *Lokal bewegen. Global verhandeln. Internationale Politik und Geschlecht.* Frankfurt a. M./New York: Campus (=Politik der Geschlechterverhältnisse 11), pp. 233-255.

Ruppert, Uta 1998b, Die Kehrseite der Medaille? Globalisierung, global governance und internationale Frauenbewegung, *Beiträge zur feministischen Theorie und Praxis* 21 (= 47-48), pp. 95-105.

Saito, Makoto 2000, Zenkoku tenkai suru NGO [NGOs Spreading across the Country], NGO no kanōsei to kadai [The Possibilities and Issues of NGOs], Ōsawa Mari (ed.): *21 seiki no josei seisaku to danjo kyōdō sankaku shakai kihonhō* [Women's Policies in the 21st Century and the Basic Law for a Gender Equal Society]. Tokyo: Gyōsei, pp. 253-264.

Sakai, Kazuko 2001, Problems of the Equal Employment Opportunity Law, Japanese Women Now. http://wom-jp.org/e/JWOMEN/kinto.html (Access January 5, 2006).

Sauer, Birgit 2004, Staat – Institutionen – Governance, Sieglinde K. Rosenberger and Birgit Sauer (eds.): *Politikwissenschaft und Geschlecht. Konzepte – Verknüpfungen – Perspektiven.* Wien: WUV, pp. 107-125.

Schöpp-Schilling, Hanna Beate 2004, Aufgaben und Arbeitsmethoden der UN-Menschenrechtsausschüsse am Beispiel des CEDAW-Ausschusses: Relevanz für CEDAW-Vertragsstaaten und Zivilgeschaft in Europa, Doris König, Joachim Lange, Hanna Beate Schöpp-Schilling, Ursula Rust (eds.): *Gleiches Recht - gleiche Realität? Welche Instrumente bieten Völkerrecht, Europarecht und nationales Recht für die Gleichstellung von Frauen?* Rehburg-Loccum: Loccumer Protokolle 03/ 71 (also in ZESAR 5-6 (2004), pp. 234-244.)

Shirafuji Eiko 2000a, Women's Rights are Human Rights, Working Women's Network (ed.): *Kokuren josei 2000nen kaigi to WWN* [The UN Women's Conference 2000 and WWN]. Osaka, pp. 23-25 (= Josei no kenri wa jinken, pp. 21-22), (booklet).

Shirafuji, Eiko 2000b, Zadankai. Rōdō undō feminizumu no kanōsei [Discussion Round. The Possibilities of Working Women's Movement], *Josei Rōdō Kenkyū Shitsu* (The Bulletin of the Society for the Study of Working Women) 38, pp. 42-69.

Shire, Karen A. 2003, Gesellschaft, Paul Kevenhörster, Werner Pascha and Karen A. Shire (eds.): *Japan. Wirtschaft – Gesellschaft – Politik.* Opladen: Leske + Budrich, pp. 179-257.

Shire, Karen A. and Jun Imai 2000, *Flexible Equality: Men and Women in Employment in Japan*, Duisburg Working Papers on East Asian Studies, No. 30.

Shōji, Reiko 1996, Hajime ni. Kono hon o yomu anata ni [Introduction. To the Readers of this Book], Miyachi Mitsuko: Byōdō e no onnatachi no haisen?- kintōhō jidai to josei no hataraku kenri [Defeat of Women on the Way to Gender Equality? – The Age of the EEOL and the Women's Rights to Work], Tokyo: Akashi Shoten, pp. 3-9.

Shoji, Reiko and Koedo, Shizuko 2005, Wakingu Uimenzu Nettowaku to tomo ni [Together with the WWN], Working Women's Network (ed.), *Miyachi Mitsuko kanshu: Danjo chingin sabetsu saiban 'kōjo ryōzoku' ni makenakatta onnatachi: Sumitomo denko, Sumitomo kagaku no sei sabetsu soshou* [Women who Didn't Lose against the 'Public Order and Good Morals' Sumitomo Electric and Sumitomo Chemical Wage Discrimination Court Cases], Tokyo: Akashi Shoten.

Takahara, Nobuo 2000, 2005nen made ni joseigiin o 50% ni' [Raising Female Parlamentarians up to 50% until 2005], Working Women's Network (ed.): *Kokuren josei 2000nen kaigi to WWN* [The UN Women's Conference 2000 and WWN]. Osaka, pp. 44-45, (booklet).

Takenaka, Emiko 2001, Working Environment and Social System Regarding Women in Japan, DAWN, December 2001. http://www.dawncenter.or.jp/english/publication/edawn/0112/envir.html (Access January 4, 2006).

Tanaka, Kazuko 1995, The New Feminist Movement in Japan, 1970-1990, Kumiko Fujimura-Fanselow and Kameda Atsuko (eds.): *Japanese Women. New Feminist Perspectives on the Past, Present, and Future.* New York: The Feminist Press, pp. 343-352.

UNO 2005, Fourth World Conference on Women Platform for Action http://www.un.org/womenwatch/daw/beijing/platform/plat1.htm (Access December 15, 2005).

Weather, Charles 2005, Equal Opportunities for Japanese Women – What Progress?, Japan Focus, October 05, 2005, pp. 1-4, http://www.zmag.org/content/showarticle.cfm?ItemID=8877 (Access November 15, 2005).

Weber, Claudia 1998, *Chancengleichheit auf Japanisch. Strukturen, Reformen und Perspektiven der Frauenerwerbsarbeit in Japan.* Opladen: Leske und Budrich (=Bildungs- und Beschäftigungssystem in Japan 3).

Wichterich, Christa 2000, Strategische Verschwisterung, multiple Feminismen und die Glokalisierung von Frauenbewegungen, Ilse Lenz, Michiko Mae and Karin Klose (eds.): *Frauenbewegungen weltweit. Aufbrüche, Kontinuitäten, Veränderungen.* Opladen: Leske und Budrich (= Reihe Geschlecht und Gesellschaft 18), pp. 257-280.

Wijers-Hasegawa, Yumi 2003, Group to Push for Greater Gender Equality in Japan, *The Japan Times*, July 1, 2003.
http://www.japantimes.jp/cgi-bin/getarticle.pl5?nn20030701d1.htm (Access January 5, 2005).

WWIN Working Women's International Network (ed.) 2001c, *WWIN News.* August 2001 (=10).

WWIN Working Women's International Network (ed.) 2002a, *WWIN News*, Oktober 2002 (=11).

WWIN Working Women's International Network (ed.) 2003, *WWIN News*, November 2003, (=14).

WWIN Working Women's International Network 2006b (ed.), *The List Exemplar Forms of Indirect Discrimination.* The Actual Situation in the Workplace in Japan, information sheet, May 16, 2006.

WWIN/HP Working Women's (International) Network Homepage (ed.) 2002-2006, http://www.ne.jp/asahi/wwn/wwin/ (Access December 15, 2005, September 27, 2006).

WWN Working Women's Network (ed.) 1997, *WWN Went to the ILO. Nihon no shokuba no danjo byōdō o kokusai kikan ni uttaete* [WWN Went to the ILO. To Appeal for Equality between Men and Women in the Japanese Workplace at the International Institutions]. Osaka, (booklet).

WWN Working Women's Network (ed.) 2000a, *Kokuren josei 2000nen kaigi to WWN* [The UN Women's Conference 2000 and WWN]. Osaka, (booklet).

WWN Working Women's Network (ed.) 2000b, *Josei sabetsu teppai jōyaku wa Nihon de ikasarete iru ka. Māsha ga Nihon no saibansho ni tsutaeta koto* [Is the CEDAW Realized in Japan? Marsha Freeman's Commentary to the Japanese Courts]. Osaka, (booklet).

WWN Working Women's Network (ed.) 2001a, Josei undō no *'90nendai katsuyaku' soshite mirai* [Activities of the Women's Movement during the 1990s and Its Future], (information).

WWN Working Women's Network (ed.) 2001b, *Saiban ni okeru jendā baiasu o nakusu tame ni. Rin Schafuransan ni kiku Amerika de no kokoromi* [To Abolish Gender Bias in the Court: A Talk with Lynn Schafran about the Procedures against Gender Bias in the United States]. Osaka.

WWN Working Women's Network (ed.) 2002b, *WWN Nyūsuretā* [WWN Newsletter], 2002/1 (=26).

WWN Working Women's Network (ed.) 2004a, *CEDAW to Sumitomo Denkō saiban* [CEDAW and the Sumitomo Elektric Court Case]. Osaka, (booklet).

WWN Working Women's Network (ed.) 2004b, Counter Report to the Japanese Governement's Fourth and Fifth Report on Implementation of Convention on the Elimination of All Form of Discrimination Against Women, September 2002 Working Women's Network (ed.): *CEDAW to Sumitomo Denkō saiban* [CEDAW and the Sumitomo Electric Court Case]. Osaka, pp. 11-26, (booklet).

WWN Working Women's Network 2005 (ed.), *Danjo chingin sabetsu saiban 'kōjo ryōzoku' ni makenakatta onnatachi: Sumitomo denko, Sumitomo kagaku no sei sabetsu soshō* [Women who Didn't Lose against the 'Public Order and Good Morals' Wage Discrimination Court Case] Tokyo: Akashi Shoten.

WWN Working Women's International Network 2006a (ed.), Working Women's Situation in Japan and WWIN's Activities, information sheet, powerpoint presentation May 16, 2006.

Yokohama-shi, Josei Kyōkai [Yokohama City Women's Association] (ed.) 1997, *Josei mondai kīwādo 111* [111 Key Words on the Women's Issue]. Tokyo: Domesu.

Yamamoto, Kazu 2000, Sumitomo Seimei Nyūyōku shitenmae de no biramaki [We are Distributing Flyers in front of the Sumitomo Life Insurance Branch in New York], Working Women's Network (ed.): *Kokuren josei 2000nen kaigi to WWN* [The UN Women's Conference 2000 and WWN]. Osaka, p. 42, (booklet).

Yamazaki, Hiromi 1996, Military Slavery and the Women's Movement, AMPO Japan Asia Quarterly Review (ed.): *Voices from the Japanese Women's Movement.* New York: ME Sharpe, pp. 90-100.

Yoneda, Masumi 2000, Japan, Marilou McPhedran et al. (ed.): *The First CEDAW Impact Study. Final Report.* New York: The Centre for Feminist Research, York University und the International Women's Rights Project, pp. 63-76.

Yoneda, Masumi 2002, International Standards of Gender Equality and Japan – the Impact on Japan, DAWN, Dezember 2002. http://www.dawncenter.or.jp (January 5, 2005).

Young, Brigitte 1998, Genderregime und Staat in der globalen Netzwerk-Ökonomie, *PROKLA. Zeitschrift für kritische Sozialwissenschaft* 28/2, pp. 168-198.

Young, Brigitte 1999, Die Welt ist zehn Jahre alt. Der Prozess der Globalisierung ist auch ein geschlechtsspezifischer Prozess, Jungle World, June 16, 1999. http://www.nadir.org/nadir/periodika/jungle_world/_99/25/16a.htm (Access January 5, 2005).

Interviews (pseudonymes except experts)

Tanaka, Naoko, activist, July 10, 2001, Osaka, Japan; Yamanaka, Emiko, activist, July 12, 2001, Osaka, Japan; Suzuki, Yumiko, activist, July 12, 2001, Osaka, Japan; Koyama, Kazuko, activist, July 12, 2001, Osaka, Japan; Murano, Toshiko, activist, July 12, 2001, Osaka, Japan; Kitano, Iseko, activist, August 1, 2001, Osaka, Japan; Mori, Takako, activist, August 1, 2001, Osaka, Japan; Harano, Sachiko, laywer, August 2, 2001, Osaka, Japan; Flowers, Kate activist, August 4, 2001, Osaka, Japan; Toda, Setsuko, activist, August 5, 2001, Sakai, Japan; Tsujimoto, Yōkō, journalist, August 7, 2001, Osaka, Japan; Nonaka, Yūkō, activist, August 9, 2001, Osaka, Japan; Sumida, Michiko, activist, August 9, 2001, Osaka, Japan; Robertson, Alison, activist, August 21, 2001, Kyoto, Japan; Yoneda, Masumi, international human rights law expert, August 22, 2001, Osaka, Japan.

Japanese Comfort Women - Sex Slaves or Prostitutes?
An Issue of Feminist Politics and Historiography

Ulrike Wöhr

1   Introduction

In this paper, I explore the historiographical issue of how members of a nation which, in a particular historical context, has clearly taken the role of aggressor or coloniser might address instances of victimisation suffered, in that same historical context, by their own or other groups belonging to that nation. I ask how this can take place without playing down or relativising the atrocities committed by one's own country, or one's own responsibility as a citizen of that country.[1]

My interest in this problem results, not least, from my background as a member of the nation that is guilty of having committed the holocaust, the most cruel, perfectionist and large-scale crime against humanity that was ever committed by a people. The relevance of this issue to contemporary German politics and society is indicated by the debate that peaked in 2003 on how to deal with the history and memories of the Germans who fled and were expelled from Eastern Europe, in the aftermath of the War.[2]

In theorising my own perspective on how to account for the history of 'victims in a country of perpetrators' (Frevert 2003), I was influenced by Atina Grossmann's work on the rape of German women by occupation soldiers, which occurred after World War II. From her perspective as a feminist historian of Jewish descent, Grossmann (1995) criticised the way in which two German feminist film makers subsumed this case under the category of militarised sexual violence against women, without paying attention to the specific historical circumstances by which these members of a nation that had only just been forced to stop its crusade against humanity were turned into victims.[3] Since my own field is the modern history of women and feminism in Japan, my approach to this problem takes as its subject the ongoing discourse on Japanese victims of militarised sexual violence, which evolved in Japan as part of a larger debate on the so-called 'comfort women' system (*ianfu seido*).[4]

This particularly coercive system of prostitution was established by the Japanese military during the Asia-Pacific War and, significantly, victimised mostly women from Asian nations other than Japan. Of an estimated total of 50,000 to 200,000 women forced into prostitution for Japanese soldiers,[5] a large majority came from Korea and China.[6] Only a minority of the comfort women (*ianfu*) came from Japan.[7] The history of the comfort women was first brought to worldwide public attention by the coming-out of survivors from Korea, who were supported by Korean women's groups. The issue gained momentum in Japan when, in 1991, three of these women took legal action against the Japanese government, demanding an official apology and the payment of individual reparations.[8] It is a well-known fact that at least the latter of these claims still has not been met. In Japan, feminist groups, including groups and individuals from the Korean minority, have been the most dedicated supporters of the survivors from Korea and other Asian nations. But even within these movements, recognition of the existence of Japanese comfort women constituted a taboo that lasted through most of the 1990s.

In the following paragraphs, I refer to texts by feminists living and writing in Japan, including women of Japanese nationality as well as Korean resident women. Seven articles by Japanese feminists, related to the topic of the Japanese comfort women, will be analysed in detail and with regard to the following questions. First, what are the functions, and what might be the dangers of raising the issue of Japanese comfort women and other instances of militarised sexual violence against Japanese women within national as well as transnational contexts? Second, how can we find ways to communicate across the lines of 'first world' and 'third world', 'majority' and 'minority' without limiting members of the former to confessions of guilt? That is, how can we allow for discourses in which the 'majority' may explore its culpable involvement in the victimisation of the 'minority', but also the experiences of victimisation that it might be sharing with the less privileged minority?

Of course it is also important to see that a discourse that only allows for the two dichotomous positions of 'perpetrator' and 'victim' also restricts the 'victims' to explorations of their status as objects of exploitation and discrimination. One might, therefore, ask the corresponding question of how the victimised side could become free to explore instances of its own involvement in colonisation or victimisation, without subsequently being pressured into giving up its claims of compensation for the injustice it has suffered. This problem has actually been addressed by feminist sociologist Jung Yeong-hae (e.g., Oka and Jung 1995: 16-18), a Korean resident of Japan. For my part, I take it as my task to explore the former issue, which is more relevant to my own position as an heir to the guilt of Nazi Germany, as being born into one of the privileged societies of the 'first world', and as living and working in another.

In the following I will first address some theoretical questions that feminist movements have been confronted with in a globalising world. In this context, I will introduce findings by Vera Mackie, which provide the framework of my analysis. Second, I will give an account of some of the questions raised in Japan with regard to the complex issue of comfort women of Japanese nationality. I will then analyse important contributions by Japanese feminist authors to the topic of militarised sexual violence against Japanese women. Finally, I will review the implications of the discussion with regard to the questions raised above.

2   Feminisms in a Globalising World

In rapidly globalising societies, transnational collaboration between nationally or locally based women's movements and collaboration between feminists of different ethnic backgrounds becomes an imperative, as more and more of the problems confronted by these movements are of a global nature. Feminists can address issues like, for instance, the plight of migrant workers in the sex industry or militarised prostitution only if they are prepared to cross the borders between nations and ethnic groups in their concepts and actions. However, crossing borders is not such an easy thing to do in a world where the nation state is not only the basic organisational unit but also the source of rights, privileges and, not least, identities. Moreover, national or ethnic belonging usually determines our access to essential goods, education and protection by the rule of law, and influences our lives in ways that grant wealth and freedom to some, but take away the most basic human rights and means of subsistence from many others.

Women's movements and feminist theories in privileged countries of the Western world have, for many decades, tried to do away with this gap. Their approaches have postulated gender discrimination to be the primary basis of oppression, and have focused on the universal oppression of women by patriarchy. However, their concept of a 'cross-culturally singular, monolithic notion of patriarchy or male dominance' (Mohanty 1988: 63) has come under severe criticism during the last two decades. The assumption of 'women' as an already constituted and coherent group has served to homogenise and colonise the experiences of women in third world countries, thereby suppressing the 'constitutive complexities' characterising their lives (ibid.). Paradoxically, while maintaining the notion of the 'sameness' of women's oppression (ibid. 65), Western feminists have, in their discourse, created what Chandra Mohanty calls the 'third-world difference' (ibid. 63), which reduces third world women to 'objects' debilitated by generalised 'third world' political, economic and cultural constraints in addition to sexual constraints, while holding Western society as the norm (ibid. 65, 79-80).

This image of the 'third-world woman' is not only paternalistic and degrading, but also misleading in that it evades the global political and economic contexts that constitute a crucial factor in the relationships between women of different nations, ethnicities or other social groups within nations and, indeed, separate the lives and experiences of these women. Feminists in both the 'first' and 'third' worlds have come to criticise such hegemonic feminist discourses and have, simultaneously, explored ways to reach across national borders and across the differences that are signified, or created, by these borders.

Vera Mackie, who investigated recent examples of transnational feminist movements in the Asian context, has found that there are two different types of transnational collaboration. The first one is grounded on 'a notion of similarity based on social location rather than nationality, ethnicity or a simple binary notion of gender' (Mackie 2001: 194). As one example, Mackie (ibid. 194) cites links between women in the Philippines, South Korea and Okinawa. These women address problems of militarised prostitution and sexual violence committed by soldiers, which emerged due to the deployment of American military in their communities. The second type of collaboration is not based on similarity but on 'a recognition of mutual imbrication in structures of inequality, which privilege some while placing others in a situation of oppression' (ibid. 195). To illustrate this, Mackie (ibid. 195-196) refers to the Tokyo-based Asian Women's Association, which stresses an involvement in chains of production and consumption that privilege Japanese women while exploiting other Asian women.

Mackie (ibid. 196-197) points out that 'there are likely to be difficulties where potential collaborators are differently positioned according to hierarchies which are gendered, racialised, ethnicised and classed.' It might be inferred that difficulties arise, particularly in situations where one group stresses similarities, whereas the other group expects its partners to recognize their own involvement in the exploitation or victimisation suffered by that group. Such situations should, however, not be dismissed as failed attempts to unite across the divide between 'first world' and 'third world', 'coloniser' and 'colonised' or 'majority' and 'minority'. Rather, some of these clashes may be understood as being part of ongoing negotiations in which the metaphors of 'first world woman' and 'third world woman' are re-contextualized and, at the same time, deconstructed to a certain extent. Indeed, Mohanty and some other postcolonial feminist theorists have themselves been criticised for a simplistic discourse coupling an ahistorical concept of postcoloniality with the category of woman, thereby 'elevat[ing] the racially female voice into a metaphor for the good' (Suleri 1992: 759).

Feminist discourses centring on the subject of the military prostitution system established by Japan during the Asia-Pacific War exemplify such a negotiation across ethnic differences, and this has, indeed, been disrupted by conflict and tension. The feminist links from which these discourses emerge are links between women of Japanese and other Asian backgrounds. With regard to the history of the comfort women, the former may be seen to represent the 'coloniser' or 'victimiser', whereas the latter are commonly perceived to embody the 'colonised' or 'victimised.' Accordingly, one might expect to find that recognition of a history of engagement in colonial power structures at two ends of the hierarchies forming these structures provides the common ground of efforts to unite across national and ethnic borders. Instead, I found that these discourses oscillate between – in Mackie's terms – notions of similarity and recognitions of 'mutual imbrication.' Surely, the writings reviewed for this article revealed notions of such an imbrication and a consciousness of existing inequalities, even on the side of the former colonisers. At the same time, however, a relationship of what Mackie calls 'similarity based on social location' was postulated. Such an approach tended to coincide with a focus on the history of the Japanese women who were forced into serving as comfort women. It was, primarily, Japanese contributors to the debate who constructed the history of Japanese and other Asian comfort women in terms of similarity – basing their argument on what they considered a shared experience of militarised sexual exploitation.[9]

3   Japanese Comfort Women and Their Significance for (Feminist) Politics

In this section, I will trace the beginnings of the discourse on Japanese comfort women, which evolved during the 1990s. This discourse constitutes the background for the feminist texts about military sexual violence against Japanese women that will be analysed in the following section. Two opposing but interdependent contexts need to be introduced here as important vantage points and frames of reference for these feminist accounts of the victimisation of Japanese women. These contexts are, on the one hand, the transnational feminist discourse on the comfort women, which has been going on since the early 1990s, and, on the other hand, strong tendencies within contemporary Japanese society to reinterpret Japan's war-time history as one of glory, and its post-war history as one of victimisation and humiliation.

This recent demand within Japanese society for a nationalistic reinterpretation of history is most conspicuously represented by the Japan Society for History Textbook Reform (*Atarashii Rekishi Kyōkasho o Tsukuru Kai*; hereafter: Textbook Society), which was founded by well-known intellectuals and academics in December 1996. This group protests against mentioning the comfort women system and other Japanese atrocities in history textbooks, as it deems these facts part of a 'masochistic' or 'self-tormenting history' (*ji-gyaku shikan*) forced upon Japan after the war by both camps of the Cold War system.[10]

The relationship between the historical revisionists' claims and feminist writings on Japanese victims of militarised sexual violence appears, at first sight, to be a rather straightforward one of nationalism versus anti-nationalism, and of overt sexism versus the condemnation of sexual violence and gender injustice. My discussion will show, however, that the connections between these discourses are somewhat more complicated and that, for feminists in Japan, to raise the issue of the Japanese comfort women actually constitutes a precarious balancing act.

Regarding the transnational feminist discourse on Japan's wartime system of military prostitution, it is quite obvious that Japanese feminists' treatises of military sexual violence committed against Japanese women constitute a somewhat self-conscious and potentially controversial contribution to this discourse. The transnational discourse was sparked by Korean survivors and supported by Korean volunteer groups. From the beginning, these groups stressed elements of colonialism and ethnic discrimination as primary features and causes of the comfort women system (Yamashita 1996). They were, thus, implying that the forces dividing nations and ethnicities outweighed the similarities of gendered experience. The assertion that Japanese women were also victimised by this system clearly challenges this view. Japanese feminists who emphasise the similarities between Japanese and other Asian comfort women may appear to be relativising the atrocities committed by Japan and to be denying the responsibility of Japanese women who partook and, arguably, still partake in their own nation's colonial privileges and power.

Not surprisingly, the existence of Japanese comfort women was not, at first, emphasised by Japanese feminists but by the Japanese government in statements it made in 1992 and 1993, following the official investigation of the comfort women issue.[11] The South-Korean women's movement reacted with strong indignation to the Japanese government's assertion that Japanese women were equally victimised by the Japanese military. This movement emphasised that Japanese comfort women needed to be distinguished from other comfort women as their being used in military brothels was only an extension of their previous work within Japan's licensed prostitution system. This argument was based on the allegedly contractual character of the licensed prostitute's work, including regular payment and the freedom to quit. In contrast, Korean comfort women were considered to have been forced into sexual slavery by the Japanese state and military (Yamashita 1996: 44; see also Soh 2004: 179-183). This part of the Korean activists' response to the Japanese government reports was never translated into Japanese, as it met with strong criticism within the Korean movement (Yamashita 1996: 55, note No. 16). Its tenor, however, became known to Japanese feminists – at least those within academia – through an article by Yamashita Yeong-ae, a feminist historian born from a Japanese mother and a Korean father (Yamashita Y. 2000).[12] Yamashita (1996: 44-45) pointed out that the prominence of nationalism in the South-Korean discourse on the comfort women had led to the suppression of arguments representing the viewpoint of gender, even within the Korean women's movement. She concluded that the evasion of sexual discrimination as a major cause behind the comfort women system resulted in the movement's failure to address the androcentrism of Korean society. Yamashita maintained that this same androcentrism was the reason why it had taken fifty years for the Korean survivors of the comfort women system to raise their voices and gain public attention.

More than a year before the publication of Yamashita's article, feminist sociologist Ueno Chizuko had raised the topic of Japanese comfort women at a workshop held at the

NGO forum of the Beijing Women's Conference in 1995. The essence of her argument was that the issue of Japanese comfort women could not be resolved as long as feminism was divided by nationalism, and she made an appeal for feminism to overcome nationalism. Apparently, Ueno's words were (or, maybe, had to be) understood to imply a critique of the nationalist discourse prominent in the South-Korean women's movement. Her stance was countered by a Korean-American woman in the audience who asserted that for Asian feminists, whom colonialism had deprived of their identity, nationalism in the sense of self-determination or sovereignty constituted a necessity, and that Ueno's statement reminded her of the kind of ethnocentrism characterising Western feminism (Yamazaki 1995: 65). This controversy was transmitted to the Japanese public through reports by participants of the Beijing conference, which were published in various books and journals (e.g. Kim 1996 and Yamazaki 1995: 65). These reports sparked a heated debate among intellectuals and activists in Japan that continued through the second half of the 1990s. The primary adversaries were Ueno and Korean resident, feminist and historian Kim Puja. A number of Japanese feminist academics, male Japanese academics and male members of the Korean minority joined Kim in her criticism of Ueno's point of view.[13] To be sure, the actors in this debate were all declared opponents of the historical revisionists. Below, I will trace the main arguments of the controversy between Kim and Ueno.

Referring to the above quoted article by Yamashita Yeong-ae, Ueno (1998: 129) pointed out that the nationalistic logic of the South-Korean support movement, characterising Korean comfort women as sex slaves and Japanese comfort women as prostitutes by their own free will, led to a discourse that was discriminatory against prostitutes in general. In the same context, Ueno (1996: 37; 1998: 124-125) criticised the creation of an innocent 'model victim' (moderu higaisha), as this would result in the exclusion of cases that did not exactly fit this model, and would reproduce the patriarchal norm of female chastity.[14] Ueno (1998: 129-131) further maintained that to create an opposition between Korean and Japanese comfort women would result in subsuming feminism under nationalism, which was, ultimately, another variety of patriarchy. She postulated that only by transcending nation and ethnicity would feminism be able to reveal that patriarchy had victimised Japanese and Korean women alike and, in fact, constituted the basis of constructs like ethnicity and nation. Consequently, Ueno refused to take on Japan's guilt and rejected colonialism as a useful category to approach the comfort women issue (Nihon no Sensō Sekinin Shiryō Sentā 1998: 62). Ueno's position, nevertheless, included some self-reflexivity. It was with regard to the post-war silence of both Japanese and non-Japanese comfort women that Ueno (1997: 166) admitted 'our "guilt"' (watashitachi no 'tsumi). It is important to note, however, that the 'we' of 'our "guilt"' was not just Japanese society, or Japanese women, but referred to South Korean society as well.[15]

Kim Puja (1998: 194-196) countered that even though both Korean and Japanese comfort women were victims of patriarchy, the differences in their situations, which resulted from colonialism and ethnic discrimination, had to be taken into account. For a member of the victimising nation not to make this distinction was to deny her own responsibility and, ultimately, to reinforce the discourse of Japanese nationalists who were claiming that, during the war, both Japanese and Koreans had suffered alike. In this context, Kim (1998: 197-198) introduced an ethics of standpoint, emphasising the importance of how the speaker as well as the addressee are positioned within a certain discourse. She explained that when Yamashita criticised the Korean women's movement she had the right to do so, since she was a member of that community. Ueno, on the other hand, who was not the addressee of Yamashita's reflections, did not have the right to cite and utilise these reflections in order to substantiate her own point of view.

It is not my purpose here to discuss the respective merits and faults of these positions.[16] Rather, I cite these positions as an example of the difficulties arising in discourses which cross the historical boundaries drawn by imperialism and colonialism. Many Japanese feminist supporters of the comfort women's struggle understood the argument which arose between Ueno and the Korean-American woman at the Beijing conference of 1995 to point to Japanese feminists' lacking awareness of their country's colonialist and imperialist history (e.g., Yamazaki 1995: 65). Apart from this problem, however, this incident and the ensuing debate exemplify the dilemma of raising the issue of the Japanese comfort women within the context of a transnational feminist discourse.

Nevertheless, a number of feminist authors in Japan turned their attention to the topic of militarised violence against Japanese women, including the wartime comfort women. Japanese comfort women, including those who were after the war recruited for sexual service to the U.S. occupation army (*senryōgun ianfu*), became the topic of a number of journalistic accounts and efforts to collect testimonies, some published as early as the 1950s.[17] In this article, however, I concentrate on the discourse evolving after 1995 or, more accurately, after 1996, when the vociferous appearance of the historical revisionists complicated the issue. I focus on feminist academics and the feminist movement in support of the struggle of the comfort women – two groups which, in many cases, overlap and which have most actively engaged in transnational activities and discourse (Germer 2003, Mackie 2003: 202-231, Wöhr 2004). These groups might therefore be expected to be keenly aware of the vicissitudes of transnational feminist politics.

In Japan, the transnational feminist alliance opposing militarised sexual violence against women and supporting the victims of such violence, particularly the survivors of the Japanese comfort women system, is represented by VAWW-Net Japan (Violence-Against-Women-in-War-Network Japan), an organisation founded in 1998. This alliance also organised the Women's International War Crimes Tribunal on Japan's Military Sexual Slavery System, an NGO tribunal that was held in Tokyo in December 2000 to investigate the crimes committed against the comfort women and pass judgement on the perpetrators. When the issue of Japanese victims of the comfort women system surfaced again in the late 1990s, a controversy took place within the transnational feminist alliance and even among the members of VAWW-Net Japan. The issues dividing these feminists were whether Japanese comfort women should be defined as victims of the comfort women system, and whether licensed prostitution could be viewed as the historical basis and background of that system. Disagreement on this issue existed not only between Japanese groups and South-Korean groups or between Japanese groups and Korean resident groups, but also between South Koreans and Koreans residing in Japan, and even among Japanese members of VAWW-Net Japan (Fujime 2001: 90-91).

Ulrike Wöhr

4 Japanese Feminists on Japanese Comfort Women, After the Onslaught of Historical Revisionism

Renewed interest in Japanese victims of militarised sexual violence was documented by two articles on this subject which appeared in 1997, two years after Ueno Chizuko's provocative reference to the Japanese comfort women. One of the factors encouraging the authors of these accounts to take up this controversial topic may have been the publication of Yamashita's article in December 1996. However, none of the texts on Japanese comfort women that appeared after 1996 and will be analysed below cites Yamashita, nor do they refer to the theoretical debate that was, at the same time, evolving between Kim Puja and Ueno Chizuko. In contrast, all but one of these articles (i.e. Nishino 2000a) make explicit reference to the nationalistic tendency which, as already mentioned, became evident in late 1996, when the historical revisionists started their movement to stop the advancement of what they perceived as a 'masochist' or 'self-tormenting view of history' (*jigyaku shikan*). Indeed, the majority of these feminist studies of Japanese women's sexual exploitation by the military and the nation state do not seem to be intended as responses to or continuations of the existing transnational discourse (although they can be read from a transnational perspective). Rather, they may be interpreted as introspective analyses of Japanese society, written in direct opposition to the revisionists' claims.

The articles reviewed here were written by three prominent feminist authors, namely, sociologist Ehara Yumiko who is known for her work on sexuality and prostitution; historian Fujime Yuki who has published widely on the modern Japanese history of sexuality and the state; and journalist Nishino Rumiko. The latter two are actively involved in the movement supporting the former comfort women, Nishino being president of VAWW-Net Japan.[18] Fujime established herself as an authority on Japanese comfort women when she delivered an expert's testimony 'On the Actual Conditions of Recruitment and the Class Background of Japanese Comfort Women' (Fujime 2002) at the Women's International War Crimes Tribunal in 2000. The articles analysed here were chosen for their theoretical impact and importance with regard to the debate on Japanese comfort women. Taken together, Nishino's and Fujime's writings on Japanese comfort women make up most of the existing feminist literature on this issue.

4.1 Positions

Ehara Yumiko has not published much on the topic of comfort women but, according to my findings, the article analysed here (1997) was the first Japanese feminist text referring to the existence of Japanese comfort women in direct reaction to the historical revisionists' claims.[19] Three articles by Fujime Yuki were chosen to be analysed here. The earliest (1997) and the latest (2001) of these article are mainly concerned with the prewar system, whereas the one published in 1999 focuses on militarised sexual violence against Japanese women in the post-war context. Nishino Rumiko, whose achievements in documenting the history of the comfort women extend to victimized women in many Asian nations (see e.g. Nishino 2003), is represented in this chapter with two articles reporting the results of primary research on Japanese comfort women (Nishino 2000a and 2000b). Another text by Nishino that will be quoted below is an epilogue to the proceedings of a symposium on

'Nationalism and the "comfort women" issue.' It summarises important points of the debate, including the problem of the Japanese comfort women (Nishino 1998).

In all these texts, criticism of nationalism and analyses of sexism and misogyny are closely intertwined. In the article by Ehara (1997), this double-edged analytical tool is directly applied to the political discourse of the historical revisionists. Ehara (1997: 27) states as her objective to 'scrutinize the "Textbook Society's" claim that reference to the "comfort women issue" in textbooks arises from a "self-tormenting view of history."' Her discussion shows that the 'self' in 'self-tormenting' can only be understood to refer to an amputated trunk or an extremely exclusive conception of Japanese society. Automatically excluded are all those 'Japanese' who were themselves forced into prostitution or were, in other ways, subjected to sexual violence. To them, Ehara's argument (1997: 30-31) goes, the emergence of the comfort women as a topic of public debate will not mean torment, humiliation and perversion, but liberation. That is, restoration of the comfort women's dignity will also restore the self-esteem of other women whom the sexual double standard of Japanese society has, so-far, compelled to silence and self-hatred. As prime examples of such existences, Ehara (1997: 29-30) refers to the Japanese women who were forced into prostitution for the U.S. occupying troops after the war, and to the women of Okinawa who were victimised by the Japanese troops during the war and, later, by American soldiers, during the long occupation and even until today. Just like the comfort women, such Japanese 'selves' and their histories appear to be excluded from the nationalists' version of 'Japanese history' – although these people claim that theirs is the suppressed version of history, 'which the textbooks do not teach' (ibid. 28-29).

Ehara's emphasis is on the universal nature of sexual violence against women, and on the necessity to address this issue in a global rather than a national context. Her universalist approach is underscored by her discussion of the relationship between prostitution and sexual violence against women, in general. Here, Ehara (1997: 31) challenges the revisionists' assertion that the case of the comfort women poses 'no problem' if it can be shown that they were actually prostitutes who received money for their services. She demands that the comfort women system be discussed not only with regard to whether it was legal or not, at the time, but within a universal framework of human rights (ibid. 31).

Like Ehara, Fujime (1997: 2, 5) makes direct reference to the historical revisionists' claim that the comfort women were licensed prostitutes and, therefore, did not need to be compensated by the Japanese government. She shows that this argument reproduces and makes use of existing prejudices against prostitutes in order to disgrace the former comfort women and, therefore, constitutes a twofold crime. To counter the logic of the revisionists, Fujime (1997: 3-5) goes on to prove in detail that the Japanese system of licensed prostitution (*kōshō seido*) and, indeed, all similar systems were (or are) in themselves criminal and exploitative instruments of power. Most of the women who became licensed prostitutes had, previously, been victims of poverty and social discrimination. The ways in which they were coerced into this system and the slave-like conditions they had to endure are evidence for Fujime (1997: 5, 6) to maintain that all women who were exploited under this system should be entitled to compensation. The revisionists' allegation that the Japanese state need not compensate the comfort women because they were licensed prostitutes (implying that they had entered their jobs voluntarily, enjoyed a regular legal status, received payment, and were free to quit) is thus shown to be a contradiction in terms. Furthermore, Fujime (1997: 6) shows that the nationalists' rhetoric results in intimidating the survivors of this

111

system, making it impossible for any woman who ever took a penny from her 'employers' or 'customers' to come out as a victim.

Fujime not only criticises the rhetoric of those who deny the former comfort women's right to compensation, but also analyses the line of reasoning prevailing among those who argue for the comfort women to be compensated by the Japanese government. In opposition to the revisionists' claims, these people maintain that the comfort women were not licensed prostitutes. Their treatment was illegal even at the time and should, therefore, be atoned for by the Japanese state. Fujime (1997: 2, 7; 2001: 90) shows that, just like the logic of the revisionists, this kind of reasoning reproduces general prejudices against prostitutes and cannot, therefore, truly restore the former comfort women's dignity. Although Fujime (2001: 105) admits that Japanese comfort women were generally better treated than victims from other Asian countries, she cautions that to position the comfort women system against the system of licensed prostitution and to assert the relatively better situation of licensed prostitutes necessarily results in legitimising the use of the licensed prostitution system by the Japanese state and by privileged dealers as a means of exploiting women's sexuality (Fujime 1997: 8). In an extension of this argument, Fujime (1997: 6; 2001: 99-100) also warns that the construction of two opposing types of *ianfu* – sex-slaves versus prostitutes – not only contradicts historical evidence but also continues to prevent countless numbers of former comfort women from coming out and making their suffering known to the public. Fujime (2001: 105) reminds her Korean readers,[20] in particular, that to restore the dignity of those victims of the comfort women system who had previously been licensed prostitutes is of importance not only for Japanese survivors but also for those Korean women who, at the time, were not 'innocent virgins' but had, prior to their being made into comfort women, been victimized by the Japanese system of licensed prostitution, which had spread to the colonies long before the *ianfu* system was established.

Although undertaken from a historical approach, the main thrust of Fujime's criticism can, just as in the case of Ehara, be seen to be against post-war and contemporary Japanese society, which has continued to abuse and silence the victims of sexual violence and – potentially – all of the women who are members of this society (Fujime 1997: 8). The pivot of Fujime's argument, which serves to connect pre-war, post-war and present, is the Anti-Prostitution Law (*Baishun bōshihō*) of 1956, which resulted in criminalising those women who were, after the war, exploited as comfort women for the U.S. occupation troops and never managed to return to a 'normal' life. Fujime (1997: 8-9) shows how the Anti-Prostitution Law follows the pre-war logic of protecting the state, the prostitution business and the men buying prostitutes, while putting the blame on the victimised women and preventing compensation for the damage they suffered. According to Fujime, the logic of this law still informs Japanese people's general opinion about prostitutes, and it is this same public opinion that not only supports the revisionists but also shapes the arguments of their adversaries.

Regarding the influence which public discourse has exerted on the lives of the Japanese comfort women, Fujime (1997: 6-7) shows that Japanese survivors of militarised sexual violence have been silenced not only by the sexual double standard of Japanese society, but also by the attempts of the revisionists to glorify these women as 'professional saviours of the nation' who 'turned the warfront from a state of lawlessness into a state of order'. Moreover, the revisionists have praised the silence kept by Japanese women about wartime experiences, like rape by Russian soldiers in Manchuria, as proof of their heroism.[21] Fujime (ibid.) counters these commendations by reminding us that it was the Japanese state that inflicted these sufferings and preyed on them again after the war, when it turned those same women into comfort women for the occupation forces.

As Nishino Rumiko (2000a: 70-71) shows, the kind of rhetoric celebrating the sexual victimisation of women as a sacrifice for the nation did not start with the historical revisionism of the 1990s, but was already employed during the war, in order to make these women submit to the will of those who tormented them. Nishino's interpretation of the effects of nationalistic rhetoric on the Japanese comfort women's lives is most clearly expressed in the following sentence: 'something that needs to be especially mentioned with regard to the Japanese "comfort women" is how their spirit of "loyalty and patriotism" (*chūkun aikoku*)[22] was shrewdly taken advantage of' (ibid. 70). Nishino shows that, in some cases, the wish to 'give this humble life [*chiisana nikutai*]' for Tennō and country made even young girls decide to sign up as comfort women (ibid. 70). Further, the sources quoted by Nishino prove that Japanese comfort women were made to believe that in case of their death at the front they would be enshrined in the Yasukuni Shrine, and would be worshipped just like the souls of fallen soldiers (ibid. 70-71). Nishino comments that

> [o]f course … the history of the 'holy war' [*seisen*] neglected and erased the lives of these women as the 'disgrace' [*chibu*] of the imperial army …. The silence [forced upon these women], after the war, shows that Japanese women, too, were existences consigned to the darkness of oblivion, whose past was taken away from them by the ideology of chastity. The reality of their continuing silence [reveals that their postwar experiences] were no different from the postwar [experiences] of the [former] Korean [comfort] women. (ibid. 71)

Back in the context of wartime Japan, Nishino also tells the story of a young Korean woman who was living in Japan with her mother and grandfather, and was recruited to work as an auxiliary nurse in a military hospital in Nagasaki. She never arrived in Nagasaki but, instead, was shipped to a 'comfort station' (*ianjo*) in order to work there, together with one hundred Japanese women who had been deceived in the same way. Part of the reason this Korean woman stated for having agreed to work in a military hospital was that she saw this as an opportunity 'to serve the country, even as a woman' (Nishino 2000a: 86-87). Nishino presents this case in order to show that '[like Japanese women,] Korean women [living in Japan] were also tricked into becoming "comfort women" as the result of their accepting some job offer' (ibid. 85). Both the experience of this woman as a Korean immigrant and her utterance about wishing to serve the Japanese country seem to call for closer examination and interpretation. However, Nishino misses the chance to discuss the different implications that such an invocation of 'the country' (*kuni*) might have implied for Koreans as compared to Japanese, but merely emphasizes the similarities between the experiences of these women.

4.2 Discussion

As can be seen from the above reconstruction of the three authors' arguments, an emphasis on 'similarities' constitutes a common feature. Admittedly, the 'difference' created by colonialism (or ethnicity) is explicitly mentioned in two of the reviewed articles. These are the most recent one by Fujime (2001), which was first published in the South-Korean journal *Dandae pipyeong* ("Contemporary Review"), and Nishino's epilogue to the symposium on 'Nationalism and the comfort women issue' (Nishino 1998), which was organized as a follow-up on the controversy that had evolved between Kim Puja and Ueno Chizuko and in which, apart from Kim, another intellectual with Korean background participated. For an author not to mention the impact of ethnicity and colonialism would, in these contexts, have been to outrage the Korean side. However, even in these texts, it is emphasised that 'when one approaches the issue of the comfort women primarily as a problem of Japan's crime of invading Asia, one easily loses sight of the Japanese "comfort women" who were Japanese citizens [*kokumin*] and members of the invading people' (Fujime 2001: 90). Both authors, implicitly, agree with Ueno Chizuko, Nishino (1998: 240) stating that the question as to whether feminism can overcome nationalism should be linked with the question as to why the history of the Japanese "comfort women" has hardly been investigated even though [feminists] have been aware of the existence of that problem. Nishino maintains that the standpoint from which this problem should be dealt with is that of sexism, and that such an approach will grant a continued and expanded discussion.

Like Ueno, all three authors examined here problematise the silence surrounding the Japanese comfort women, and blame the sexism prevalent in Japanese society for this silence. Consequently all three, like Ueno, postulate the primacy of suppression on grounds of gender over suppression on grounds of ethnicity.[23] Of course, it is not their intention to deny the crimes committed by Japan as an imperialist and colonial power in Asia. The objective of these authors to critically analyse and change their own society (explicitly stated by Nishino 1998: 243, and Fujime 2001: 100) could even be seen to justify their preoccupation with sexism. A connection between these authors' emphasis on gender and their introspective view of Japanese society is also suggested by the fact that they criticise the historical revisionists primarily for their sexism, and mention their nationalism only insofar as it colludes with sexual discrimination against Japanese women. This approach could be taken to imply that oppression within a certain society is limited to sexism, whereas ethnic discrimination occurs not within but only between countries. Indeed, issues concerning ethnic minorities and the interrelatedness of sexual and ethnic discrimination do not seem to be of much interest to these authors. This shortcoming is exemplified by Fujime's and Nishino's discussions of the comfort women who were recruited from the licensed quarters of Naha in Okinawa. Both authors subsume these women under the category of 'Japanese comfort women' without mentioning that Okinawan women were also subject to ethnic discrimination by 'mainland' Japanese (Fujime 2001: 92–94, Nishino 2000b: 128-129).[24]

In a way, this neglect of ethnic diversity contradicts the assertion by all three authors that Japanese society is structured by diverse categories, namely, gender and class. Fujime (2001: 105) explicitly deconstructs the 'nation' which, according to her, 'is not homogeneous' but divided by 'power relations of gender and class.' Nishino (2000a: 90) asserts that 'the fact that women from the poorest and lowest classes became the target of recruitment shows clearly the extent to which the "comfort women" system was based on women's discrimination as well as class distinctions.' Ehara (1997), as has been shown, deconstructs the 'nation' into people who will be 'tormented' and people who will be liberated by the entry of the comfort women issue into school textbooks.

Another characteristic of these texts that could be understood to result from their introspective approach is the difference in attention paid to discursive constraints of apparent relevance to Japanese society as compared to discursive realities that seem to be external. Ehara, for instance, who postulates that both national borders and the dualistic division between the 'virgin' and the 'whore' should be overcome, does not discuss these terms with equal confidence. With regard to the issue of "virgin and whore", she seems to be rather uneasy with her own strategy of treating comfort women in the same context as Japanese and Okinawan prostitutes of the occupation army, conceding that it might be denigrating to the comfort women to be put into the same category with prostitutes (Ehara 1997: 32). Her reluctance may be seen to result from her insight into issues relevant to her own society, e.g. existing prejudices against prostitutes, and the problem of how to conceive of the relationship between prostitution and sexual violence.[25] However, when Ehara (1997: 34) asserts the obsolescence of nationalism and the universality of sexual violence against women, she does not take discursive realities into account in the same way. She refers to the comfort women issue's universal dimension of gendered sexual violence without even mentioning its particular dimension of ethnic discrimination, and thus ignores the importance which the latter dimension has to the survivors and many of their supporters.

The deconstruction of established categories like 'nation' and of binary oppositions like 'virgin–whore' is an important discursive strategy employed in all these texts. Similarly, Nishino, Fujime and, albeit less explicitly, Ehara oppose the creation of a 'model victim' (although none of the three authors uses this term, which was introduced into the debate by Ueno Chizuko). The topic is most clearly addressed by Fujime (2001: 90) when she maintains that to view the issue of the comfort women as a problem of 'the victimisation of innocent non-Japanese virgins who were made into comfort women against their will' is to contribute to rendering the Japanese comfort women invisible. Nishino's account of the life of one Japanese comfort woman who told her deeply distressing story in a book that came out in 1971 (Nishino 2000a: 71-77, Shirota 1971) and, again, in an anonymous radio interview, in 1985, is also an argument against the creation of a 'model victim'. The testimony of this woman remained almost unnoticed, not only before but also after the coming-out of the first Korean comfort women and the formation of a support movement in Japan. Nishino (2000a: 76-77, 2000b: 128) points out that this woman was excluded from the category of 'victim' because she was Japanese, and because she had been a prostitute before she 'volunteered' to become a comfort woman.

However, one might ask if Nishino is not herself in danger of creating a 'model victim', namely, by asserting that the category of class – together with that of gender – constituted the basis of the comfort women system as a whole (Nishino 2000a: 90). Apart from the question whether we can legitimately locate the lowest social stratum of colonial Japan on the same level as the lowest social stratum of colonised Korea – a problem that has, for example, been addressed by Kim Puja (1998: 199–200) – the assumption of lower class and poverty as a determining factor in the history of the comfort women also constitutes a problem. As Tanaka Yuki (2002: 80) has shown, there were, for instance, Indonesian women who ended up as comfort women precisely as a result of their relatively privileged status as daughters of local public servants. Through their fathers, they had primary access to the information that the Japanese were offering to take young Indonesian women to Tokyo to study Japanese. This information was, of course, false, and the women ended up boarding

115

the ships that transported them to comfort stations in Singapore and other places in Southeast Asia.

A basic problem flawing the analysed texts by Ehara, Fujime and Nishino seems to lie in the fact that the new categories which are, implicitly or explicitly, constructed in place of the old, discredited ones are not subjected to the same critical analysis and, therefore, are in danger of constituting yet another ideology.

This is also true of the new category of 'Asian people' or 'Asian woman' introduced by Fujime in at least two of her articles. In one of these (Fujime 1999), she traces the atrocities committed by members of the U.S. forces against Japanese women during the occupation and the Korean War. During these years, Japan was literally turned into a 'comfort base' ('*ian' kichi*) for American soldiers fighting in Korea (Fujime 1999: 124-127). Moreover, Japanese women working at U.S. bases in Japan were taken to the warfront in Korea, where they were exploited as comfort women, and many of them were killed either in bombings, or by retreating American troops (ibid. 128-130). Fujime examines the complicity of the Japanese government and the privileged strata of the Japanese bureaucracy and industry in this unprecedented victimisation of Japanese women. She reminds us that integration into the U.S. anticommunist containment policy was not simply imposed on Japan, but was also in the interest of the conservative elites of Japan. Their war crimes remained unpunished, and rather than ousting them from power, the U.S. policy worked to confirm their authority (ibid. 131). Fujime (1999: 135) asserts that

> there is a connection between Japanese women's suffering of sexual violence during the years when the cold-war system took shape, and the ordeals suffered by the people of East Asia, who became victims of the U.S. cold-war policy during that same period. Moreover, these experiences are in continuity with the experiences of the Asian women who were enslaved by the Japanese military during the Asia-Pacific War, and with the present sufferings of sexual violence inflicted on women by American troops stationed in Asia, including the Japanese main islands and Okinawa. The ruling classes of the U.S. and Japan have linked the chains of imperialism and sexual violence to expand like a web into all directions, and have sacrificed the women of East Asia to the military. These connections are obscured and misrepresented by those who use the sexual exploitation of Japanese women after Japan's defeat as a pretext to argue that there is no need [for the Japanese government] to recompense the [war-time, non-Japanese] 'comfort women'. This is a vicious argument as it exploits the Japanese women who were already in the past exploited for the sake of the nation, for a second time. This time, this happens to scorn those other Asian women who stood up to testify [to the crimes committed against them], and to divide Japanese women and other Asian women into two camps.

As this quote demonstrates, Fujime postulates a community of Asian women, which includes Japanese women and is based on the shared experience of militarised sexual violence. This new category of 'Asian woman' rests on Fujime's analysis of militarised sexual violence against Asian women as being a problem of class and of race. To include Japanese women on an equal level of victimhood, Fujime needs to distinguish between guilty 'elites', or 'ruling classes', and innocent 'people' (see also Fujime 2001: 96-97, 105-106), as well as between 'Asians' and 'non-Asians'. As a result, she collapses the past into the present, and Japan into Asia. The consequence is, again, a disregard of ethnic discrimination and colonialism, realities that are being emphasised by the former comfort women and their supporters. Paradoxically, Fujime could thus be accused of employing a discursive strategy not so different from the one that she criticises with regard to the historical revisionists. As Fujime (1999: 117) tells us, these people claim that the crimes that Japan inflicted on Asia have already been atoned for through Japan's own sufferings during and after the war.[26]

Ultimately, the way in which the feminist authors discussed here approach the issue of the Japanese comfort women might be associated with the 'victim consciousness' (*higaisha ishiki*) which John Dower detected even among 'progressive' Japanese intellectuals, shortly after the war. These intellectuals protested against the incorporation of Japan into U.S. cold-war policy and against rearmament, but they attempted 'to nurture antiwar sentiments in Japan by appealing directly to the suffering experienced by the Japanese in the recent war' (Dower 1993: 10).

5   Conclusion

The main objectives of the texts analysed above may be summarised, firstly, as an opposition to nationalistic tendencies in Japanese society; secondly, they address the misogyny of Japanese society in the past and present (namely, the sexual double standard and the dualistic norm of 'virgin'/'mother' versus 'whore'); and, thirdly, they imagine new communities defined by gender, class and race, in order to overcome Japan's (or Japanese women's) isolation within Asia. These objectives are, as such, honourable and sincere and, from an exclusively Japanese viewpoint, offer much-needed social criticism. However, from the perspective of a transnational feminist movement based on the recognition of mutual but unequal 'imbrication', the discourse on Japanese comfort women which is represented by these contributions is problematic in several respects.

The most obvious and basic problem lies in the generalisation of concrete historical cases into an abstract concept of sexual violence, which obscures more specific mechanisms and categories of discrimination like, for instance, that of ethnicity. For the same reason, it also seems problematic to ignore categories which historically divided women – for instance, the division between 'internal' (*naichi no*) and 'external' (*gaichi no*) subjects of the Japanese empire – in order to create other, seemingly comprehensive, categories – like 'lower class,' 'Asian woman,' or just 'woman.' The above discussion has also shown that even seemingly inclusive categories necessarily result in new exclusions that must be accounted for.

In concrete terms, it is the following two strategies of the reviewed essays on Japanese comfort women, which, in my view, are problematic and need to be reconsidered. First, Japanese victims of militarised sexual violence are discussed in isolation, that is, without clarifying their (unequal) relationship to other women victimised by the Japanese army. While similarities are emphasised, differences are neglected. Second, Japanese women are only looked upon as victims, and not from the perspective of their active and, often, patriotically inspired support of the war and the colonial system.

The solution, of course, does not lie in disregarding the history of Japanese comfort women altogether. As Japanese, as Germans, as Americans, we can of course easily avoid any blame by simply concentrating on retelling the suffering that our nations have inflicted on others. By concerning ourselves exclusively with our nation's crimes against others, we can prove our impeccable morality, our political correctness, so to speak. But an approach that neglects the oppressed in our own society cannot truly solve the problem.

The history of the Japanese comfort women needs to be written, just like the history of the atomic bombings of Hiroshima and Nagasaki and of their victims, and the history of the German women who were raped by Russian soldiers after the end of World War II. For the sake of a more complex view of history, and if we are really driven by a humanist desire to analyse the causes of discrimination and violence against the 'other', we will have to turn our eyes to those 'others' whom we have discriminated against within our own society. Also, the foremost task which the most suppressed groups of people from the 'third world' (or of the postcolonial world) have set us inhabitants of the 'first world' is to change our own society. If this is so, then it is indeed our duty to expose the mechanisms of sexual violence at work in our society, and to examine how sexual violence in our own country is being concealed and justified. The essays by Ehara, Fujime and Nishino are certainly dedicated to this task, but in the process they seem to lose sight of what should be their frame of reference.

Luckily, the privilege of inhabitants of the 'first world' to set the agenda and impose their categories of analysis is, increasingly, being challenged. We tend to assume that the 'similarities' of our experiences of discrimination must form the basis of our transnational collaborations. However, we are being reminded that, as our starting point we may have to accept our 'mutual imbrications', or our involvement in global structures and processes that are based on hierarchies and inequalities. With regard to the Japanese comfort women, we are requested to write their history in view of their 'imbrication' in structures of inequality of their time – a truly transnational framework.

Notes

[1] The first version of this chapter was presented at the EAJS conference in Warsaw, in 2003, a second version was presented at the VSJF conference on Gender Dynamics and Globalization, in Berlin, in 2004. I thank all those people whose comments helped improving this text, especially Andrea Germer, Ilse Lenz, Vera Mackie and Carol Rinnert.

[2] See, for instance, the critical appeal by an international group of academics (Hahn et al. 2003) against the 'Centre against Expulsions' (Zentrum gegen Vertreibungen) which has been promoted by the 'Federation of Expellees' (Bund der Vertriebenen), an organisation representing the interests of Germans displaced from their homes in historical Eastern Germany and other parts of Eastern Europe, and an essay on the topic by historian Ute Frevert (2003).

[3] See also Grossmann 1998.

[4] For stylistic reasons I will, hereafter, use the term 'comfort women' without indicating the contentious nature of this term by quotation marks, even though this contradicts the convention governing most Japanese texts.

[5] See Yoshimi 2000: 91-94. There are, however, also estimates as low as 20,000 (see note 7).

[6] Most authors assume that the overwhelming majority – about 80 percent – of the comfort women came from Korea (e.g., Tanaka 2002: 31). Yoshimi Yoshiaki (2000: 96), however, stresses that 'the number of Chinese comfort women was probably larger than is usually assumed.'

[7] Whereas most authors speak of a small minority of Japanese comfort women, Fujime's (2001: 97) estimate is 'several tens of thousands' (*sūmannin*). She concedes, however, that the lack of

historical sources and survivors' testimonies makes it impossible to estimate the exact number. Another author who estimates the number of Japanese *ianfu* to have been high, at least in relative terms, is conservative historian Hata Ikuhiko. According to Hata (1999: 410), about 40 percent of the *ianfu* came from Japan (he uses the term *naichijin*). He claims, however, that the total number of comfort women did not exceed 20,000 (Hata 1999: 406).

[8] The three women were part of a group of Koreans that filed a class action suit against the Japanese government demanding compensation for the violation of human rights of certain categories of Koreans under Japanese colonial rule.

[9] However, one feminist historian of Korean descent also strongly emphasised the aspect of similarity (see Song 1997).

[10] The establishment of the Japan Society for History Textbook Reform was preceeded by that of the Liberal Historiography Research Association (Jiyūshugi Shikan Kenkyūkai) in September 1996. Both were initiated by Tokyo University professor Fujioka Nobukatsu, who was joined by other influential academics and intellectuals. Both groups attack existing forms of history education from a nationalist perspective (see Kersten 1999).

[11] As early as 1990, Korean women's groups had requested the Japanese government, which stubbornly denied the involvement of the state and the military in the establishment and management of the comfort women system, to disclose the historical facts (Yun et al. 1992: 253-258). However, the government only responded to this demand in 1992, after Japanese historian Yoshimi Yoshiaki had discovered and published documents proving the direct involvement of the Japanese army in setting up 'comfort stations' (*ianjo*) (Yoshimi 2000: 35–36).

[12] About how Yamashita's transnational background shaped her identity as a scholar and a feminist, see Wöhr 2004: 79-81.

[13] See, especially, the symposium on 'Nationalism and the "comfort women" issue' (Nihon no Sensō Sekinin Shiryō Sentā 1998).

[14] See also Ueno 1997: 168. Although Ueno developed her historiographical argument on the comfort women system in several publications from 1996 onward, I mostly refer to her book *Nashonarizumu to jendā* (Ueno 1998), where she summed up her own position.

[15] This becomes clear from Ueno's (1997: 166) explanation that the main factor suppressing the voices of the former comfort women was patriarchy, which governed both Japanese and South Korean societies (*Nikkan no kafuchōsei*).

[16] For a reconstruction and discussion of the controversy between Kim Puja and Ueno Chizuko, from the viewpoint of feminist identity politics, see Wöhr 2004: 71-79.

[17] Some examples of journalistic accounts and (anonymous) memoirs are Tomida 1953, Akashi 1957, Shirota 1971, Hirota 1975, Yamada 1992 and Inoue 1995. See also the bibliography in Kamiyama 2004.

[18] When Nishino published the articles that are reviewed in this chapter, she was vice president of VAWW-Net Japan.

[19] Ehara was also one of the first academics to respond to the lawsuit of 1991 that was launched by three former Korean comfort women (Ehara 1992; see also Wöhr 2004). The article by Ehara which is analysed in this chapter was cited by Fujime (1997: 9, note No. 2) to correspond to her own view of the relationship between '*ianfu*' and 'public prostitutes'.

[20] Fujime 2001 was first published in the South Korean journal *Dandae pipyeong* ("Contemporary Review") 14 (Spring 2001). See Fujime 2001: 107.

[21] Fujime cites *manga* writer Kobayashi Yoshinori, one of the most prominent members of the Textbook Society.

[22] In Nishino's text, this is rendered as *chūkoku aikoku*. However, I strongly suspect that this is a misprint as, to my knowledge, no such expression existed.

[23] An interesting question to be asked is why Ueno has been criticised for this assertion, but not

[24] Fujime or Nishino (the latter being, after all, the top representative of the Japanese side in the transnational feminist movement in support of the comfort women). This question cannot be pursued, and certainly not answered in this paper. Part of the reason may lie in the recent history of Japanese feminism, in which Ueno took a leading but contested role (see Yamashita, A. 2000).

[24] Ehara (1997: 29-30), at least implicitly, acknowledges the combination of ethnic and sexual discrimination that Okinawan women suffered from Japanese soldiers during the war. An author who particularly emphasises the ethnic aspect of the history of Okinawan comfort women is Urasaki Shigeko (2000: 95-96).

[25] Ehara's own interpretation of this relationship is ambiguous. On the one hand, she warns against identifying sex workers with victims of sexual violence, but on the other, she seems to deny the existence of anything like 'voluntary prostitution' (Ehara 1997: 32-33).

[26] This strategy of the revisionists has also been critically commented on by Takahashi Tetsuya ('Konpasshon wa kanō ka?' Taiwa Shūkai Jikkō Iinkai 2002: 18-19).

References

Akashi, Seizō. 1957. *Kisarazu kichi: Jin'niku no ichi* [Kisarazu Military Base: Trade in Human Flesh]. Tokyo: Yōyōsha.

Ehara, Yumiko. 1992. 'Jūgun ianfu ni tsuite' [About the Military Comfort Women]. In: *Shisō no kagaku* 159 (December): 32–41.

-----. 1997. '"Jūgun ianfu mondai" no kyōkasho kisai ni yotte seishinteki ni ijikesaserareru "Nihonjin" to wa, dare no koto ka?' [Who Are the 'Japanese' Who Are Being Psychologically Stunted by the School Textbooks' Reference to the 'Comfort Women Issue'?]. In: *Jōkyō* (April): 27–34.

Frevert, Ute. 2003. 'Die Rückkehr der Opfer im Land der Täter: Über den Erinnerungsboom und die Chancen der Historisierung' [The Return of the Victims in the Country of the Perpetrators: On the Memory Boom and the Chances of Historicisation]. In: *Neue Züricher Zeitung*. August 30.

Fujime, Yuki. 1997. 'Joseishi kara mita "ianfu" mondai' [The Issue of the 'Comfort Women' as Seen from the Perspective of Women's History]. In: *Kikan sensō sekinin kenkyū* (Winter): 2–17.

-----. 1999. 'Reisen taisei keiseiki no beigun to seibōryoku' [The U.S.-Army and Sexual Violence During the Formation of the Cold-War System]. In: *Josei, sensō, jinken* 2: 116–138.

-----. 2001. 'Nihonjin ianfu o fukashi ni suru mono' [What is Rendering the Japanese 'Comfort Women' Invisible]. In: *Sabakareta senji seibōryoku*, ed. VAWW-Net Japan. Tokyo: Hakutaku-sha: 88–108.

-----. 2002. 'Nihonjin ianfu no chōshū no jittai to shusshin kaisō nado ni tsuite' [How Japanese 'Comfort Women' Were Recruited, and Which Social Stratum They Came from]. In: *Josei kokusai senpan hōtei no zen-kiroku*, vol. 1, ed. VAWW-Net Japan. Tokyo: Ryokufū Shuppan: 217–220.

Germer, Andrea. 2003. 'Feminist History in Japan: National and International Perspectives'. Intersections: Gender, History and Culture in the Asian Context 9 (August). http://wwwsshe.murdoch.edu.au/intersections/issue9/germer.html (accessed August 2, 2004).

Grossmann, Atina. 1995. 'A Question of Silence: The Rape of German Women by Occupation Soldiers', In: *October* 72 (Spring): 43–63. [This article also appeared in Japanese translation: 'Chinmoku to iu mondai.' In: *Shisō* 898 (April): 136–159].

-----. 1998. 'Trauma, Memory, and Motherhood: Germans and Jewish Displaced Persons in Post-Nazi Germany, 1945-1949.' In: *Archiv für Sozialgeschichte* 38: 215–239.

Hahn, Hans Henning et al. 2003. 'For a Critical and Enlightened Debate About the Past'. http://www.bohemistik.de/zentrumgb.html (accessed July 29, 2004).

Hata, Ikuhiko. 1999. *Ianfu to senjō no sei* [Comfort Women, and Sexuality at the Warfront]. Tokyo: Shinchōsha.

Hirota, Kazuko. 1975. *Shōgen kiroku: jūgun ianfu, kangofu: senjō ni ikita onna no dōkoku* [A Record of Testimonies: A Comfort Woman and Military Nurses: The Lamentations of Women Who Experienced Life at the Warfront]. Tokyo: Shin-Jinbutsu Ōraisha. (Reprinted 1993).

Inoue, Setsuko. 1995. *Haisen hishi. Senryōgun ianjo: Kokka ni yoru baishun shisetsu* [The Hidden History of the Defeat. Comfort Stations for the Occupation Army: Prostitution Facilities Established by the State]. Tokyo: Shin-Hyōron.

Kamiyama, Noriko. 2004. 'Nihonjin "ianfu" ga "chinmoku" suru genjō ni kansuru kōsatsu' [A Study of the Present-day Circumstances of the 'Silence' Kept by the Japanese 'Comfort Women']. In: *Karin karin: joseigaku, jendā kenkyū* 4 (March): 57–66.

Kersten, Rikki. 1999. 'Neo-nationalism and the "Liberal School of History."' In: *Japan Forum* 11, 2: 191–203.

Kim, Puja (Jap. transcription: Kimu). 1996. 'Sekai josei kaigi hōkoku (2): "ianfu" mondai o chūshin ni' [Report on the World Conference of Women (2): Focusing on the 'Comfort Women']. In: *Daisan sekai no hataraku joseitachi*, ed. Ajia Keizai Kenkyūjo. Tokyo: Akashi Shoten: 253–261.

-----. 1998. 'Chōsenjin "ianfu" mondai e no shiza: feminizumu to nashonarizumu' [The Issue of Korean 'Comfort Women' from the Perspectives of Feminism and Nationalism]. In: *Shinpojiumu. Nashonarizumu to 'ianfu' mondai*, ed. Nihon no Sensō Sekinin Shiryō Sentā. Tokyo: Aoki Shoten: 193–202.

'Konpasshon wa kanō ka?' Taiwa Shūkai Jikkō Iinkai, ed. 2002. *Konpasshon wa kanō ka? Rekishi ninshiki to kyōkasho mondai o kangaeru* [Is Compassion Possible? Reflections on Historical Consciousness and the Textbook Problem]. Tokyo: Kage Shobō.

Mackie, Vera. 2001. 'The Language of Globalisation, Transnationality and Feminism'. *International Feminist Journal of Politics 3*, 2: 180–206.

-----. 2003. *Feminism in Modern Japan*. Cambridge, UK: Cambridge University Press.

Mohanty, Chandra T. 1988. 'Under Western Eyes: Feminist Scholarship and Colonial Discourses.' In: *Feminist Review* 30 (Autumn): 61–88.

Nihon no Sensō Sekinin Shiryō Sentā, ed. 1998. *Shinpojiumu: Nashonarizumu to 'ianfu' mondai* [Proceedings of the Symposium on Nationalism and the 'Comfort Women' Issue]. Tokyo: Aoki Shoten.

Nishino, Rumiko. 1998. 'Shinpojiumu ga teiki shita mono: "Nihonjin" toshite sekinin o ukeru to wa.' [The Problem Posed by the Symposium: What It Means to Take Responsibility as a "Japanese".] In: *Shinpojiumu: Nashonarizumu to 'ianfu' mondai* ed. Nihon no Sensō Sekinin Shiryō Sentā. Tokyo: Aoki Shoten.

----. 2000a. 'Nihonjin "ianfu": Dare ga dono yō ni chōshū sareta ka' [Japanese 'Comfort Women': Who Was Recruited How]. In: *'Ianfu', senji seiboryoku no jittai (I): Nihon, Taiwan, Chōsenhen*, ed. VAWW-Net Japan. Tokyo: RyokufūShuppan: 66–91.

----. 2000b. 'Okizari ni sarete kita Nihonjin "ianfu": Dare ga dare ni yori dō isō sareta ka – Kainantō no baai [The Japanese 'Comfort Women,' Who Were Left Behind: Who Was Transported by Whom, and How – The Case of Hainan Island]. In: *Sekai* 682 (December): 128–132.

----. 2003. *Senjō no 'ianfu:' Ramō zenmetsusen o ikinobita Paku Yonshimu no kiseki* ["Comfort Woman" at the Warfront: Tracing the Life of Bak Yeong-sim, Survivor of the Battle of La Meng, which Ended in the Crushing Defeat of the Japanese Army]. Tokyo: Akashi Shoten.

Oka, Mari and Jung, Yeong-hae (Jap. transcription: Chon Yonhe). 1995. 'Zadankai: Gurōbaru feminizumu no kanōsei' [Roundtable Discussion on the Possibility of Global Feminism]. In: *Inpakushon* 94 (November): 4–24.

Shirota, Suzuko. 1971. *Mariya no sanka* [The Hymn of Maria.]. Nihon kirisutokyōdan shuppankyoku.

Soh, C. Sarah. 2004. 'Aspiring to Craft Modern Gendered Selves. "Comfort Women" and Chongsindae in Late Colonial Korea.' In: *Critical Asian Studies* 36, 2: 175–198.

Song Young-ok (Jap. transcription: Son, Yonoku). 1997. 'Nihonjin "ianfu" ga nanoriderarenai wake' [Why the Japanese 'Comfort Women' Have not Been Able to Come Out with their Stories]. In: *Buraku kaihō* 422 (June): 116–120.

Suleri, Sara. 1992. 'Woman Skin Deep: Feminism and the Postcolonial Condition.' In: Critical Inquiry 18 (Summer): 756–769.

Tanaka, Yuki. 2002. *Japan's Comfort Women: Sexual Slavery and Prostitution During World War II and the US Occupation*. London and New York: Routledge.

Tomida, Kunihiko, ed. 1953. *Senjō ianfu: Misaka Miwako no shuki* [Comfort Woman at the Warfront: The Memoirs of Misaka Miwako]. Tokyo: Fuji shobō.

Ueno, Chizuko. 1996. '"Kokumin kokka" to "jendā": Josei no "kokuminka" o megutte' [The Nation State and Gender: On Turning Women into Citizens]. In: *Gendai shisō* 24, 12 (October): 8–45.

-----. 1997. 'Kioku no seijigaku: Kokumin, kojin, watashi' [Politics of Memory: The Citizen, the Individual and the I]. In: *Inpakushon* 103 (August): 154–174.

-----. 1998. *Nashonarizumu to jendā*. Tokyo: Seidosha. (English translation: *Nationalism and Gender*. Melbourne: Trans Pacific Press, 2004).

Urasaki, Shigeko. 2000. 'Okinawasen to gun "ianfu"' [The War in Okinawa and Military 'Comfort Women']. In: *'Ianfu', senji seiboryoku no jittai (I):* Nihon, Taiwan, Chōsenhen, ed. VAWW-Net Japan. Tokyo: Ryokufū Shuppan: 92–116.

Wöhr, Ulrike. 2004. 'A Touchstone for Transnational Feminism: Discourses on the Comfort Women in 1990s Japan'. In: *Japanstudien* 16: 59–90.

Yamada, Meiko. 1992. *Senryōgun ianfu: Kokusaku baishun to onnatachi no higeki* [Comfort Women of the Occupation Forces: Official Prostitution and the Tragedy of Women]. Tokyo: Kōjinsha.

Yamashita, Akiko. 2000. 'Sengo Nihon no feminizumu to "ianfu" mondai: Mejā to mainā no kessetsuten' [Post-war Japanese Feminism and the 'Comfort Women' Issue: A Point of Intersection Between Major and Minor Currents]. In: *Kagai no seishin kōzō to sengo sekinin*, ed. VAWW-Net Japan. Tokyo: Ryokufū Shuppan: 264–288.

Yamashita, Yeong-ae (Jap. transcription: Yon'e). 1996. 'Kankoku joseigaku to minzoku: Nihon-gun "ianfu" mondai o meguru "minzoku" giron o chūshin ni' [South Korean Women's Studies and Ethnicity: Focusing on the Debate on 'Ethnicity' that Evolved in Connection with the Issue of the Japanese Military 'Comfort Women']. In: *Joseigaku* 4: 35–58. (English translation: 'Nationalism in Korean Women's Studies'. In: *U.S.-Japan Women's Journal*, English Supplement 15, 1998).

-----. 2000. 'Nihon no feminizumu: Aidentiti to feminizumu' [Japanese Feminism: Identity and Feminism]. In: *Onnatachi no 21 seiki* 21 (January): 27–30.

Yamazaki, Hiromi. 1995. 'Beijin josei kaigi to "Nihongun seiteki dorei seido"' [The Beijing Women's Conference and the 'Japanese Army's System of Sexual Slavery']. In: *Inpakushon* 94 (November): 62–68.

Yoshimi, Yoshiaki. 2000. *Comfort Women: Sexual Slavery in the Japanese Military During World War II*. New York: Columbia University Press.

Yun Jong-ok (Jap. transcription: Jon'oku) et al. 1992. *Chōsenjin josei ga mita 'ianfu mondai'* [The 'Comfort Women Issue' Seen from the Perspective of Korean Women]. Tokyo: San'ichi Shobō: 168–206.

Physical Education and the Curriculum of Gender Reproduction

Wolfram Manzenreiter

1   Introduction

Critical inquiries into the world of sports have disclosed that sports have always been a "sexual battlefield" in which familiar stereotypes of men and women are communicated and reinforced (Boyle/Haynes 2000:127). Male domination in sports was established as early as the 19th century, when sports emerged as a social institution created by and for men. Biological scientism and the social organisation of modernity, in particular the spatial and functional segregation of gender roles, provided the ideological nutrient for the legitimisation of gender discrimination in sports. Female subordination was based on taken-forgranted view of sports as "natural domain" of men because of the innately different biological and psychological natures of men and women. In contrast to and as complement of the adventurous and competitive-victorious ideal of masculinity, the modern idea of femininity was conceptualised around domestic services provided by women as wives and mothers.

In Japan, as elsewhere (Dunne/Leach 2003), compulsory schooling effectively contributes to the production and reproduction of gender roles. For a number of reasons, physical education classes have been and continue to be at the core of an ideological programme reinforcing the dominant gender order. First of all, the subject of physical education is located at the intersection of the two social institutions of school and sports. Secondly, the wide uniformity of school education, including instructor manuals and teaching styles, guarantees that generational cohorts throughout the country become familiar with similar ideas and messages about being a girl or a boy. Thirdly, the long duration of twelve years, in which more than 90% of Japan's children attend school, coincides with periods of maturation and human development which are crucial for the development of attitudes, values, norms and ideas of selfhood. Fourthly, Japan's education industry is fuelled by a societal want of hierarchy, and despite the myth of the classless society, it has always created and continues to produce hierarchical differences between educational institutions with farreaching consequences (Saitō 2000). Within this institutionalised system of ranking and differentiation based on educational credits, sports arguably serves as a trade mark or marketing tool of schools of secondary education which are vying for the same customer base. Sports practice is also related to the reproduction of social stratification insofar as membership in school sports clubs has often been used either as a criterion for the assessment of team work capabilities of job applicants, or more bluntly as a pipeline for personal recruitment through alumni networks. However, for the overwhelming majority of Japanese students enrolled in compulsory education, sports are first of all part of a regular school subject, and as such a basic component of class room routine. Seen from the perspective of the education system, physical education (PE) is a standard element of the curriculum for a sound and healthy upbringing of pupils. Yet it also reproduces social inequality based on gender differences.

In this paper I am going to deconstruct physical education as a practice field in which four or five rather independent currents converge and contribute to the production and re-production of what I call "body regimes". Body regimes are here defined as mind sets of orientation which are incorporated into the (physical) body, consciously as well as uncon-sciously, by the members of a social community. As they speak through the body to the individual and to the collective, body regimes provide standards of bodily appearance and behaviour, categories of distinction and difference, but also of sameness and similarity. Constituting an embodied knowledge about society and one's place within society, body regimes bear structural analogies to the idea of 'habitus' (Bourdieu 1987). This central notion of Pierre Bourdieu's sociology, to which my work is heavily indebted, denotes 'a system of structured (and) structuring dispositions, which is constituted in practice and is always oriented towards practical functions' (Bourdieu 1990:53). As part of humans' habi-tus, body regimes are constructed through and manifested in the shapes of bodies, gestures and everyday usages of the body ranging from sitting and eating to ways of walking, run-ning and using the body in sport. They are normative, but not necessarily mandatory. To a certain degree, they are experienced as coercive though no regime rules absolutely uncon-fined.

In order to comprehend the impact of physical education on the construction of femin-inities and masculinities in contemporary Japan, we have to give equal consideration to five different contexts which have always been closely interconnected throughout the modern history of school sports and cannot be dealt with separately. Body regimes are contextual-ised by institutional, organisational, ideological, transcultural and corporeal currents. We first have to look at the education system as a social institution, at its historical formation and the way in which the official ideas of what constitutes a 'grown-up' in Japan are trans-lated into educational curricula and spread by the schools' teaching staff. Secondly, we have to look at how sportive experience is organised in class room formations and extra-curricula club activities. Thirdly, we will be concerned with the ideological and termino-logical packaging of sportive experience: what are the dominant ideas of the merits of sports education, and what ideas of gender relations and the relationship between individual and society work behind the practice of school sports. Fourthly we have to be aware of the transcultural context of sports. In the introductory part I already referred to the inherent gender logic of sports. In the age of globalisation, the local sports experience can hardly be disconnected from the rules monitored by governing transnational organisations and the images transmitted and sold by multinational media corporations. Fifth, and finally, the body, which is the primary target of physical education, is a powerful mnemonic device, as Marcel Mauss demonstrated in his essay on Body Techniques (1934). The sociologist ar-gued that the entire inventory of body movements is formed by 'education' and 'contact' (with the social environment), and he called people's knowledge of how to employ their bodies in response to situational requirements in their respective societies the "techniques of the body". Observers of Japanese pre-school institutions have shown how the teaching staff is consciously making use of this corporeal capability in daily life and work routines (e.g. Ben-Ari 1997).

My argument is based on two general assumptions; first, the principal observation of the structured arrangement of economic and cultural capital, which can be gained or lost on the sports ground as well as in any other socially embedded situations, and second, the reading of sports as a projection screen for the symbolic display of gender order, which itself is a function of power relations in the social fabric of public and private life. What makes sports so peculiar in this regard are its physical appeal and the role of the body that constitutes 'the fundamental principle of division of the social and symbolic world' (Bourdieu 1995:93). A modern subject's notion of self is composed of multiple components, but the body is probably the component most intimate to the self and immediate to the other. Phenomenology teaches us that we *have* a body and at the same time *are* bodies. We can reflect upon our own corporeality, we can dress up, trim our bodies or slim them down; at the same time, we are bodies, for they are the interface to the world we are living in. Without consciously or unconsciously acting upon our bodies and its externalities, there are no meaningful encounters with others (Kameyama 1991). Sport, which can be understood as a particular kind of body performance, is affected by the same antagonistic principle: Athletes train and shape their bodies in training sessions in order to be superior to contenders in competitive encounters.

For analytical purposes, my discussion centres on three different features of sports at school: regular PE classes as required by the curriculum, extracurricular club activities as suggested by the curriculum, and the impact of the so-called 'hidden curriculum of physical education'. As I will show, choice and practice are deeply tainted by the impact of the gendered worldview of Japanese society.

2   Physical Education in the Prewar School System

Sports emerged as a conservative domain for the representation of gender since it became adapted to the needs of compulsory education. At Japanese public schools, the Education System Order of 1872 (*gakusei*) introduced the subject of gymnastics at elementary school level as early as 1872. Two adversary currents of interest determined the physical education policy in Imperial Japan. Liberal-minded educationalists (Izawa Shūji, 1851-1917, and Tsuboi Gendō, 1852-1922, among others) sympathised with humanist philosophy and advocated a holistic approach that acknowledged the unity of mind, body and soul. Physical education thus was seen as an indispensable part of educating the individual character (Irie 1988:37-40). In contrast to the individual-centred pedagogy, a second school focussed on the individual body as ingredient of the national body. Invented and promoted by the influential thought of social evolutionism, its proponents emphasised the merits of physical education for the nation as a whole. The basic ideas of this school of thought were summarised in the Report to the Throne On Military Style Physical Education (*Heishiki taisō ni kansuru jōsōbun*), written by Minister of Education Mori Arinori (1847-89) around 1887:

> The wealth and strength of the country will rise to the same extent as the spirit of loyalty to the Emperor and love of our nation prospers. Therefore it is the task of the Minister of Education to nurture this spirit. Physical education has been recognised as being of utmost importance for this purpose and has been added to the curriculum. However, as yet there is no result to be seen because only a few military men have been summoned as instructors and the great majority of school teachers have only had one or two occasions to learn exercises from military men.

Generally speaking, the will of school teachers cannot even be spoken of in the same way as that of the military men. The ordinary school teachers do not know how to cultivate an attitude of obedience to a superior authority, to develop an attitude of courage like that of the samurai, nor do they understand how to teach young people to strictly observe rules and regulations. [...] The subject of physical education should be separated from the [jurisdiction of the] Ministry of Education and placed under the management of the Ministry of the Army, and pure military style physical education should be carried out by military officers. [...] If this was done and the regulations strictly enforced, we will see the development of physical education. Students will take on the superior character of military men. A spirit of loyalty to the Emperor and love of the country will be encouraged. The vital energy for persevering under hard labour will be born. And some day in future when these students are selected for conscription, the results of the military style physical education will be most conspicuous. (Monbushō 1972: Chap. 3.1 [1] c)

Hence since the late 1880s, physical education was clearly seen as being in the interest of the collective, the nation or the state. The emphasis on military-style exercises, including marching, armed exercises and repetitive drills, prepared the male students for compulsory military service (introduced in 1873). The communion with the nationalist emperor state-ideology indicated that the ultimate purpose of physical education was seen in the formation of 'diligent workers and strong soldiers' as the male supplement to the "good wife and wise mother". Their future superiors were trained and shaped within the framework of elite schools at secondary level. Donald Roden (1980) described in his historical account of *Schooldays in Imperial Japan* how team games in particular and sports in general were regarded as essential training fields for physical power, controlled aggressiveness, leadership capabilities and moral standards; all of them qualities that differentiated the boys from the men.

Table 1: **Attendance rate at ordinary elementary schools, 1875-1915**

	Total [%]	Boys [%]	Girls [%]
1875	35.4	50.8	18.7
1880	41.1	58.7	21.9
1885	49.6	65.8	32.1
1890	48.9	65.1	31.1
1895	61.2	76.7	43.9
1900	81.5	90.4	71.7
1905	95.6	97.7	93.5
1910	98.1	98.8	97.4
1915	98.5	98.9	98.0

Source: Monbushō 1972

Girls were largely excluded from these nation-centred perceptions within school education. Mass enrolment of female students started only at the end of the 19th century (cf. Table 1). At the turn of the century Inokuchi Aguri and others introduced 'sweden gymnastics' to Japan as a new variant thought of as more suitable to the Japanese physique in general and to girls in particular. For the following decades, both military and Sweden gymnastics co-existed side by side with games. The first Syllabus of School Gymnastics, proclaimed by the Ministry of Education in 1913, was comprised of these core elements. However, the male body continued to be of primary concern. The Diet passed a by-law in 1917 on the promotion of military gymnastics, following recommendations by the Council for Education: male 'students above middle school should be trained to be a soldier with patriotic conformity, martial spirit, obedience, and toughness of mind and body' (Abe, Kiyohara and Nakajima 1992). The female body was also excluded from the field of martial arts which were added to the school curriculum in 1931 had eventually been ending a decade-long debate between militarists, *budō* teachers[1] and pedagogues on the suitability of martial arts for the juvenile body. The liberal climate of the Taishō years (1912-1925) allowed substantial improvements for girls' participation in sport. A survey of the Prime Minister's Office among 2,153 schools (594 boys' schools, 949 girls' schools, 610 vocational schools) showed that athletics, tennis, table tennis and volleyball were quite common at the majority of girls' elite institutions of advanced education (cf. Table 2).

Table 2: **Middle school sports clubs in early Shōwa Japan**

	Boys middle schools	Girls middle schools	Vocational schools	Total
Kendo	569	1	508	1,078
Judo	476	0	311	787
Kyudo	119	132	98	349
Sumo	155	0	166	321
Track and Field	550	517	453	1,520
Swimming	377	199	197	773
Tennis	546	600	481	1,627
Volleyball	175	563	81	819
Basketball	213	451	127	791
Baseball	450	2	260	712
Table tennis	47	424	114	585
Football	210	0	52	262
Rugby	24	0	5	29
Rowing	73	3	25	101
Ski	72	56	48	176
Skate	10	8	8	26
Others	210	403	220	833
Total	4,276	3,359	3,154	10,789

Source: Monbu Daijin Kanbō Taiiku-ka 1932, quoted in Sakaue 1998:32

During the increasingly chauvinist interwar years, girls' participation in physical education classes was redirected towards gymnastics, outdoor games and other activities guiding them towards their future as roles mothers. In the course of general mobilisation after 1937, some of the differences in the treatment of the sexes disappeared. The 1942 Syllabus of Physical

Discipline (*tairen*) emphasised physical activities dedicated to national defence such as throwing hand grenades instead of rounders, running with gas masks or with the freight of sandbags or stretchers. With less and less male students available, girls as well were prepared for semi-militarist deployment.

Postwar reforms immediately prohibited all militaristic physical exercises. *Budō* sports followed suit on November 6, 1945 because of its martial quality and feudalist character in the eyes of the Occupation Forces. Instead, a new understanding of sports was emphasised, stressing its educative qualities for the promotion of democratic attitudes. For the first time, women were given the right to enjoy equal opportunities in education with men, following Article 26 of the Constitution:

> All people shall have the right to receive an equal education correspondent to their ability, as provided by law. All people shall be obligated to have all boys and girls under their protection receive ordinary education as provided for by law. Such compulsory education shall be free.

3 Sports in Contemporary Curricula

When the new school curricula were promulgated in 1947, the physical education subject was expanded to denominate a broader health program (*hoken taiiku*). Since then, course programs have been revised about every ten years. Ministry guidelines specify the same amount of time for boys and girls in callisthenics, gymnastics, track and field, swimming, and health education. In principle, PE subjects at school are roughly the same for both sexes, regarding the number of hours, but with slight differences in the kind of subjects. PE curricula generally state that the subject is meant to raise interest in sports among the students. To accomplish this goal, all curricula neatly register an overall aim and content of classes, according to phase and year of school. A sketchy guideline for the achievement of the goal is also included.

3.1 Physical education and the lifecourse at school

As with other school subjects, sports curricula reflect a developmental and hierarchical structure: basic knowledge and techniques are provided first, followed by more detailed instructions or more specialised exercises in later years. For example, during the first two years in elementary school pupils are expected to become familiar with rudimentary exercises and simple team games, in order to build up physical strength, and to be good friend with others. As in all later stages, a fifth of the entire five hours of physical education per week is dedicated to health education and theoretical knowledge (including sports theory in much later phases). Over the next stages, more skills, exercises and games are added to the catalogue as well as more elaborated ethical and moral standards. During the third and fourth grade, boys and girls are freshly introduced to swimming, apparatus gymnastics, and expressive movements. Teachers are expected to pay attention to the awakening awareness of sexual differences, and students shall adapt to the imperatives of rules, develop respectfulness, spirit of cooperation, fairness and the ability of 'giving it all' (*saigo made ni doryoku suru taido*). This list is further extended during the final two years at elementary school when pupils get acquainted with track and field athletics, new exercises in gymnastics, fitness training, ball sports and creative expressivity.

In order to maintain the effectiveness of class room teaching and orderliness, teachers instruct their pupils how to follow commands, to keep still, line up according to height, and similar routines. While curricula explicitly recommend teachers to pay full attention to local traditions and environmental conditions, the ultimate decision on the extent to which folk games or outdoor activities such as skating, skiing, or playing in snow should be included into the course program is left to the school and the teacher.

3.2 PE curricula in secondary education

Until children leave elementary school, boys and girls have been practicing sports together. At secondary level, there is no general guideline recommending either co-educative or separated sports education. However, until very recently physical education classes were usually divided into courses for male and female students, based on the general notion that students should be educated according to their physical abilities and interests. Physical education was thus an outstanding field in the education system where students were confronted with the issue of gender identity. As we will see later, this policy is currently undergoing changes (Itani 2003).

Table 3: **Health and physical education at junior high school**

A Fitness training	E Ball games
(1) stretching and release	(1) basketball, handball
(2) increase in physical strength	(2) football
	(3) volleyball
B Apparatus gymnastics	(4) tennis, table tennis, badminton
(1) mat exercises	(5) softball
(2) horizontal bar exercises	
(3) balance beam exercises	F Martial arts
(4) vaulting horse exercises	(1) judo
	(2) kendo
C Track and field	(3) sumo
(1) running (short, long distance, hurdles, relay)	G Dance
(2) wide jump, high jump	(1) creative dance
	(2) folk dance
D Swimming	(3) contemporary rhythmic dance
(1) crawl	
(2) breast stroke	H Health education
(3) backstroke	

Source: Monbushō 1999a

Since national guidelines were revised in 1999, junior high school students of the second and third year have been garanted some freedom of choice, and the array of elective subjects has been widely enlarged for high school students (cf. Kreitz-Sandberg 2000).[2] In the lower secondary phase, the subject of physical education (*taiiku*) is renamed to health and physical education (*hoken taiiku*). The course outline features eight subgroups, i.e. fitness training, apparatus gymnastics, track and field, swimming, ball games, martial arts, dance, and health education (cf. Table 3), which are all compulsory during the first year. Fitness training, which is basically geared towards acquiring strength and stamina, and basic sports

129

theory are mandatory in the following years, while students can choose one or two disciplines of apparatus gymnastics, track and field, and swimming, and two more out of ball games, martial arts, and dance. Health education, which is most clearly pronounced during the final stage of compulsory education, prepares students to take responsibility for their own health and well-being. During the first year, students acquire knowledge about the physical and chemical processes within the maturing body, basic sex education and ways to mental and spiritual well-being. The larger relationship between health and the living environment is addressed in the second year, with an emphasis on healthy nutrition, hygiene instructions, appropriate and reasonable handling of resources, waste reduction, and sound lifestyles. Students also receive guidance in first-aid practices. The final year offers tutorials on managing a healthy lifestyle which includes explanations about the dangers of consuming tobacco, alcohol and drugs, as well as basic information on AIDS and sexually transmitted diseases.

4   Extracurricular Sports Activities

The sporting experience is not limited to the class room. A far larger proportion of time, interest and enthusiasm is spent on extracurricular club activities (*bukatsudō*) which constitute an essential part of school life at the secondary level.

4.1   Junior Sports Club Network

Elementary school students who want to deepen their sports involvement can join the nation-wide network of kids' sports clubs (Monbushō 1999c). The respective organisation *Supōtsu Shōnendan* was established in 1962, just prior to the Tokyo Olympics, for the purpose of sparking interest in sports among the younger Japanese. The name is misleading, as *Supōtsu Shōnendan* does not exclusively target young boys. Membership is not restricted to elementary school grades, though the majority is likely to stem from this age group. Clubs are open to everyone up to the age of 25, regardless of sex and educational status. Kids' sports clubs focus on sports activities but they also engage in outdoor activities like camping and hiking, cultural activities such as painting, singing, and crafts, and social activities including volunteering and participation in community projects. The local communities provide basic resources such as training space and voluntary instructors. A statement published on the homepage of the governing body Japan Amateur Sport Association (*Nihon Taiiku Kyōkai*) reveals the perception of sports enrolment as a useful tool for socialisation into community affairs: 'There is considerable interest in clubs as institutions providing important experiences to boys and girls in becoming commendable members of society.' (NTK n.y.)

Kids' sports clubs usually feature a single sport; only a minority of about 5,000 cover more than one kind of sports. Most members are enrolled in sports activities that also rank highest among junior and senior high school students: football, followed by *nanshiki yakyū*, a modified version of baseball, basketball, and *kendō*. While the choice at hands depends largely on the goodwill of people from the local community, the overall concern with male-dominated sports may be one explanation for the low participation rate of girls who comprised only 20 percent of club members in 2003 (NTK 2003).

4.2   Roots and traditions of school sports clubs

When students enter junior high school, they are likely to join one of the self-administered school clubs, which are usually divided into sports clubs and culture clubs. Membership at the *undōbu* or *bunkabu* is voluntary, but the social pressure to join a club and maintain membership status throughout the three years of junior high or senior high school years is immense. Club membership demands a huge amount of time from participants. Sports clubs in particular meet on a daily basis for training sessions, sometimes twice a day before and after classroom hours. Training periods cover the whole week, often Saturdays and Sundays, too, and usually stretch well into school vacation. Physical education curricula also advise teachers to adjust their teaching programme to the local array of extracurricular club activities. The spectrum of clubs depends on school traditions as well as on the availability of supervisors from the teaching staff (*komon*) and a minimum of student members. In recent years, both the fading popularity of school sports clubs as well as the increase of alternative sports organisations beyond school has caused at some schools a decrease in numbers of clubs and of students enrolled in these clubs. Demographic trends will accelerate this process in the near future.

The origin of *bukatsudō* goes back to the early days of the establishment of the modern education system in Meiji Japan and the boarding school system at the national high schools. The quantitative discrepancies between the universal elementary school and the intensely limited institutions of higher education created elitist perceptions, hierarchical structures, severe competition, inter-school rivalry, and a new self-image of a privileged youth standing at the top of the social order. As Donald Roden (1980) has pointed out, the backbone of the educational system at higher schools was a Social Darwinist ethic that was most obvious in the daily routines of dormitory life and club life. The meaning of sports created and reproduced within this social framework was strictly instrumental. Participation in sports activities and competitions was devoted to the honour of the home institution which served as the primary locus of identification.

Stoic endurance, strict obedience, and self-sacrificing rigour were core qualities of the elite ethos furnished within the sports clubs which at that time were only addressing men. The tradition of autonomous self-administration and physical self-discipline, which was borrowed from the English public boarding school system, and the neo-confucianist, samurai class background of students and teaching staff merged into the ethos of 'muscular spirituality' (Kiku 1984:10-11; Shimizu 2002:130-134). While the "budofication" of Western sports certainly helped to facilitate the adoption of sports, it also fatally shaped the way sports in Japan have been assessed ever since. The Ichikō baseball club at the First Higher School in Tokyo became particularly prominent for its rigorous training sessions, stoic endurance and perseverance. These attitudes, as well as the social organisation and the spiritual connotation, became a role model for most kind of sports inside and outside the school system (Taniguchi 2003:81). The overemphasis on winning, dedication to and identification with the team, the school, and the nation were not restricted to the so-called "Pride Baseball" but a characteristic feature of all club sports. Rituals of masculinity and exercises of asceticism forged the collective solidarity of the student community. In every respect, club life maximised the individual's feelings of dependence on, first the team, then the school, and ultimately, the nation.

131

Women, by contrast, were hardly considered to be a serious contender in sports, althought at some of the secondary educational institutions for women clubs had been opened as well since the Taishō years. The progress of women's sport, albeit very slow, was propelled by three different dynamics: state concerns with national health first encountered the peda-gogical orientation of liberal-minded educators and their experiences from abroad, and in a later stage these currents met the rise of an urban middle class with new lifestyle interests. However, club activities were limited to those sports deemed to be suitable to the female body, such as tennis, hiking, bicycling or skating. If freetime practice only allowed women to 'adopt good manners and get a cheerful spirit' (*yōgi ni totonae, seishin o kaikatsu ni,* Kōkō jogakkō-rei segyō kisoku 1901), educators did not see any reason to speak out against women's participation in sport.

From the early 20th century, a rising number of articles in journals devoted to physical education such as *Undōkai* (The World of Sports') or *Taiiku to Kyōgi* ('Physical Education and Competition') echoed a new understanding of sports that was no longer exclusively male-oriented. But these professional discourses reflected a deep-rooted belief in the innate difference between men and women, and these differences were now employed to explain male superiority in sports. Ōtani Takeichi stated in 1922 that women were lacking the fight-ing spirit of men. As they did not posses the natural desire for throwing things or wrestling, they should not engage in such activities. In another article, the same authority related the spirit of sportsmanship to the Japanese tradition of *bushidō*. This analogy to the male-centred cultural ideal was also used to explain women's inferiority in sports (Taniguchi 2003:82).

The tradition of the *bukatsudō* survived the postwar reforms of the education system. As my research on mountaineering has shown, school and university sports clubs remained deeply tainted by their prewar legacy until the late 1960s (Manzenreiter 2000). The con-tinuation of clubs relied on the reactivation of former members and instructors as well as on Old Boys' networks that helped to maintain the character of a 'ritual community, set apart from the mundane world around it by its own internal rules and values' (Cave 2004:390). Fierce competition among schools and intense training demand continued to emphasise the values of hierarchy, strict subordination and moral improvement. The downside of a prac-tice which blurs the line between hierarchically ordered discipline and bullying has been documented most drastically in a number of tragic incidences that culminated in the death of junior members by the hand of their seniors. Furthermore, when form prevails over sub-stance, practice for the sake of practice may dominate or suppress the joyful experience, as Dalla Chiesa (2002) observed in his years with several football teams at Japanese schools. 'When the goal is not the goal', participation in a football sports club does not impact posi-tively on the youngsters' body and health. The particular lesson students learn from being inside the Japanese institution of *bu* is that total dedication to the team will earn them a safe place on the rooster (or on the social ladder) in the future, no matter how far their physical capabilities are developed (Dalla Chiesa 2002:196-197). School activities thus help schools to attain the goals of adjusting students to a social environment structured by vertical rela-tionships, increasing control over their students, consuming their physical energy, and con-trolling the value orientation of the peer group (Dalla Chiesa 2002:195-196).

However, as Cave has argued, there is also a brighter side to club activities because of their flexible nature and their multifaceted appeal. 'They are a means of school manage-ment and control in the widest sense, supplementing the classroom as an arena that allows both discipline and relaxation, and which lets students develop enthusiasms and abilities neglected by the formal curriculum' (Cave 2004:414). Because of the pervasiveness of a club system that managed to cope with decades of immense social change, clubs form the cornerstone in Japan of the wide-spread acceptance of *seishin kyōiku* (character education), achieved by perseverance (*gaman*), endurance against hardship, self-perfection through emulation and repetition, and mutual dependence.

4.3 Making sense of gendered club membership

For reasons waiting to be explained, boys are much more susceptible to the pleasures and hardship of sports club membership than girls, as membership data to the nationwide federations of school sports clubs exhibit.

Table 4: **Top 10 club sports activities at junior high school level**

rank	boys	girls
1	*nanshiki* baseball (21.2%)	soft tennis (22.4%)
2	football (15.0%)	volleyball (19.9%)
3	soft tennis (14.0%)	basketball (16.3%)
4	basketball (12.2%)	table tennis (9.9%)
5	table tennis (12.0%)	badminton (8.5%)
6	track & field (7.2%)	track & field (8.2%)
7	kendo (5.1%)	softball (5.9%)
8	volleyball (4.1%)	kendo (4.2%)
9	judo (2.8%)	swimming (1.8%)
10	badminton (2.5%)	judo (1.2%)

Source: Chūtairen 2004

In 2004, 1.87 boys and 1.79 million girls were enrolled at Japan's junior high schools. From the 3.67 million students, 2.39 million or two out of three students have joined a school sports club (Chūtairen 2004). As the remaining 35% have very likely entered some culture club, this distribution shows the relatively larger appeal of sports to the students and to their social environment. In terms of sex differences, boys outnumber girls not only in total numbers but also in share of enrolment: only every second girl, but three out of four boys are members in a sports club. Sex differences prevail also in terms of sports activities pursed by the students. The National Junior School Sports Association (*Nihon Chūgakkō Taiiku Renmei*) features eighteen sport-specific sections, ranging from gymnastics, martial arts, and team sports to track and fields. Until 2001, football and *nanshiki yakyū* were not allowed for girls; since then, however, girls' participation in these sports activities has met with approval. At the same time, rhythmic gymnastics (*shin taisō*, which is best characterised as variant of gymnastics that places aestheticism over athleticism) has been opened for boys for the first time. Comparing the kind of sports activities boys and girls are attracted by (cf. Table 4) girls favour soft tennis, which is practised by 22.4% of all girls enrolled in school sports club activities, followed by volleyball (19.9%), basketball (16.3%), table tennis (9.9%) and badminton (8.5%): each of these sports activities were found acceptable for female students many decades ago. By contrast, *nanshiki yakyū* attracts a fifth of the entire male sports population (21.2%) and is thus most popular with boys, followed by football (15.0%), soft tennis (14.0%), basketball (12.1%), and table tennis (12.0%). Among the top five sports activities, three are shared by boys and girls. Yet the overwhelming concern of boys with baseball and football causes imbalances in the respective sex ratios.

The sex ratio is most clearly unbalanced in the previously exclusively male domains of baseball and football where boys will continue to outnumber girls for the foreseeable future. Table 5 shows two different methods of comparing sports involvement of the sexes. The first column depicts the membership ratio which simply compares numbers of students of a given sports activity. A value of 1 would indicate perfect balance, a value higher than 1 specifies male prevalence and a lower value female prevalence. The same principle is applied to the appeal ratio which takes into account the aforementioned difference in population size of male and female club members.

Table 5: **Sex differences in sports enrolment at junior high school level**

Sport activity	Membership ratio (m/f)	Appeal ratio (m%/f%)
track & field	1.3	0.9
gymnastics	0.5	0.4
rhythmic gymnastics	0.1	0.01
swimming	1.3	0.9
basketball	1.1	0.7
volleyball	0.3	0.2
table tennis	1.9	1.3
soft baseball	480.8	334.9
handball	1.5	1.0
football	109.5	76.3
softball	0.01	0.01
badminton	0.4	0.3
soft tennis	0.9	0.6
sumo	37.0	25.8
judo	3.4	2.3
ski	1.5	1.0
skating	4.6	3.2
kendo	1.8	1.2
total	1.4	1.0

Source: Chūtairen 2004; own calculations

Since this value pays attention to the generally lower appeal of sports for girls, the appeal ratio thus is better suited to compare the relative attractiveness of a sports activity for the respective sex. The left column indicates that the number of boys in track and field is 1.3 times higher than the number of girls. But given that boys generally outnumber girls in school sports clubs, this activity seems to be more attractive to girls. Similarly, we can see from the comparison that the conspicously low participation rate of male students in rhythmic gymnastics is actually an expression of a very low appeal.

Gendered differences in sports participation become more pronounced with rising age. At senior high school level, the variety of sports activities offered increases considerably, though in terms of popularity, there is hardly any noticeable shift (cf. Table 6). According to membership data provided by the All Japan Senior High School Sport Federation (*Zenkoku Kōtō Gakkō Taiiku Renmei*), eight of the ten most popular junior high school sports activities remained among the top ten of both sexes. Boys sympathise most strongly with baseball and football (both slightly less than 16%), followed by basketball (9.9%), tennis (8.3%) and track&field (6.0%). Women's sports is largely made up of the team sports volleyball (14.9%) and basketball (13.4%), followed by badminton (11.6%), tennis and soft tennis (about 9.4% each).

Table 6: **Top 10 club sports activities at senior high school level**

rank	boys	Girls
1	baseball (15.8%)	volleyball (14.9%)
2	football (15.4%)	basketball (13.4%)
3	basketball (9.9%)	badminton (11.6%)
4	tennis (8.3%)	tennis (9.4%)
5	track & field (6.0%)	soft tennis (9.4%)
6	table tennis (5.4%)	kyudo (7.4%)
7	soft tennis (5.2%)	track & field (6.7%)
8	volleyball (5.1%)	softball (5.1%)
9	badminton (4.4%)	kendo (4.4%)
10	kendo (3.8%)	table tennis (3.9%)

Source: Zen-Kōtairen 2004 + Kōyaren 2004

Most eye-catching is the change at the top position of male sport. The junior high school boys' favourite sport vanished entirely from the list and has been replaced by baseball, which is the 'real thing' in comparison to *nanshiki yakyū,* the variant played at middle school level. High school baseball has been the most popular spectator sport at amateur level for the last century, particularly since the national newspaper Asahi Shinbun initiated the well known national baseball tournament in 1916. For largely historical reasons – baseball was the first sport to be organised nation-wide, and the first professionally managed sport as well – high school baseball is supervised by a distinct federation.

Unfortunately, data of the Japan High School Baseball Federation do not differentiate between male and female students, and thus my calculatoions concerning gender differences in high school sports are not as reliable as I would wish them to be. I adjusted official numbers by taking into account average membership size (2004: 38 per club) and Tom Blackwood's information that since 1997, the year of the first all-female national championship, there have been around 20 female teams throughout the country (2003: 23). I also tried to figure in female managers and supporters of the male teams, estimating conservatively slightly less than two female students per team (total of 8,000).

Sports participation rates considerably decline when students enter high school. A total of 1.45 million students (approximately 50%) continues doing sports. Compared to a participation rate of 65% at junior high school level, the drop-out rate is quite large and particularly high among girls, as the membership sex ratio of 2.0 indicates. The number of sports activities at offer is twice the number of junior high, but out of 40 sports and games, at least eight are formally secluded for women.

Male-only sports activities are water ball, football, rugby, cycling, boxing, weight lifting, *sumō* and wrestling, while *naginata*, a martial art traditionally associated with female members of the warrior aristocracy, is exclusively open to females (cf. Table 7). In both cases, discrimination is not necessarily based on formal criteria of exclusion. The baseball federation rejects female players because the sport is too dangerous and the federation can not bear the risk of injury (Blackwood 2003:22). In the case of other sports, it is more likely that the lack of same-sex qualified teaching staff reduces the opportunity of girls to maintain a club of their own. Lastly, the exclusiveness may be due to a lack of interest on the part of the students who have similar or more attractive sports to choose from (like *kendō* instead of *naginata*, for example). For a more detailed depiction of the gendered structure of sports participation at senior high school level, see Table 7.

Table 7: **Sex differences in sports club enrolment at senior high school level**

sports activitiy	membership ratio	appeal ratio	sports activity	membership ratio	appeal ratio
baseball	17.4	8.8	sumo	M	M
nanshiki yakyū	M	M	judo	4.2	2.5
track&field	1.8	1.1	ski	2.4	1.5
gymnastics	1.0	0.6	skating	4.2	2.5
rhythmic gymnastics	0.2	0.1	rowing	1.8	1.1
swimming	1.3	1.3	kendo	1.8	1.1
dive jump	1.2	0.7	wrestling	M	M
waterball	M	M	cycling	M	M
basketball	1.5	0.9	boxing	M	M
volleyball	0.7	0.4	hockey	1.2	0.7
table tennis	2.7	1.6	weightlifting	M	M
soft tennis	1.1	0.7	sailing	2.1	1.3
handball	1.6	1.0	fencing	1.1	0.7
football	M	M	karate	1.9	1.1
rugby	M	M	archery	1.6	0.9
badminton	0.7	0.4	naginata	F	F
softball	0.2	0.2	paddling	2.7	1.6
			total	2.0	xx

M signifies male only, F female only; own calculations.
Source: Zen-Kōtairen 2004 + Kōyaren 2004

Rohlen observed in the 1970s that girls belonged to many high school sports clubs but they generally practiced and competed separately (Rohlen 1983:188). This is still the case in most sports disciplines, although borderlines have become less strict. Blackwood found out that at least five female players had joined baseball teams in 2002, even though they knew that they could not play at tournaments. But in the shadow of the male performers on the ground, there are in fact quite a substantial number of female members of baseball and other team sports clubs. Instead of acting front stage, they are usually involved in support roles for the male players, washing their uniforms, preparing snacks and meals, putting away equipment (Kameda 1995:115). According to a survey by the Japan Highschool Baseball Federtion, 71% of all high school baseball clubs had female 'managers' in charge of all the tedious but badly needed work. Baseball is not unique in this regard. The supportive role of females seems to be a rather common feature of team sports clubs (Itō 2001; Blackwood 2003). When girls are not available for the manager's duties, the behind-the-scenes work is usually executed by someone of lower rank within the club hierarchy, a junior member or someone with little chance to ever play in games.

5   Society and the Hidden Curriculum

The discussion so far has shown that patterns of sports participation of Japanese students are significantly gendered. These patterns impact the decision whether to get involved in sports and, if yes, in what kind of sports. The outcome of this process of decision-making in turns impacts the way sports and gender are interrelated. Parental adults as role models and peer groups as pressure group have always been important factors influencing the individual's decision; nowadays the media have come to join them, as Sugimoto correctly observed on the impact of the media on the latent curriculum (*senzai karikyuramu*) of physical education (1995:161-163). I also argue that the media's impact is particularly strong because in the age of media sports the media appeal of a discipline is decicive for its financial support (e.g. in form of sponsorship), on the one hand, and its capability to draw media audiences, and foster fan loyalities, on the other hand. The question of who is represented in the media is no less important than the question of how an athlete is represented.

While cultural industries have been comparatively open to the employment of women, the sports writers' world seems rather closed. Virtually everywhere, argues Jennifer Hargreaves (1994:151), men figure much more than women as media-sports professionals, sports writers and academics in all sports-related fields. The Japanese case is no exception. Among the 46 Japanese newspaper journalists that covered the Sydney Olympics in 2000, Iida (2002:81-83) identified only 3 women, who contributed a mere 4.1% of 635 articles and not a single photo to the Japanese print media display of the Olympics. While the coverage of women's and men's sports in three national dailies was quite evenly balanced in quantitative terms, it differed considerably in qualitative terms, i.e. the kind of sports featured and its contextualisation. Women got a frequent press coverage in disciplines that had gained social acceptance long ago, such as track and field or swimming, or in "typically" feminine sports, such as synchronised swimming and beach volleyball (Iida 2002:79). The women's beach ball team did not advance very far in 2000, yet its photo shots were, together with the synchro swimmer teams, most often displayed on the sports pages. Hence the observable gains women made in the media representation did not always work to their advantage, if the increase were primarily based on the permissive (or compelled) disclosure

137

of the female body to the male gaze. As Alina Bernstein (2002) has commented, the sexualisation of female athletes trivialises their achievements and in fact robs them of athletic legitimacy, thus preserving hegemonic masculinity.

Research on the role of sports media in the reproduction of gender stereotypes has found that the coverage is often framed within stereotypes which emphasise social expectations toward the athlete as women rather than as athletic achievers (cf. Iida 2003). According to Hirakawa's analysis of sports-related TV commercials (2002), women were clearly underrepresented (comprising 14.4 per cent of images) in the spots and staged in comparatively passive or overdetermined roles that can easily be associated with the dominant normative destination of female existence: as wife and mother. While male athletes were typically shown in action, in actual competition, or surrounded by fans and admirers, women rarely appeared hardly as active performers, and if they did, then in fairly domestic contexts, running the dog, or playing with children. Masculinity was valorised by the celebration of the sports hero in very condensed heroic situations, whereas the sports heroines were deprived of all their heroic features. Again, this narrative technique is far from being exclusively Japanese as Whannel has observed in comparative work on sports heroes and heroines. He also noted that 'sport characteristically provides a space for the eradication, marginalisation and symbolic annihilation of the feminine' (Whannel 2002:45). It seems that the success of the female athlete causes alert or a sense of crisis in the world of masculine domination. Iida also found that female athletes were often called by pet names and endearing terms stressing their cuteness and 'lovely' dependence on men. As male athletes are referred to in a much more detached and honourable way, the verbal annexation of the female athlete is a linguistic practice that reinforces gender-based status differences.

The prominence of a sport in the media guarantees its retention as we can see in the correlation of media visibility and appeal of a sport to the young Japanese. If a mass sport is also played on a professional level, it usually should command over a substantial amount of capable and certified instructors. This observation is closely connected with one of the basic problems frequently associated with gender inequality in Japanese sports. In August 2001, the Council of Education explained the low participation rate of girls in kids' sports clubs with the lack of qualified female sports instructors. Girls were said not to shun sports in general but to be disgusted and repelled by the unattractive supply of male-dominated sports games.[3] Looking at the broader picture, Kawaguchi et al. (1999) stated that more and more female athletes are performing on the world stage, yet 90 percent of their coaches are male. More and more women take actively part in sports classes of social education, yet only 3.5% of their instructors are female. Furthermore, while the number of female teachers is increasing, they are overrepresented in certain subjects and underrepresented in senior positions. Many women teach home economics and Japanese, but few teach science and physical education. 60% of teachers at primary schools are female, but the number of women promoted to senior positions is very low, given the share of 1% female principals out of the total. In short, concludes the Japan NGO Alternative Report on Women 2000, girls simply lack positive role models among the teachers close to them. There are still many obstacles to overcome in the education system until gender equity will be achieved (Japan NGO Report Preparatory Committee 1999).

If we looked more into the actual practice of PE classes, more concrete examples would emerge showing how the actual experience of sports engraves gender differences into the body. An often heard criticism is the name call issue. Teachers have alphabetically ordered name lists (*meibō*) for boys and girls (Itō 2001:128); traditionally, girls had to stand still and wait until the teacher had checked the attendance of their male class mates. This routine seems to be still widely in practice, as well as the habit of having students line up according to body height. This does not necessarily give advantage to the boys as some girls are big and taller than boys, but in general this ritualised form of behaviour tends to emphasise the physical superiority of boys. Another point of complain is the overall concern with the quantitative measurement of individual development (Iida 2000). The basic model is the Ministry's physical strength test (*tairyoku chōsa*), which has been conducted annually since 1964 to ascertain the present conditions of the nation's physical fitness and abilities.[4] Originally this test covered only students at the levels of primary and secondary education, but the coverage has been extended to include the adult population, and on pre-school level many institutions mirror the national survey. PE curricula advise teachers to adjust the PE programme to the schedule of the test, which is likely to heat up training activities before the day of the survey. Again, the design of the survey, the measurement standards of performance and the way results are computed for public display seem to prove the superiority of the male body.

6 Conclusion

The discussion has shown that physical education is an important site for the construction and consolidation of gender identities within schools. It goes without saying that the Japanese body regime rather comply with collective norms than with the totality of individual choices. Class room lessons and self-administered club activities function as sites for the gendered display of hegemonic forms of both femininities and masculinities. Differences in sports club enrolment clearly show the tension between dominant and subordinate masculinities and femininities and that these are played out through the acceptance and refusal of different forms of sports activities. Comparing the gendered sports supply at school institutions of early Shōwa Japan and the present, the consolidation of a gendered worldview in sports is remarkably perennial. Sports remained to be primarily a 'homosocial institution enforcing and reproducing the ideals of masculinity' (Okada 2004:42). As Jennifer Hargreaves (1994:279) observed, 'the longer men practically and ideologically have appropriated an activity, the more difficult it is for women to get inside'.

This result contrasts with the general observation of social change. The spread of liberal democratic ideology in the latter half of the 20th century triggered tremendous changes in patterns of leisure and consumption, and in the relation between the sexes. It is equally true that the advance of consumer society opened new opportunities for women's participation in sports. Globalisation impacts have put masculine hegemony under scrutiny again: The East Asian economic crises, the loss of job security, men's dissatisfaction with corporate employment and the modest increase in career opportunities for women have challenged the gendered division of labour. But the willingness to take sides with neoliberalism has weakened familial patriarchy while social patriarchy gained ground. Looking at women's participation in football in China, Japan and Korea, I argued that capitalism and democracy, on the one hand, and the commercialisation and spectacularisation of football, on the other hand, have brought about contradictory effects of "civilising" and "suppressive" power. While the globalisation of sports has given some impetus to changing gender relations in several nation-states, male sports continues to flourish as the unquestioned standard of sports. In consequence to economic market principles overgrowing traditional culture-based principles of gender discrimination in sports, power relations between the sexes were disguised and the male prerogative was preserved (Manzenreiter 2004).

Spielvogel (2003) argues that social inequalities between the sexes contribute to the ubiquituous dieting in high schools, on campuses, and in fitness clubs where most aerobics instructors and members reflect the national preoccupation with weight and slim. Given the Japanese ideological emphasis on the fluid boundaries between self and the other, dieting and food refusal serve women as powerful means to resist and comply with gender inequality and age-appropriate gender roles. Her study reconfigures the Japanese fitness club as a confluence of historical transformations, in which constructions of sports shifted from expressions of patriotism and national solidarity to those of individuality and lifestyle directed particularly at the female body (Spielvogel 2003:60). The emphasis on youth, associated with sexiness and vulnerability, good proportions and shapely legs, is prescriptive, distinctively Japanese and nonetheless intentionally constructed by drawing on Western standards of physical beauty. Club management attempts to counter the hegemonic notion of beauty by emphasising health over appearance are doomed to fail because it is the desire for the right look that drives the majority of club members into the studio. Thus the fitness industry capitalises on the desire for appropriate appearance, with good health, well-being, and exercises serving as the means to achieve good looks. But female consumers shun the hard work of exercise and prefer catered service, quality leisure, and ultimately the beauty industries' tricky promises of slimming or toning up any body part in isolation. Being trapped into the functional chain of consumerism, both members and instructors of aerobics classes find themselves "shaping up" to an unrealistic ideal denying them private fulfilment and actual empowerment in the end.

The school as a social institution proves to be incapable of establishing counter-trends to the hegemonic body regime. Cultural discourses on the "reproductive capabilities" and "domestic destiny" of the "fair sex" confront girls with social responsibilities overshadowing the private realm of personal pleasure and physical sensation. Female subordination and male domination are codified at political and administrative levels, exploited in economic relations, symbolically reproduced in popular cultural forms, and most pervasively performed in school sports everyday life.

Notes

[1] In 1914 Nishikubo Hiromichi published a series of articles arguing that the Japanese martial arts should be called *budō* ('martial way') rather than *bujutsu* ('martial techniques'). The police official recommended the martial way as effective tool to teach schoolchildren to be willing to sacrifice their lives for the Emperor. When Nishibuko became head of the martial arts college of the Dai Nippon Butokukai in 1919, he ordered its name changed from Bujutsu Senmon Gakkō to Budō Senmon Gakkō. The Dai Nippon Butokukai adopted the new phrase in its publications and the Ministry of Education followed suit in 1926. Since 1931, the word *budō* began to refer to compulsory instruction in the Japanese public schools. The Dai Nippon Butokukai was established at the occasion of the foundation of the Butoku-den, a consecrated shrine for martial arts at Heian Jingu in Kyōto in 1895. The Butokukai was patronized by the Royal family. The organisation aimed to revive *bushidō*, to 'promote *bujutsu* to future military men,' and to make Japan 'a nation of mili-

tary prowess'. Enjoying rapid growth, branches in forty-two prefectures reported about 1.3 million members by 1906. As the most forceful, influential, and chauvinistic sport governing body, it was dissolved by the Allied Occupation Forces in September 1946. For more on this topic, see Nakamura 1994.

2   The reduction of compulsory subjects is in line with the general shift of emphasis towards a society of lifelong learning (*shōgai kyōiku shakai*) in which individual interests, rather than institutional coercion, are meant to build the platform of self-cultivation.

3   See the online minutes of the Council's discussion in its fourth and fifth meeting on August 9 and 27, 2001 at http://www.mext.go.jp/b_menu/shingi/12/hoken/.

4   The survey is a sampling survey covering pupils and students attending public elementary, lower secondary and upper secondary schools, national technical colleges, public and private junior colleges, and national colleges and universities as well as working adult of 20-64 years old and elderly persons 65-79 years old. Pupils and students are surveyed annually in May to October through schools, and others by the local boards of education. The 2001 survey covered about 75,000 persons.

References

Abe, Ikuo; Kiyohara, Yasuharu and Nakajima, Ken. 1992. 'Sport and physical education under fascistization in Japan'. *International Journal of the History of Sport* 9/1. 1-28

Ben-Ari, Eyal. 1997. *Body projects in Japanese childcare: culture, organization and emotions in a preschool*. Richmond. Curzon Press

Bernstein, Alina. 2002. 'Women in sports media: time for a victory lap?'. Paper delivered at the 3rd Play-The-Game Conference, Denmark, 10-12 November 2002. Online http://www.play-the-game-org. Accessed 20 October 2003

Blackwood, Thomas. 2003. 'The reproduction and naturalisation of sex-based separate spheres in Japanese high schools: the role of female "managers" of high school baseball teams.' *Social Science Japan* 25. 22-26

Boyle, Raymond and Richard Haynes. 2000. *Power play. Sport, the media and popular culture*. Harlow. Longman

Bourdieu, Pierre. 1987. *Die feinen Unterschiede. Kritik der gesellschaftlichen Urteilskraft* [Distinctions. A social critique of the judgement of taste]. Frankfurt. Suhrkamp

Bourdieu, Pierre. 1990. *The logic of practice*. Stanford. Stanford University Press

Bourdieu, Pierre. 1995. *Sociology in question*. London. Sage Publications

Cave, Peter. 2004. '*Bukatsudō*: The educational role of Japanese school sport clubs.' *Journal of Japanese Studies* 30/2. 383-415

Chūtairen [Nihon Chūgakkō Taiiku Renmei]. 2004. *Kameikō, kamei seitō sū chōsa shūkeibyō Heisei 16nen* [Membership table of schools and pupils 2004]. Tōkyō. Chūtairen

Dalla Chiesa, Simone. 2002. 'When the goal is not the goal. Japanese school football players working hard at their game.' Joy Hendry and Massimo Raveri. eds. *Japan at play. The ludic and the logic of power*. London. Routledge. 186-198

Hargreaves, Jennifer. 1994. *Sporting females. Critical Issues in the History and Sociology of Women's Sports*. London. Routledge

Hirakawa, Sumiko. 2002. 'Supōtsu, jendā, media imēji. Supōtsu CF ni egakareru jendā' [Sport, gender, media image. Gender depictions in sport TV commercials]. Hashimoto, Junichi. ed. *Gendai media supōtsu ron*. Kyōto. Sekai Shisō Sha. 91-115

Iida, Takako. 2000. 'Monbushō supōtsu tesuto' ga tsukuru danjosa' [Differences in body strength of men and women created by The Ministry of Education's sport test]. Paper delivered at the Sym-

Wolfram Manzenreiter

posium Kyōto supōtsu to josei fōramu, Kokuritsu Fujin Kyōiku Kaikan, Kyoto, 6-8 October 2000

Iida, Takako. 2002. 'Media supōtsu to feminizumu' [Media sports and feminism]. Hashimoto, Junichi. ed. *Gendai media supōtsu ron*. Kyōto. Sekai Shisō Sha. 71-90

Iida, Takako. 2003. 'Shinbun hōdō ni okeru josei kyōgisha no jendā-ka. Sugawara Kyōko kara Narazaki Noriko e' [The gendering of female athletes in newspaper reports. From Ms Noriko Sugawara to Mrs Noriko Narazaki]. *Journal of Sport and Gender Studies* 1. 4-14

Itani, Keiko. 2003. 'Josei taiiku kyōshi e no mensetsu chōsa kara mita gakkō taiiku no jendā sabukaruchā' [The gender subculture of school physical education as viewed through interviews of women physical educators]. *Journal of Sport and Gender Studies* 1. 27-38

Itō, Kimio. 2001. 'Supōtsu kyōiku to jendā' [Sports education and gender]. Sugimoto Atsuo. ed. *Taiiku kyōiku o manabu hito no tame ni*. Kyōto. Sekai Shisō Sha. 124-141

Japan NGO Report Preparatory Committee. 1999. 'B. Women and education.' Japan NGO Report Preparatory Committee. *Women 2000, Japan NGO Alternative Report*. Online http://www.jca.apc.org/fem/bpfa/NGOreport/B_en_Education.html. Accessed 10 October 2004

Kameda, Atsuko. 1995. 'Sexism and gender-stereotyping in schools.' Kumiko Fujimura-Fanselow and Atsuko Kameda. eds. *Japanese women. New feminist perspectives on the past, present, and future*. New York. The Feminist Press. 107-124

Kameyama, Yoshiaki. 1991. 'Seisei suru shintai - sakusō shintai, seido shintai to kakuchō shintai, shintō shintai' [The becoming body – intricative body, institutionalised body and expanding body, immediate body], *Soshioroji* 111 (36/1). 17-29

Kawaguchi, Chiyo; Ikeda, Hiroe and Miki, Hiromi. 1999. Women's education and physical education in Japan: past, present, and perspective. Unpublished paper presented at the 50th Anniversary Conference, International Association of Physical Education & Sports for Girls and Women, Smith College, Northampton, Massachusetts, 7-10 July 1999

Kiku, Kōichi. 1984. 'Kindai no puro supotsu no seiritsu ni kansuru rekishi shakaigakuteki kōsatsu. Wa ga kuni ni okeru senzen no puro yakyū o chūshin ni' [A historical-sociological study on the development of modern professional sports – particularly on the development of professional baseball in Japan before World War II]. *Taiiku Supōtsu Shakaigaku Kenkyū* 3. 1-26

Kōyaren [Nihon Kōtō Gakkō Yakyū renmei]. *Buin sū tōkei* [Membership statistics]. Online: http//www.jhbf.or.jp/renmei33.doc

Kreitz-Sandberg, Susanne. 2000. Reformen im japanischen Schulwesen [Reforming the Japanese school system]. Friederike Bosse and Patrick Köllner, eds. *Reformen in Japan*. Hamburg. Institut für Asienkunde. 265-285

Manzenreiter, Wolfram. 2000. *Die soziale Konstruktion des japanischen Alpinismus. Kultur, Ideologie und Sport im modernen Bergsteigen* [The social construction of Japanes mountaineering. Culture, ideology and sports in modern mountain climbing]. Wien: Abtl. für Japanologie des Instituts für Ostasienwissenschaften 2000 (= Beiträge zur Japanologie; 36)

Manzenreiter, Wolfram. 2004. 'Her place in the 'House of Football': globalisation, sexism and women's football in East Asian societies' Wolfram Manzenreiter and John Horne. eds. *Football goes east. business, culture and the people's game in East Asia*. London/New York. Routledge. 197-221

Mauss, Marcel. [1934] 1989. 'Die Techniken des Körpers' [Body techniques]. Marcel Mauss. *Soziologie und Anthropologie 2*. Frankfurt a.M. Fischer Taschenbuch. 197-220

Monbushō. 1999a. *Chūgakkō gakushū shidō yōryō* [Outline of teaching instructions at junior high school]. Tōkyō: Monbushō. Online http://www.mext.go.jp/b_menu/shuppan/sonota/990301c/990301g.htm. Accessed 12 November 2004

Monbushō. 1999b. *Kōtō gakkō gakushū shidō yōryō* [Outline of teaching instructions at senior high school]. Tōkyō: Monbushō. Online http://www.mext.go.jp/b_menu/shuppan/sonota/990301/03122603/007.htm. Accessed 12 November 2004

Gender and Education: Perspectives on Schooling in Japan and Comparisons from the Philippines

Susanne Kreitz-Sandberg

1   Introduction

School is one of the places, which are seen as comparatively gender equal. Many studies have, however, pointed out various matters of discrimination, both of boys and girls, and an enormous amount of adjustment is still needed if equality between or equal opportunities for the sexes are to be realised. The change of the gender order in (post-) modern societies seems to be accompanied by a certain discomfort and asks not only for understanding but also for appropriate measures of support (O'Donnell/Sharpe 2000). Schools play a vital role in this context and increasingly realise their responsibility in the context of gender education. In social sciences the approach of a *socially constructed character of gender* provides us with tools for analysis, something that has been developed by many authors in women's studies as well as men's studies (e.g. Connell 1995).

Which role does gender play in Japanese education today, more than a decade after gender-free education (*jendā furīna kyōiku*) became a catch phrase in 1995? Gender can be understood as the personal, social and cultural assignment of being male or female. This definition includes differences between men and women in connection with their specific roles and division of labour as well as variations within the group of women or the group of men. Gender identities are shaped by a wide range of factors from interactions in the family, the school, peer groups and youth culture, with strong influences by music idols, sports icons and many others. And on top of this, actual power relations in society are often reflected in the gender order.

Gender is an extended research area in educational studies. Early studies focussed on factors reproducing inequality between the sexes. Diverging behavioural patterns, interests and personal traits of boys and girls were explained in connection to their social environment. Later studies point out that boys and girls even contribute themselves actively to this process of acquiring gender identities. Detailed studies describe how teachers and schools contribute to the process of "doing gender", taking into account that gender is not a personal trait but developing in the process of interaction. These analyses are usually connected to discussions on gender equality, which builds on equal rights, duties and possibilities for both men and women.

In addition to obvious international convergences concerning gender equality in major industrial countries relevant specifics can also be observed. Each country and research culture has its own discourses on gender and education. These are closely connected to historical and social developments within the respective society in general, and the school system in particular. A detailed comparison of the dominant discussions, e.g. in the Anglo-Saxon, German or Scandinavian research on gender and education, would definitely be

143

very enlightening in order to understand that there is not a single discourse on the topic but a multiple variety of familiar topics being brought up. Presumably, gender order in the respective societies is reflected in the perspective on gender in educational science literature, while at the same time international discourses are influenced by the reasoning of researchers within gender studies.

Instead of choosing a particular Western discourse as ground for this article I will build this study on a brief analysis of Japanese sociology of education literature on gender in education.[1] My further comparative analysis builds on qualitative empirical material in order to base my reasoning on descriptions of the reality in Japanese schools through the eyes of gender-sensitive researchers.

Gender-free education (*jendā furīna kyōiku*) has been a catch phrase in Japan in the 1990s.[2] Many initiatives and semi-governmental institutions were engaged in a debate whether education should be gender-free and discussed how this could be achieved. For example Tōkyō Josei Zaidan (1995) became very active publishing materials for young teachers in order to raise consciousness on gender in education.[3] At the same time an international comparative study claimed a 'modernisation gap' (Windolf 1997: 2–8) concerning gender in Japanese higher education, with reference to the low participation of women at universities with BA and MA. Such somehow contradicting foci on gender in Japanese education demand additional attention on conditions for boys and girls in the Japanese school system.

Aim of the study and structure of the article

The aim of this study is to shed light on the situation around Gender and Education in Japan. Therefore the situation of girls and boys in the school system and the reasoning of gender researchers will be analysed. A comparative perspective will contribute information to the question if and how Japanese education provides a somehow specific experience concerning gender roles. My aim with this contribution is to answer to a variety of questions concerning the role of gender in Japanese schools and our possibilities to do research on related topics. First of all, I will describe the situation concerning gender in Japanese schools building on basic education statistics and on research findings especially from the Japanese Society for Sociology of Education, which hardly has been referred to in Western studies on Gender and Education (Section 2). Through the eyes of mainly Japanese researchers I aim at characterizing the recent discussion. In Section 3 the method of the comparative study is described and the aim is to investigate if and how an international comparative perspective can contribute to an even deeper understanding of the situation of boys and girls in Japanese schools. In detail I am interested in what additional insights we can gain – if any – by including results from studies in other Asian countries into our understanding of Japan. Therefore, I will introduce case studies on gender and education in order to find evidence on similarities and specifics in two Asian nations. This analysis builds on material by researchers from the respective countries (Section 4). I am aware that both studies are only examples and that we should be careful with any type of generalisation. The core question is whether we find convergences from the situation in Japan with other societies and research cultures and what we possibly could describe as specifics in the Japanese educational system. How can we characterize the reproduction of gender in the school and in the family? And finally, what further research strategies should we choose in order to gain and ground innovative knowledge on Gender and Education in Japan?

2   Gender and Education as a Topic in the Japanese Education Discussion

Which role does gender play, if we want to understand the reality in the Japanese school system? In terms of participation in the school system, the relation between boys and girls is rather balanced in Japan.[4] After completing compulsory education with graduation from junior high school, 97.5 percent of the pupils continue their studies at a senior high school (Ministry of Education, Culture, Sports, Science and Technology 2005: 46–47). This included 96 percent of the male and 97.8 percent of the female middle school graduates in 1998 (*kōkō shingakuritsu*) (Ministry of Education, Science, Sport and Culture 1999: 47).[5] Already in the mid-eighties the quota of girls had exceeded the one of boys. Comparatively more boys than girls started working at this early stage, but generally it can be stated that high school education had become necessary in order to earn a certain social status and income. About 73 percent of girls and boys attend schools with a general curriculum (*futsūka*). Within the professional track we can distinguish gender specific choices: Girls are more likely to specialise in a commercial course, in home economics, nursing and welfare studies, while boys more often select technical high schools with courses for industry, agriculture and fishery (Ministry of Education, Culture, Sport, Science and Technology 2005: 54–55).

The tension between a formal equality combined with specific gender differences proceeds all the way up through high school and university. Advancement to university (*daigaku shingakuritsu*) has increased from 30 percent of the high school graduates in 1985 to 45 percent in 2004 (Ministry of Education, Culture, Sport, Science and Technology 2005: 60–61). This quota, however, includes also the advancement to two-year junior colleges. That is why the figures for male and female students present such a favourable picture for women: 43.6 percent of young men and 47.1 percent of young women continue their training at so-called higher education institutions.[6] Japanese governmental reports point out these favourable results in terms of participation in higher education. However, the topic 'Women in higher education' was also one of the first gender-related discussions in Japanese educational sociology (Amano 1986, 1988, 1997, Fujimura-Faselow 1985), where feminists presented the gender bias in these data. An international comparative study on universities with BA level and higher even proves a 'modernisation gap' (Windolf 1997: 2–8) concerning the participation of women in higher education. In fact, in Japan 38.9 percent of the male high school students advanced to universities with a BA level (four years of studies) in 1994, while only 21 percent of the female high school graduates entered a four-year university. Another 24.9 percent entered the so-called junior colleges, two or three year courses of study (Sōrifu 1995, cf. Hōnuki 1996: 35). More recent data show that the application rate to universities is steadily increasing. It has reached 47.4 percent of high school graduates in 2004. The gap between the sexes has, however, only gradually decreased with 55.3 percent of the male and 39.4 percent of the female graduates aiming at entering BA courses, while an additional 14.7 percent of the young women chose to apply to one of the junior colleges, which are providing education almost exclusively for women (Ministry of Education, Culture, Sports, Science and Technology 2005: 62–63).[7]

These explicit differences in the educational system are connected to what is called *danjo tokusei kyōikuron*, a discourse on education that addresses women and men differently. These *tokuseiron* have played an important role in the development of the Japanese educational system, where segregation according to gender is still quite common. However, in Japan, there is a strong appreciation of education as contributing to the equality of society. In comparison to other public fields, school education is seen as the area where equality of the sexes could be realised. Among the six fields, family life, work place, cultural customs, educational, political and legal institutions, the schools earned the highest recognition for 'equality' (with 65 percent agreement) in a governmental survey on public opinion (Sōrifu 1995, cited by Hōnuki 1996: 34). Many Japanese share the view that school might be the area of society, where most attention is paid to equality of the sexes. However, the school system harbours contradicting roles. Kimura Ryōko (1990, 1999), who published widely on gender and school culture, states that schools are on one hand comparatively egalitarian, but that on the other hand many discriminating factors must be taken into account.[8] The following descriptions try to shed light on these contradicting elements.

Many of the studies introduced below provide us with information on how the gender roles are cemented in the school system rather than change being introduced. In educational research special attention is paid to questions of gender role acquisition and sex stereotyping of children and youths. Quite some attention is placed on defining how the term gender should be understood. Tsuruta Atsuko (1998: 315) defines gender as 'historically, culturally and socially formed sex' (*rekishiteki, bunkateki, shakaiteki ni keisei sareta sei*). Fujita Hidenori (1992: 258) refers to gender questions as 'social and cultural phenomena related to questions of sex differences and sex relations' (translation by the author). Gender researchers discuss the relation between a pure difference and discrimination (*seisa* versus *sei sabetsu*), and various concepts on gender/sex role (*sei-yakuwari*) and division of labour (*sei-bungyō*) are seen as related but not always clearly distinguished from each other. Fujita Hidenori (1999: 8), a leading researcher in Japanese sociology of education builds his introduction on gender and education on the closeness of gender concepts and feminism, which both are aiming at overcoming sex discrimination in society.

Examples of gender related discrimination in the form of stereotyping could be found in various studies describing multiple gender bias in teaching materials (Morimoto 1998). Some of these studies build on international comparisons (Tomo 1999, Tomo et al. 1996, 2002). Intercultural differences could be observed not only when comparing Japan with "Western" cultures but also among Asian cultures (Tomo/Tung 1997: 67–84). The expected behaviour styles are, however, not rigidly fixed but may also change within one country. In newer Japanese textbooks, for example, we might observe female characters who are much more assertive and persistent than in books published two decades earlier (Tomo 1999: 206). Therefore, we can understand that gender stereotypes are undergoing a constant change.

International research obviously triggers also discourses in Japanese research. Often, however, we find a clear gap in topics being raised with a certain time lag. It was only in the late 1980's and 1990's that Japanese educational scientists brought up gender discourse more actively. Review articles in the Japanese Journal of Sociology of Education leave no doubt that the discussion entered Japanese research circles only gradually (Mori 1992).[9] 'Gender and Education' was used for a long time as a successor or quasi-synonym for women's or girls' education in Japan. Two groups were especially interested in the new discourse. Researchers who had been working on the topic of women's education in its traditional functions rather reinterpreted the aims and used them in order to strengthen their position as regards women's education; and feminists – who identified strongly with the ideas of the second international women's movement – took a rather radical stand in order to realise their ideas on equal opportunities for boys and girls via education.

One example of long preserved gender segregation, which included a hierarchy between boys and girls, is the use of separate name lists for boys and girls, which give the names in the order of the *hiragana* "alphabet" with all the boys first, followed by a list with all the girls. Nowadays such lists are in use in very few schools while in the majority of the schools mixed lists were introduced through the initiatives of teachers and parents for equal education for boys and girls (e.g. Danjo Byōdō Kyōiku o Susumeru-kai 1997).

A long prevailing segregation of women and men in the daily life in the society has attracted quite some international attention (Lenz/Mae 1997). In youth studies segregation became especially obvious through results from a survey study attesting how strongly senior high school students associate in same-gender groups (Kreitz-Sandberg 1994, 1996). A comparison of junior high school students proved that youth in Japan actually spend much more time in single-sex groups than in Germany (Toyama-Bialke 2000). This also influences gender identity (Kreitz-Sandberg 1999) and the specific experiences in school. However, we need to investigate further how this segregation influences young people.

Segregation as such can facilitate different results, as can be understood by studies of senior high schools for girls and B.A. level women's universities (Nakanishi 1993, 1998, 2002). These studies on various 'gender tracks' in education illustrate the difference between school or university cultures in different institutions. Nakanishi shows that the future life course relies stronger on the school culture than on the academic abilities of the girls. All-girls institutions (both senior high schools and universities) can strengthen female orientation to either direction: forcing women into their "traditional" feminine role as well as helping them to opt for a professional career.

On top of specific school cultures a wide range of diverse gender patterns can be described within each institution. This is connected to the influence of peer groups on respective gender identities. Miyazaki (1993) describes in her school ethnography how girls associate in different groups within one school and how these groups often represent common views concerning gender. Some were, for example, identifying with quite traditional gender roles while others experimented more actively in the field of youth culture and respective patterns of girlishness.[10]

Different expectations in education are often connected to gender stereotyping. Girls are often educated to behave in accordance with their female identity, *onna rashii*, and boys to behave *otoko rashii* (Ujihara 1996, Mori 1985). One study on sex stereotyping in school asked students and teachers whether the categories *onna rashii* and *otoko rashii* (behaving according to what is appropriate for a woman or a man) played an important role in their education. *Onna rashii* stereotyping was connected for the girls with categories like tidiness or helping others. *Otoko rashii* was associated for the boys with the ability to study, academic achievement and helping others. The study elucidates various ambivalences of the topic. Teachers claimed to use these patters equally with boys and girls. However, sex stereotyping occurred more frequently towards girls than towards boys. And boys were quite aware of being asked to behave in appropriateness with being or becoming a man, although the educators said that they did not express such intentions (Niigata-shi 1995).

However, sex stereotyping is no special characteristic of school education, as the study also showed that students had experienced sex stereotyping much more frequently in the family than at school.

Research on the development of male identity (Taga 1996, 2000, 2002a, 2003a) points to the multiple influence factors involved in the creation of 'masculinity' as a cultural attitude (see also Connel 1987, 1995). Behaviour in relation to gender and related opinions and life concepts developed during the students' family and school history, as Taga illustrates via case studies and interviews with university students.

All these studies have contributed to the fact that 'gender in education' has become part of the core curriculum in teacher education. Gender is no longer just a "hidden" curriculum,[11] as many teachers are aware about patterns and stereotypes of reproducing so-called traditional gender roles. Educators are, for example, concerned about the message transmitted to students by sex typical role distribution at school. Until now we have, however, little information about how this knowledge is being translated into educational programmes and integrated into the curriculum and daily life in school.

3   Object of the Study

The analysis will be comparative in nature. Most Western studies on Japan have been shaped by an *implicit* comparative perspective. Standards of comparison are unclear, leaving many open questions about the focus of comparison. One approach to overcome implicit Western standards is by *explicitly* comparing realities and cultural specific interpretations (Seifert/Weber 2002). However, until now very few Asian nations have been included into such comparisons.

In the following I will approach an explicit comparison via two case studies. One was carried out in Japan and one in the Philippines. Choosing a non-European society for the comparison is a very conscious decision, as I want to break – at least for this small study – with the habit of comparing Japan to one of the Western nations. I will analyse gender policies for schools in Japan and another Asian nation. This can stimulate the discussion and contribute to an understanding of realities and discourses on gender and education in two Asian countries.

I am conducting a secondary analysis of two studies of gender practices in primary schools. Both projects are documented in so-called "grey literature"; the Japanese study in a University Journal, the one from the Philippines in a journal of a human rights organisation and published on an internet site. Both analyses focus on the implementation of so-called gender-free or gender-fair education. One study has been carried out by an external advisor for a project on gender-free education in a primary school in Kyūshu in the South-West of Japan (Taga 2003b). My knowledge about the second study is based on a report on gender-sensitive education in so-called child-friendly schools in the Philippines (Women and Gender Institute, Miriam College, in the following cited as WAGI 2004). Both studies are concerned with primary schools and have been carried out in 2001. They provide us with knowledge of the realities in schools and how the respective researchers reason over the continuation of unequal approaches in the educational settings for boys and girls.[12]

4   A Comparative Perspective on Gender Policies in Primary Schools

"Difficulties in Gender-Free Education in Japan" and "Gender-Fair Education in the Philippines" could be the titles of the two case studies to be introduced and compared below. This summarises a general impression of a slightly pessimistic or maybe just critical perspective in the Japanese study and a more affirmative approach in the Philippine study. Both studies are concerned with schools, which put an effort in child-friendly and gender-sensitive education. In the Japanese study the term 'education for equality of boys and girls' (*danjo byōdō kyōiku*) is used by the school, and in research the study is introduced within the concept of 'gender-free education'. The study from the Philippines used the terms 'gender-fair education' or 'gender-sensitive education'.

This article has, until now, paid no attention to the background of schooling in the Philippines, as we are more specifically interested in the situation in Japan. Philippine education is seldom included in comparative education studies. One reason might be that different developmental standards pose obvious difficulties in a comparison between so-called developing and developed (post-)industrial countries. However, a detailed description might help to provide the context needed for the analysis. Will we find common Asian elements or can we expect a certain hybridity with European culture, as the Philippines is a former Spanish colony and strongly influenced by Christianity? Does this also influence the degree of development and the positioning towards gender questions? These are some of the questions we have to keep in mind for further analysis. And there are, obviously, limits to a direct comparison due to the differences in the general situation of the schools and even based on methodological differences in the studies. Therefore, we have to be careful with generalisations. However, let us first take a closer look at both studies and judge later whether the findings from the Philippines can contribute to a deeper understanding of the situation in Japan.

4.1 Object and method of the two case studies

The first study was carried out by a primary school in Kyūshu in Western Japan. The teaching staff of 'M' primary school decided in the year 2000 to launch a project for the whole school in the context of the special research focus proposed by the local education council (*kyōiku iinkai*) of 'L' city on 'education for equality of boys and girls' (*danjo byōdō kyōiku*). L city has 230 000 inhabitants and according to teaching staff the discussion of women's rights has been much more active in this city than in other places of the region, which is generally known as gender conservative (Taga 2003b: 67).

The primary school M is located in the outskirts of the city, where farmland has been turned into apartment blocks and one-family houses successively. 32 teachers were teaching 566 pupils in three classes each from grade 1 to 6 in the school-year 2002/2003. The study was carried out from November 2001 until October 2002, when Taga Futoshi served as an external adviser, because he is known for his studies on gender identity of male university students. The findings are based on a variety of sources, like interviews with the teaching staff, the head master, a few parents and pupils, materials provided by the school, and a survey carried out by the school with the respective six graders before and after the project. The author also engaged in participant observations in the school and recorded several school assemblies and lessons with video camera and tape recorder (Taga 2003b: 67–68).

The second study is from the Philippines and presents an example from a Southeast Asian country, one of the ASEAN nations. The study examines gender socialisation of boys and girls in grades 1, 5, and 6 in six selected public schools. The main source for the following analysis is a report by The Women and Gender Institute of Miriam College from 2002 on 'Gender Socialization in Philippine Child-Friendly Schools'. Three teachers from Miriam College carried out fieldwork from January to March 2001.[13] Various data-gathering techniques were used in the schools, like classroom observations, observations of children's play activities, analyses of messages and communication materials on campus, focus group discussions among teachers on gender-fair education, short interviews with school administrators and a survey of students' attitudes towards gender.

The research was carried out in schools, which were supported by the United Nations Children's Fund (UNICEF) to set up a 'child-friendly school system'. The study reviewed in collaboration with the national Department of Education how gender and development policies and programmes were integrated into the child-friendly school system. For this reason it explored the learning environments in six schools, which were part of the model for child-friendly schools. Fieldwork was conducted in one urban and one rural public school in three different regions. Selection of the schools was dependent on a co-ordination between UNICEF and the Department of Education.

One school was located in the mountains, teaching children of parents mostly engaged in retailing, vending, farming and mining. With 408 students from preschool until grade 6, a combined class in grade 6 is overpopulated with 65 students. The second school served 497 students. It was also located in the mountains with most of the parents engaged in farming or small-scale mining. A third school was located in a clean and friendly area close to the sea. The families of the 353 pupils had their earnings from fishing and farming. The forth mountain school could only be reached by motorcycle. Upland farming was the most common activity to earn one's income. In this school with 236 students grades 3 and 4, and grades 5 and 6 are taught together. The fifth school, hosting over 1000 students, was located in a slum area. The children came from very poor households with many of the parents doing simple jobs within the service industry. Some of the girls worked as prostitutes. The sixth school, located in another remote mountain area served 222 children of mainly indigenous people (WAGI 2004: 117–118).

The description of the schools illustrates various kinds of problems schools are facing, which are quite different from well-established institutions such as the Japanese primary schools we know (White 1987, Schubert 1992, 2002). To choose only one example for the difference between the national school systems: the so-called primary pupil-teacher ratio, which indicates the number of students enrolled in primary education divided by the number of teachers (regardless of their teaching assignment). According to data from the World Development Index for the school year 2001/02 there were 35 pupils per teacher in primary schools in the Philippines, 32 in the Republic of Korea, 20 in Japan, 15 in Germany and 11 in Sweden (World Bank 2004). This obviously also influences the possibilities in teaching styles and educational outcomes. However, although, or maybe even because, there is a clear difference in the general teaching standards, it will be interesting to compare the results concerning gender, or in the terminology of the report cited, concerning measures of 'gender-free' education in Japan and 'gender-fair' or 'gender-sensitive education' in the Philippines.[14]

4.2 Character and aims of the studies

The Japanese case study addresses difficulties in so-called 'gender-free education' in primary schools. This school project can be understood in the context of 'aiming at special abilities in the context of cooperation between men and women, boys and girls'. The research outline by the school aspires to 'the creation of education for the equity between men and women in order to bring up children who can show their inner self' (*jibunrashisa ga hakki dekiru kodomo*). This aim is stated in connection with 'focussing on lessons, which teach to think and care about each other'. Individual self-understanding and understanding of each other are regarded as one process – in this case through the tool of 'education for equality of boys and girls' (*danjo byōdō kyōiku*). The school publications use the term 'education for equality of boys and girls' whereas Taga (2003b: 66–68, 76) refers to the project in the context of 'gender-free education'.[15]

The child-friendly school system and the Department of Education of the Philippines follow policies similar to Gender and Development programmes of the UNESCO. The programmes promote shared parenting, shared home management, shared decision making, and the elimination of violence against women, particularly domestic violence (WAGI 2004: 116–117) but also other aims in connection with social roles like socialisation of leadership traits and breaking down gender stereotypes in occupations. The study from the Philippines considers the need for gender-fair education, as an inter-mediation between sex role standards of students and their families (see Figure 1).

The study examines whether the reality in those schools reinforces or contradicts the aims for gender-fair education by the Department of Education. These aims focus on gender-fair family roles and gender-fair social roles, which are defined as follows:[16]

- Gender-fair family roles: Shared parenting, shared home management, and shared decision-making.
- Gender-fair social roles: Equal opportunities (particularly in mathematics and science); socialisation of leadership traits among students; breaking down of gender stereotypes in occupations; and appreciation of women's roles and value, including elimination of violence against women.

The fieldwork aimed at answering questions concerning key messages about gender, sent to students through interaction of teachers, peers, and administrators, and implications of these messages for students' sex-role standards and for the promotion of gender-fair education.

4.3 Results and analysis

In the following I will summarise some of the main topics in the context of the gender projects in the studied primary schools. The projects on 'gender-free education' gain their relevance because they are taking place in an obviously non-gender-free or a clearly gendered social context.

Susanne Kreitz-Sandberg

Figure 1: **Reinforcement and modelling of gender-fair education in the school setting**

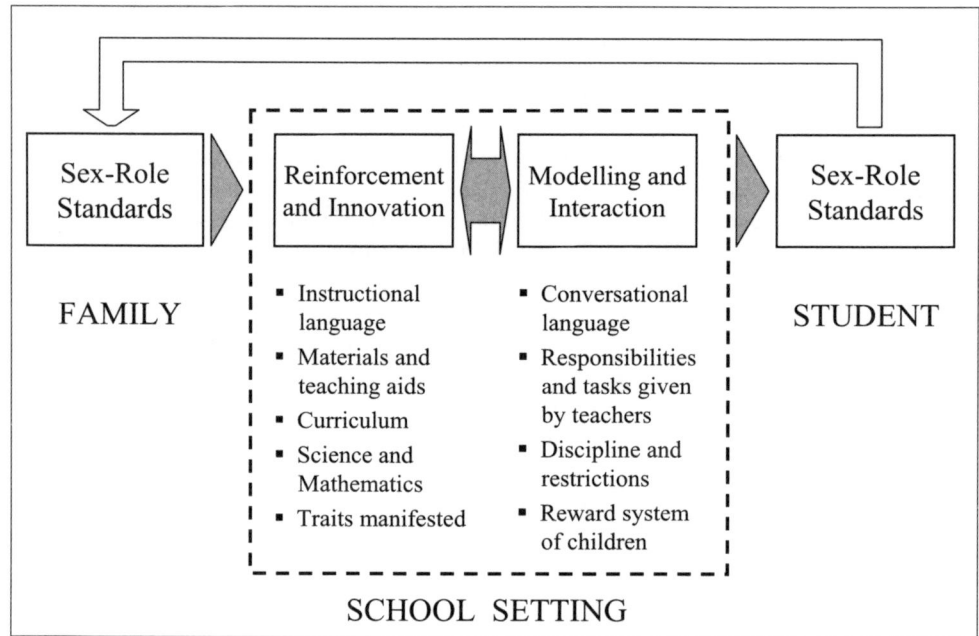

Source: WAGI 2004: 114.

Raising awareness concerning gender roles

In both countries gender stereotypes are expected to prevail in similar fields, especially concerning female attribution of home management. The project in Kyūshu aimed at raising awareness concerning gender roles. By means of a questionnaire the school surveyed the opinions of 11- to 12-year old students. Answers by the sixth graders in 2000 were compared with those of the same age group in 2002 after they had gone through the gender programme. The answers show significant differences – at least on the level of expressed opinions – in connection with the following statements: The acceptance of women's responsiblity for preparing food (21%–14%), cleaning (8%–5%), and washing clothes (29%–8%) has declined while the answers for a common responsibility have risen for preparing food (69%–72%), cleaning (81%–89%), washing clothes (56%–89%; see Taga 2003b: 69). We might discuss how important these answers are in connection to actual behaviour, but in any case this can be seen as one step towards raising gender awareness.[17]

Similar to the study in Japan, attitudes towards gender roles were investigated through a questionnaire in the child-friendly schools in the Philippines. Obviously, there is no statistical basis to compare the results directly with each other. However, they can provide us with a first impression of gender in the perspective of the children. In this questionnaire the students could choose if activities are for girls only, for boys only or for boys and girls. Responses are said not to differ according to sex.[18] Parenting, decision making and also

152

leadership roles were, with a high majority (mostly over 80 percent of the answers), assigned to both sexes. Differences were obvious in connection with household management. While about half of the students favoured shared responsibility, the other students expressed cooking, washing and marketing being responsibilities of the girls/women and fixing house structures as a responsibility of boys/men. However, according to the report personal traits like respectfulness or open-mindedness were not associated with one or the other gender. Because this study was carried out over a period of three months, we cannot gain any information about a possible change in connection with explicit gender education programmes.

Teaching materials, classroom management and language use in a gender perspective

The research in the Philippines analyses instructional language during classes and in the teaching materials, as well as activities and interactions, such as classroom management, responsibilities, and tasks assigned to students. Generally, the researchers report gender-fair practices at school, but they also analyse in detail, where they observed gender-specific instructions. They state that some of the teachers administered different tasks to boys and girls, even though they claimed to act gender-sensitively. The teaching materials were generally described as gender-sensitive 'with some exceptions' (WAGI 2004: 119). These included that boys often were shown in a more active role than girls; and women were often depicted while taking care of domestic chores. Professional activities corresponded with gender stereotypes like a man as doctor and a woman as nurse. In teaching materials the male pronoun he or 'man' was often used although a gender-neutral statement was intended. These descriptions could be interpreted more critically than in the report, as school materials not only reflected existing gender stereotypes but also transported hierarchies between the sexes, as the example with the male doctor and the female nurse illustrates.[19]

The curriculum of many subjects, e.g., home economics, was gender-sensitive working towards shared responsibilities. It was stated that no gender gaps were observed in subjects like mathematics, social studies, etc. English lessons, however, showed a gender bias, often using girls' names in their examples. In some schools science lessons were biased in favour of males. Concerning the results we rely on the interpretations of the researchers from Miriam College. Obviously, there might be other topics catching our eye, if we ourselves could visit the school. One example not brought up explicitly was mentioned in the characterization of the first school site: 'Some of the male students had to sit on top of cabinets for lack of chairs. All the girls had chairs.' (WAGI 2004: 117) So, obviously, gender was also here an important measure of distinction, but this does not yet provide us with information as regards how different opportunities were facilitated.

Concerning classroom management the researchers from Miriam College assert that leaders were chosen not on the basis of sex but responsibility, leadership qualities, social maturity, friendship, popularity, and intelligence. Cleaning and monitoring tasks were assigned to boys and girls, even if some tasks like weeding outside were rather taken care of by boys, while sweeping the floor or wiping furniture were girls' tasks. There were approaches to overcome such gender typical divisions. 'Convincing boys that there was nothing abnormal in their arranging flowers is a small but important gender-bender success.' (WAGI 2004: 121)

In the Japanese study gender specific use of language was pointed out as one of the obvious areas where change is being intended. The use of Japanese language is generally very gender specific (Mae 1993, 1996). In this school, one aims now at using the gender-neutral suffix *san* for both boys and girls, instead of the more common *kun* and *chan*. Both suffixes carry gender-specific connotations, *chan* being used for female friends and little girls or children and *kun* for male friends and young boys (Taga 2003b: 68). The gender specific use of language is not limited to the use of specific expressions and we might show some of the more complex factors related to the teachers' identity.

Earlier studies have been focussing on the active role which teachers play in attributing gender roles towards students (e.g. Amano 1988, Miyazaki 1991, Kimura 1997). However, the existence of the teachers as such can only be understood in the context of a highly gendered reality. Every teacher is acting not only as 'teacher' but obviously also as 'woman' or 'man'. In one of the interviews in the Japanese primary school a teacher provides an example of gender specific language use of male and female teachers. A male teacher might easily address his students in a high voice 'Nan ka, o-mae tachi wa!' in order to call their attention concerning some inappropriate behaviour. This colloquial and very direct, almost rough address would be widely accepted by students and also by their parents. The same behaviour from a female teacher would, however, call for critique. She might be much more closely bound to a more polite way of addressing the students. This teacher thought it might be also appropriate for himself as a male teacher, to talk to the students more politely 'anatatachi, chanto shinasai', but he appreciated having possibilities to act more directly towards the students, which was widely accepted (Taga 2003b: 70–71). Female teachers obviously needed to develop very different tactics in order to call the students' attention and might be more limited doing so in a socially accepted mode.

These difficulties are closely related to expectations by the parents towards the teacher. Changing communication patterns in school only is obviously not possible, as many of the parents expect a teacher's behaviour to conform to male and female gender roles. The schools are careful to take the conformity of the families and the reality of the children into account when addressing gender roles. Their work is seen mainly in the context of developing gender awareness and rather as prospect than as critique of "traditional" gender roles, which are often still predominant in the families.

Gender mechanisms are very influential in teachers' realities and gender conservative mechanisms are difficult to change. Taga points out that gender projects need to address also gender-typical responsibilities and opinions by male and female teachers. However, limitations became obvious in both projects. In the Philippine study it was stated that teachers often had a more developed notion of gender sensitivity and gender fairness than school principals (WAGI 2004: 122–123). The Japanese study pointed out the imbalance of the positions of female teachers and male principals. In this primary school like in many others we find a high dominance of female teachers, only two of the 18 teachers in charge of classes were male. The principal and the deputy principal are – as is often true for people higher up in the Japanese school hierarchy – men. This hierarchical distribution is one of the structural factors influencing gender identity, as students internalise such facts in their understanding of social reality. This might be seen as one example of what Kimura (1990, 1999) describes as the contradicting role of the school: On one hand, the school launches a project in order to stimulate gender awareness, on the other hand, structures are clearly transmitting a different message.

Segregation and standardisation

Segregation according to gender is, as illustrated in Section 2, an important topic in the literature on Japanese education. Many of the so-called gender-free education programmes are concerned with intermingling boys and girls, whether it is name lists, working groups or sitting orders in the class. All these are elements in education, which can be far from taken for granted until today. The situation is especially delicate, however, as many projects in Europe have, for quite a while now, been experimenting with creating learning groups according to sex, in order to give special support to both girls and boys. In the study introduced here we can distinguish three dimensions of segregation being discussed. One is related to topics associating an immanent hierarchy between the sexes, the second one can be seen in relation to identity questions and individualisations, and the third segregation becomes especially visible because of a combination with a strong standardisation of male and female patterns.

The first topic becomes evident in the context of name-lists used in schools where all boys are listed first, followed then by all the girls. Many teachers and parents were actively against these lists which they experienced as discriminating for the girls. Sex discrimination had been an important topic in Japan since the 1970s. In the mid-1980s discussions on integrated name lists in school classes (*danjo kongō meibo*) in fact helped the first female assembly member to be voted into the city council of the here mentioned city in Kyūshu (Taga 2003b: 67). In 1992 these integrated lists were finally introduced into the first municipal schools and since 2002 all 27 municipal primary schools and 11 of the 13 middle schools use such lists, where the names of boys are no longer listed before the names of the girls.

In Japan much stress is put on breaking up the dominant sex segregation in school. Students are encouraged to form groups not by sex but by interest. In connection with or maybe contrary to the intended individualisation an increasing distribution of boys and girls in single sex groups could be observed when, for example, selecting partners individually for group activities. Although the teachers tried to motivate the students to form groups according to interest rather than associating with friends from the same sex, many of the working groups turned out to be single sex groups. A teacher at a metropolitan school in Tokyo voiced similar experiences in an interview, which I carried out in 1998. She described that liberalisation in forming groups (instead of administering who should work with whom) had, at least in short term, led to very homogeneous gender groups. Possibly the strategy of individual choice was not working because it was ignored that even 'interest' is a highly gendered topic.

On the whole the project of gender-free education is part of an initiative supporting children to find their own identity and express their inner self (Taga 2003b: 67). However, we might ask how much individual choice is possible in a highly gendered and standardised context? Taga observed that the 'subjective choice' of boys and girls is strongly influenced by sex stereotypes. Limits of individual choice are illustrated with examples of the newly introduced policy of free choice of the colour of schoolbag and shoes. Before the children had no choice at all in these matters: girls had to have red schoolbags and boys black ones.

The slippers to be worn in school used to be red for the girls and blue for the boys. Now these strict regulations were lifted, but not much variation occurred. Almost all girls continued to have red schoolbags; some of the boys had chosen blue instead of black ones. As reasons students from a third grade claimed that they received the bag, that they preferred blue over red, that there were almost only red and black ones available in the shop, or that somebody from their family had taken the decision for them. The strongest variation was that two girls had bags which were rather pink than red. In none of the cases the colour chosen was the one associated with the opposite sex, and variations were obviously very rare.

Under the influence of the peer group nobody chooses 'sex-inappropriate colours' in fear of negative reactions. This is also the case concerning clothes, and a mother remarked that the possibilities of choice depend on the social position in the group. Children with a strong social standing can make unconventional choices, while weak children would most likely become victims of harassment in the same case. Trials to take away rules with clear stereotypes for boys and girls, as for example the rule of a special colour for the schoolbags and slippers, did not automatically lead to de-standardisation.

In the reality of the Japanese school described above, 'gender' as differentiation between male and female patterns seems to be closely connected to a high degree of standardisation, and segregation between the sexes influenced the possibilities of choice beyond simple recipes for change. The explicit wish to work against segregation must be seen in connection with the existing reality, where association in same-sex groups is more common in Japan both in groups of adolescents and of adults (Toyama-Bialke 1996, Lenz/Mae 1997). Sitting orders according to gender, either with all boys on one side and all girls on the other side, or strictly regulated patterns, like one line with boys and one line with girls, could be observed even a decade ago. They are the background, in front of which we have to understand the stress towards dissolving segregation. It becomes obvious, however, that overcoming this segregation is very difficult because of the strong standardisation immanent in many fields of Japanese school education.

In the context of our international comparison it might be interesting to shed light on this topic through results of the Philippine study. Compared to Japan we can state a generally critical perspective on segregation in the Philippines, at least in the interpretation of the researchers. I am quoting the study from the Philippines: 'Generally, teachers' instructions to the students were gender-fair, except at one school, where the math teacher separated boys and girls in a contest.' (WAGI 2004: 118) Here the mere separation of boys and girls is experienced as discrimination. Another matter to be discussed is that in the Philippine study sensitivity to pupils' poverty was an important point in child-friendly schools as opposed to Japan. The difference was especially obvious in this case, as the project supported by UNICEF was aiming at children in need. Teachers often spend their own money in order to give away necessities that poor families cannot afford (WAGI 2004: 121). In these schools the focus is on covering the necessities, and topics like identical schoolbags are very remote. So standardisation seems to be much less of a topic in these schools in the Philippines than in Japan.

5   Discussion and Summary of the Results

The comparison between two case studies demonstrates that discourses on Gender and Education include trans-national elements. Similar approaches towards research on Gender and Education could be observed in the studies, not least in the general methodological approach with a combination of quantitative and qualitative methods. At the same time specifics in the situation and the reflections of the researchers became obvious. This has various reasons. First of all, similar realities concerning gender in the different national school systems provoke the same topics in the research on Gender and Education. One example is the distribution of women and men in school hierarchies: with more women in teaching and more men in management positions, as well as more female teachers in primary and more male teachers in secondary schools. Another reason can be seen in the reception of international research. Many of the topics discussed in Japanese educational sociology concerning gender sound familiar if one already knows international discourses on Gender and Education. Japanese educational science reflects some international discourses. At the same time, the discussion in Japan is focussing strongly on Japan's own school system and reviews mainly literature written in or translated into Japanese. This is different in the Philippines where most of the academic discussion is taking place directly in English, allowing also a closer relation to international discussions.[20]

Reproduction of gender in the school and the family

In both studies a certain tension between education in the school and the family can be observed. The researchers in both nations quote the teachers about their lack of control over what is happening in the families. In the Japanese study this topic was mentioned in connection with gender-stereotype role distribution in the family and in the Philippine study concerning poverty and domestic violence against children and women. Obviously, cooperation between these major agents of socialisation has some limits concerning critical gender questions in both countries. The teachers experience limits as to what they think could be possibly achieved in school education. However, the researchers addressed the topic in quite different ways. While in the study from the Philippines a feeling of resignation towards possibilities of change was strong, the focus in the Japanese report was pointing out the need to accept the reality in the family and the society as kind of a natural limit of possibilities in school education.

The difference in the perspective might be connected to the aim of the study and the definition of gender-sensitivity, which in the Philippine study included a stronger stress on gender-fair family roles with shared parenting and shared decision-making, mentioning even elimination of violence against women. The open approach in the Philippines suggests that the problem of domestic violence is more obvious in the Philippines than in Japan, but for a definite judgement we would need much more detailed information. Building on the data available here we can only state that the topic is widely ignored in Japan and not problematized in gender projects in school. In general, the Philippine report gives a somewhat more outspoken overall impression, while the report by the Japanese researcher reflects in detail the consequences of educational initiative.

This comparison on gender policies in schools focussed on the primary school system in two different countries. While the comparison was primarily aiming at cultural differences or, more exactly speaking, at structural and programmatic differences within two national school systems, one further aspect became evident. This is the question of class or social standing of the pupils in the two studies. Obviously, the children in the Japanese school represented a broad middle class, so typically described in many studies on Japanese education. Even if there are differences between schools in different living quarters, nothing in the description of this particular school hinted at a specially challenged population. This was different in the Philippine study. The child-friendly schools are often aiming explicitly at groups, which need special support for receiving a well-based education. Because of this we should be extra careful in generalizing the differences observed to differences between two school systems. We should keep in mind that also social class might have an impact on the results presented here as regards reproduction of gender in the school and in the family.

What do other Asian examples contribute to our understanding of gender and education in Japan?

Including a study from another Asian nation, in this case the Philippines, into the comparison could provide us with some aspects, which both countries have in common concerning gender (un-)equal education. On top of that it became clear that the specifics of the Japanese situation, especially gender segregation and high standardisation, seemed to have no or little relevance to the school situation in the Philippines. We might want to discuss more in detail, why this is the case. Both the influence of developmental organisations like UNICEF, the strong orientation of the higher education system towards Anglo-Saxon models, and even the colonial history, might serve as arguments in order to describe a possibly stronger closeness of the gender situation in the Philippines to European "models".[21]

One last difference between the Japanese and the Philippine examples introduced above is the direct connection of the report by Miriam College to official policies adopted and defined by the Department of Education. This connection might be strengthened because the study was carried out in schools supported by a UNICEF-programme. The relation between the Japanese school project and governmental policies was less clear. Although the teaching staff in the Japanese school had started the project for gender equality in connection with an initiative of the local council for education, there was no or very little direct input by this government body. This reflects the fact that the Japanese Ministry of Education has not put much stress on questions of gender equality in the context of recently enacted educational reforms. Gender equality is dealt with only very briefly and mainly through references to forums other than schools (Kreitz-Sandberg 2000).[22] Recent trends of neo-conservative politics do not facilitate the situation for researchers and teachers working for an increasing gender fairness. Shedding light on this situation might be a task for the future, as the present political situation is characterized as 'gender-free bashing' (*Josei Tenbō*, July 2004: 6–13).

A critical analysis of our comparison might want to question whether the results would look different had we chosen another East-Asian country, like Korea or China, for the comparison, as the strong gender segregation in the Japanese society is said to be closely connected to the influence of Confucian thinking. There are collaboration projects between Japanese and Korean researchers also in the context of gender education.[23] However, I could not find information about any project on gender in primary education, which would have been comparable to the Japanese study. One possibility to find such material is by further digging into Japanese studies, as there is, in fact, much more material available in Japanese than in Western languages on Korean education (e.g. Nakamura et al. 2002).

Finally, concerning the question what further research strategies we should choose in order to gain innovative results on Gender and Education in Japan, I would like to highlight two areas. The first would be to engage into classroom studies and school ethnographies in order to collect material for analyses of doing-gender in school, or, alternatively, reanalyse the material collected in video studies.[24] The other field of interest, which occurred to me during my work with this article, is the question concerning the character of gender in teachers' education. There were various projects going on in the last decade, for example on awareness building for young teachers, simply by providing side readers with information about the topic Gender and Education by the local education council. The pace of change will depend on, a) general educational policies that apply for all students, b) private initiatives and single teachers in their attitude towards students and teaching, but also, c) schools providing children with possibilities to create individual space within the educational system. The degree to which students can develop differing gender roles will depend very much on schools allowing students to experiment and experience a wide variety of gender roles and supporting them in a possible crisis. Teachers play a central role in this context and gendering in the identity of teachers seems to be so profound that it deserves its own studies.

Notes

[1] It is often expected that societies become increasingly similar in the process of industrialisation, modernization and globalisation. However, Japan has often been described as different – even as a 'different modernity' (Hardach-Pinke 1990) throughout the 1990s. Later it has been argued that Japan is being experienced as 'different' because it is mainly compared with other industrialised nations, which for a long time meant Western nations. Most studies carried a pro-western bias (while others saw Japan as the new model). A neutral view seems almost impossible. This is even true for highly theoretical studies, as many theories analyse the social reality from a Eurocentric perspective. If one talks about 'international' discourses, this often means 'Western' theory, or even more exactly Anglo-Saxon discourses. At the same time there is a high degree of international exchange in the intellectual discussions. And many of the discourses seem to be transnational rather than national.

[2] Concerning gender-free concepts compare also Schad-Seifert and Mae in this book.

[3] This discussion draws on international discussions, especially from the US; for example Houston's 'Should education be gender free?' from 1994 is often quoted. For a characterisation of several of these movements cf. Tachi 1998.

[4] On gender in sports and education compare also Manzenreiter in this volume.

[5] The statistical abstracts from 2005 do not include figures for boys and girls. The translation junior high school, middle school and lower secondary school are used without distinction for school level with grades 7 to 9 (*chūgakkō*).

[6] The difference was even stronger in the mid-90s with 37.2 percent of young men and 47.6 percent of young women continuing their training at so-called higher education institutions (Ministry of Education, Science, Sports, and Culture 1999).

[7] For more details on the life in junior colleges cf. McVeigh 1997.

[8] Kimura argues that 'gender' should be considered a relevant element in the research of social difference, which is just as important for the reproduction of inequality as class or others.

[9] For further literature and research reviews on the topic Gender in Education see Amano 1988, Kameda/Tachi 1990, Nakanishi/Hori 1997, Fujita 1999: 55, Kreitz-Sandberg 2002.

[10] While Nakanishi's study focuses on the difference between institutions and therefore suggests conformity within one institution, Miyazaki's case study illuminates that even within the same school many different gender cultures are supported. Peer control, peer culture and also peer pressure play an important role in terms of experimenting with gender identity in this time of rapid sexual development which goes along with a search for identity and one's place in the group and, gradually, in society.

[11] In the Japanese (and international) discourse on school culture we distinguish between the regular and the so-called 'hidden curriculum' (*kakusareta karikyuramu*). While this term originally related to processes of social reproduction, feminists took up the argument and analysed the hidden curriculum concerning gender (Kimura 1990).

[12] The methodological approach and the aims of the respective studies will be described in Sections 4.1 and 4.2.

[13] I quote the Women and Gender Institute, Miriam College as author, as the only information we get about the researchers is that the fieldwork was carried out by 'three teachers from Miriam College' (see WAGI 2004: 118).

[14] The terms gender-fair and gender-sensitive are used synonymously in the report.

[15] In the Japanese discourse a wide range of terms addresses connecting concepts. The expression 'education for equality of boys and girls' (*danjo byōdō kyōiku*) is mainly used in governmental policies by the Ministry of Education and the various advisory boards. From a feminist perspective, however, these concepts are rooted strongly in the idea of difference of the sexes (Tachi 1998: 17–18). The over-all perspective of this project was, according to Taga (2003: 67), in accordance with the newer trend of 'gender-free education'. Concerning the use of the terms 'gender' and 'gender-free' cf. Schad-Seifert in this volume.

[16] WAGI 2004: 113–114.

[17] Strictly speaking we cannot be sure if this difference depends on the programme or on surveying a different cohort.

[18] Here I relate to the discussion in the text, the data in the tables show some differences, but we have no possibility to analyse the statistical significance of differences found in the results.

[19] The Japanese study introduced here did not bring up this topic, but former studies on Japanese schoolbooks showed gender-typical illustrations in schoolbooks, which reflect much of the gender-typical distribution of work, that can be observed not only in the family but also in the public sphere of the companies (Shire 1999).

[20] I am aware that we need more information about the situation in schools in the Philippines if we want to understand it properly. However, the aim in this article was only to contrast our information on Japan.

[21] For a further discussion we might find very stimulating arguments in recent cultural studies, which reflect on the lagacy of colonial rule (see Bhabha 1994 and Young 1995).

[22] Osawa (2000, 13) points out that three of six reforms related directly to gender issues: the administrative reform, the economic structural reform, and the structural reform of social security. The Basic Law for a Gender-Equal Society was enacted in 1999. Osawa does not mention educational reform in this context. The Ministry of Education is generally known for a rather conservative stance, and several authors mention that the various consultative councils (*shingikai*) ignore for example more progressive trends like questions of gender equality in their school policies (Tachi 1998: 13). Concerning reforms cf. Bosse/Köllner 2002.

[23] For example there was a meeting in August 2003 on Korean government's policies and programme on human resource development for women, the improvement of the status of the female teachers, and the strengthening of academic and career counselling for girls, as well as the promotion of gender equality education and efforts to curb sexual harassment in schools (Park 2003).

[24] Work in this direction can be found in the study by Miyazaki Ayumi quoted in Section 2. For the secondary studies I think about the wide range of video studies which were part of the Trends in International Mathematics and Science Study (TIMSS).

References

Amano, Masako (ed.) 1986. *Joshi kōtō kyōiku no zahyō* [The coordinates of women's higher education]. Tokyo. Kakiuchi Shuppan.

Amano, Masako. 1988. *'Sei to kyōiku' kenkyū no gendaiteki kadai – kakusareta 'ryōiki' no jizoku.* [Present topics in research on education and sexuality. A special reading of hidden spheres]. In: *Nihon Shakaigaku Hyōron*, 39/3, pp. 266–283.

Amano, Masako. 1997. Women in higher education. In: *Higher Education* 34, 2 (September), pp. 15–35.

Bhabha, Homi K. 1994. *The location of culture*. London: Routledge.

Bosse, Friederike / Köllner, Patrick (eds.) 2002. *Reformen in Japan* [Reforms in Japan]. Hamburg: Institut für Asienkunde.

Connel, Robert. 1987. *Gender and power. Society, the person and sexual politics*. Cambridge: Polity Press.

Connel, Robert. 1995. *Masculinities*. Cambridge: Polity Press.

Danjo Byōdō Kyōiku o Susumeru-kai. 1997. *Dōshite itsumo otoko ga saki nano? Danjo konai meibo no kokoromi* [Why do boys always come first? Questioning name lists with gender separation]. Tokyo: Shinhyōron.

Fujimura-Faselow, Kumiko. 1985. Women's participation in higher education. In: *Comparative Education Review* 29, 4 (November), pp. 471–489.

Fujita, Hidenori. 1992. Kyōiku ni okeru seisa to jendā [Sex difference and gender in education]. In: Arima, Akito et al. (eds.) *Seisa to bunka* [Culture and sexual difference]. Tokyo: Tōkyō Daigaku Shuppankai, pp. 257–294.

Fujita, Hidenori. 1999. Jendā mondai no kōzō to 'josei kaihō purojekuto' no kadai. In: Fujita, Hidenori et al. *Jendā to kyōiku* [Gender and education, Kyōikugaku nenpō 7]. Yokohama: Ijima Insatsu, pp. 5–68.

Hardach-Pinke, Irene (ed.) w.y. (1990). *Japan. Eine andere Moderne* [Japan. A different modernity]. Tübingen: Konkursbuch Verlag Claudia Gehrke.

Houston, Barbara. 1994. Should public education be gender free? In: Stone, Linda (ed.) *The education feminism reader*. London and New York: Routledge, pp. 122–134.

Hōnuki, Kaoru. 1996. *Jendā bunka to gakushū: Riron to hōhō* [Gender culture and learning: Theories and methods]. Tokyo: Meiji Tosho.

Kameda, Atsuko / Tachi, Kaoru. 1990. Kyōiku to joseigaku kenkyū no dōkō to kadai [Women's studies and Education]. In: Joseigaku kenkyū (ed.). *Jendā to seisabetsu* [Gender and sex discrimination] Tokyo: Keisō shobō. pp. 147–170.

Kimura, Ryōko. 1990. Jendā to gakkō bunka [Gender and school culture]. In Nagao, Akio / Ikeda, Hiroshi (eds.): *Gakkō bunka – shinsō e no pāsupekutibu* [School culture. A profound perspective]. Tokyo: Tōshindō: pp. 147–170.

Kimura, Ryōko. 1997. Kyōiku ni okeru jendā keisei [Constructing gender in the class room]. In: *Kyōiku Shakaigaku Kenkyū* 61, pp. 39–54.

Kimura, Ryōko.1999. *Gakkō bunka to jendā* [School culture and gender]. Tokyo: Keisō Shobō.

Kreitz-Sandberg, Susanne. 1994. *Jugend im Japan. Eine empirische Untersuchung zur Adoleszenz in einer „anderen Moderne"* [Youth in Japan. An empirical study on adolesence in a 'different modernity']. Rheinfelden, Berlin: Schäuble.

Kreitz-Sandberg, Susanne. 1996. Bildung, Konsum und Geschlechtertrennung – das japanische Jugendmoratorium [The youth moratorium in Japan: Education, consumerism, and gender segregation]. In: *Zeitschrift für Sozialisationsforschung und Erziehungssoziologie* (ZSE). 1996, vol. 16, no. 4, pp. 370–387.

Kreitz-Sandberg, Susanne. 1999. Mädchenwelten – Jungewelten. Aspekte geschlechtsspezifischen Lernens im Jugendalter [Girls' worlds – boys' worlds. Aspects of genderspecific learning in adolescence]. In: Schubert, Volker (ed.). *Lernkultur. Das Beispiel Japan* [Learning culture. The Japanese example]. Weinheim: Beltz-Deutscher Studienverlag, pp. 121–141.

Kreitz-Sandberg, Susanne. 2000. Modes of change and matters of continuity: reforms in Japanese high schools. Papers of 2000 International Symposium on Educational Reforms and Teachers Education Innovation for the 21st Century. 26 to 30 March, 2000. Waseda University, Tokyo.

Kreitz-Sandberg, Susanne. 2002. „Andere Welten?" Soziale Integration von Jugendlichen in Japan und Deutschland im Vergleich ['Other worlds?' Social integration of youths in Japan and Germany in comparison]. In: Kreitz-Sandberg, Susanne (ed.): *Jugendliche in Japan und Deutschland. Soziale Integration im Vergleich* [Youths in Japan and Germany. Social integration in comparison]. Opladen: Leske + Budrich, pp. 1–49.

Lenz, Ilse / Mae, Michiko (eds.). 1997. *Getrennte Welten, gemeinsame Moderne? Geschlechterverhältnisse in Japan* [Separate worlds, a common moderinisation? Gender relations in Japan]. Opladen: Leske + Budrich.

Mae, Michiko. 1993. Frauensprache als Sozialisationsinstrument? Ein Beitrag zum japanischen Kommunikationsverhalten [Women's language as soialisation instrument? A contribution to understanding Japanese communication]. In: Hans-Joachim Kornadt / Trommsdorff, Gisela (eds.): *Deutsch-Japanische Begegnungen in den Sozialwissenschaften* [German-Japanese meetings in the Social Sciences]. Konstanz: Universitätsverlag Konstanz.

Mae, Michiko. 1996. Das Japanische als 'Sprache der Harmonie' oder die Formalisierung der Differenzen [Japanese as "language of hormony" or formalisation of difference]. In: Schründer-Lenzen, Agi (ed.) *Harmonie und Konformität. Tradition und Krise japanischer Sozialisationsmuster* [Harmony and conformity. Tradition and crisis of Japanese socialisation pattern]. München: Iudicium, pp. 130–150.

McVeigh, Brian. 1997. *Life in a Japanese Women's College.* (Nissan Institute Routledge Japanese Studies Series). London/New York: Routledge.

Ministry of Education, Culture, Sports, Science and Technology. 2005. *Statistical Abstract, Culture, Sports, Science and Technology, 2005 edition.* Tokyo: National Printing Bureau.

Ministry of Education, Science, Sport and Culture. 1999. *Statistical Abstracts of Education, Science, Sport and Culture.* Tokyo: Printing Bureau, Ministry of Finance.

Miyazaki, Ayumi. 1991. Gakkō ni okeru 'seiyakuwari to shakaika' – saikō. Kyōshi ni yori seibetsu kategorii [Reconsideration of gender role socialization – sex categorization by teachers]. In: *Kyōiku Shakaigaku Kenkyū* 48, pp. 105–123.

Miyazaki, Ayumi. 1993. Jendā sabukarucha no dainamikusu – joshikō ni okeru esunogurafii o motoni [Dynamics of gendered subcultures. An ethnographic approach at a girls' high school]. In: *Kyōiku Shakaigaku Kenkyū* 52, pp.157–177.

Mori, Shigeo. 1985. Gakkō ni okeru seiyakuwari kenkyū to kaishakuteki apurōchi [An explanatory approach to gender role research in school]. In: *Kyōto Daigaku Kyōiku Gakubu Kiyō* 31.

Mori, Shigeo. 1992. 'Jendā to kyōiku' kenkyū no suii to genkyō [Transition and today's trend of research on "Gender in education": From "women" to "gender"]. In: *Kyōiku Shakaigaku Kenkyū* 50, pp. 164–183.

Morimoto, Eriko. 1998. Jendā to saiseisan suru bungaku kyōzai. Jiko keiseiki no kodomotachi ga yomitoru mono no [The reproduction of gender roles in reading material: What children read during the period of building self-identity]. In: *Joseigaku.* vol. 6/1998 (Nihon Joseigaku Gakkai ed.), pp. 30–45.

Nakamura, Takayasu; Fujita, Takeshi and Arita, Shin. 2002. *Gakureki, senbatsu, gakkō no hikaku shakaigaku—kyōiku kara miru nihon to kankoku* [Comparative sociology of the school, selection, and credentials: Seeing Japan and Korea through their education]. Tokyo: Tōyōkan Shuppansha.

Nakanishi, Yūko. 1993. Jendā torakku – seiyakuwari ni motozuku shinrō bunka no mekanizumu ni kansuru kōsatsu [Gender track. Gender-specific mechanisms concerning school entry]. In: *Kyōiku Shakaigaku Kenkyū* 53, pp. 131–154.

Nakanishi, Yūko. 1998. *Jendā torakku. Seinenki josei no shinro keisei to kyōiku soshiki no shakaigaku* [Gender Track: Sociology of educational institutions and the formation of educational tracks of female youth]. Tokyo. Tōyōkan Shuppansha.

Nakanishi, Yūko. 2002. Gender tracking. Schulkultur und Bildungsgänge junger Frauen in Japan. In: Kreitz-Sandberg, Susanne (ed.) *Jugendliche in Japan und Deutschland. Soziale Integration im Vergleich.* Opladen: Leske + Budrich, pp. 153–177.

Nakanishi, Yūko and Hori, Takeshi. 1997. 'Jendā to kyōiku' kenkyū no dōkō to kadai: Kyōiku shakaigaku, jendā, feminizumu [Recent and future studies on "Gender in Education": Between sociology of education and feminism. In: *Kyōiku Shakaigaku Kenkyū* 61, pp. 77–100.

Niigata-shi Josei Kōdō Keikaku Suishin Kaigi. 1995. *Ima, kokokara hajimaru danjo byōdō kyōiku. Gakkō ni okeru danjo byōdō kyōiku kenkyūkai hōkokushō.* Niigata: Nigata-shi Sōmukyoku.

O'Donnell, Mike / Sharp, Sue. 2000. *Uncertain masculinities. Youth, ethnicity and class in contemporary Britain.* London and New York: Routledge.

Osawa, Mari. 2000. Government approaches to gender equality in the mid-1990s. In: *Social Science Japan Journal*, Vol. 3, No. 1, pp. 3–19.

Park Koonae. 2003. Japan-Korea Exchange on Gender-Equal Society. In: Asia Pacific News, Newsletter by HURIGHTS Osaka, December 2003 Volume 34 See: http://www.hurights.or.jp/asia-pacific/no_34/07.htm; 27 sept 2004.

Schubert, Volker. 1992. *Die Inszenierung der Harmonie. Erziehung und Gesellschaft in Japan* [Production of harmony. Education and society in Japan]. Darmstadt: Wissenschaftliche Buchgesellschaft.

Schubert, Volker. 2002. Jugend und Schule in Japan. Zur kulturellen Konsturktion des Jugendalters [Youth and school in Japan. The cultural construction of adolescence]. In: Kreitz-Sandberg, Susanne (ed.) *Jugendliche in Japan und Deutschland. Soziale Integration im Vergleich* [Youths in Japan and Germany. Social integration in comparison]. Opladen: Leske + Budrich, pp. 71–90.

Seifert, Wolfgang / Weber, Claudia, eds. 2002. *Japan im Vergleich* [Japan in comparison]. München 2002: iudicium.

Shire, Karen. 1999. Socialization and work in Japan. The meaning of adulthood of men and women in a business context. In: *International Journal of Japanese Sociology*, no. 8, pp. 72–78.

Sōrifu (Prime Ministers Office). 1995. *Danjō byōdō ni kansuru seiron chōsa* [Survey on equality of men and women]. Tokyo: ōkurashō Insatsukyoku.

Tachi, Kaoru. 1998. Gakkō ni okeru jendā furii kyōiku to joseigaku [Gender-free education in primary and secondary schools and its linkage to women's studies]. In: *Joseigaku* (Nihon Josei Gakkai Gakkaishi) Vol. 6: Tokushū: Kyōiku no ba kara jendā o tō, pp. 8–29.

Taga, Futoshi. 1996. Seinenki no danseisei keisei ni kansuru ichi kōsatsu – Aidentiti kiki o taiken shita daigakusei no jirei kara [A study on the formation of masculinity during adolescence: Through the cases of university students who experienced an "identity crisis"]. In: *Kyōiku Shakaigaku Kenkyū*, No. 58, pp. 47–64.

Taga, Futoshi. 2000. *Dansei no jendā keisei – otokorahisa no yuragi no naka de* [Gender formation of men. Masculinity in change]. Tokyo: Tōyōkan.

Taga, Futoshi. 2002. Der Wandel von Geschlechterrollen und männliche Konflikte. Eine Biographiestudie mit jungen Männern in Japan [The change of gender roles and male conflict. A biography stydy with young men in Japan]. In: Kreitz-Sandberg, Susanne (ed.) *Jugendliche in Japan und Deutschland. Soziale Integration im Vergleich* [Youths in Japan and Germany. Social integration in comparison]. Opladen: Leske + Budrich, pp.179–205.

Taga, Futoshi. 2003a. Rethinking male socialization: Life histories of male Japanese youth. In: Kam Louie / Loow, Morris (eds.) *Asian masculinities. The meaning and practice of manhood in China and Japan*, London and New York: RoutledgeCurzon, pp. 137–154.

Taga, Futoshi. 2003b. Jendā furī kyōiku no konnan [Difficulties in "gender-free" education]. In: *Kurume Daigaku Bungakubu Kiyō* (Jōhō Shakai Kagaku, ed.) June 2003, pp. 65–78.

Tōkyō Josei Zaidan (ed.) 1995. *Jendā furīna kyōiku no tame ni* [Aiming at gender-free education]. Tokyo.

Tomo, Rieko / Tung , Chao-Huei. 1996. Content analysis of Japanese and Taiwanese textbooks: Sex role and child rearing behavior. In: *Journal of Koshien Junior College* 16, pp. 67–84.

Tomo, Rieko. 1999. A content analysis of interpersonal coping-behavior in Japanese and German primary school textbooks. In: *Japanstudien*; 11, pp. 193–209.

Tomo, Rieko / Kimura, Atsushi / Tung, Chao-Huei. 2002. Interpersonal coping-behavior in Asian and European textbooks. In: Teichler, Ulrich / Trommsdorff, Gisela (eds.): *Challenges of the 21st century in Japan and Germany*, pp. 125–141.

Toyama-Bialke, Chisaki. 1997. Alltagsstruktur und Schulleistung. Eine Untersuchung zur Sozialisation von deutschen und japanischen Jugendlichen [Scholastic achievement and the structure of everyday life: a study of the socialisation of adolescets in Germany and Japan]. In: *Japanstudien*; 8, 1996 (1997), pp. 319–335.

Toyama-Bialke, Chisaki. 2000. *Jugendliche Sozialisation und familiäre Einflüsse in Deutschland und Japan* [Adolescent socialization and family influences in Germany and Japan]. Köln, Weimar, Wien: Böhlau.

Tsuruta, Atsuko. 1998. 'Danjo kyōgaku' kara 'danjo byōdō kyōiku (jendā ikuiti no kyōiku)' e [From 'coeducation' toward 'the gender-equity education']. In *Kyōikugaku Kenkyū* 65,4, pp. 315–323.

Ujihara, Yōko. 1996. Chūgakkō ni okeru danjo byōdō kyōiku to seisabetsu no sakusō: Futatsu no 'kakureta karikyuramu' reberu kara [The complexity of gender equality and sexism in junior high school: Two hidden curriculum levels]. In: *Kyōiku Shakaigakku Kenkyū* 58, pp. 29–45.

White, Merry. 1987. *The Japanese educational challenge. A commitment to children.* Tokyo, New York, London: Kodansha International.

Windolf, Paul. 1997. *Expansion and structural change. Higher education in Germany, the United States, and Japan, 1870–1990.* Boulder / Colorado / Oxford: Westview.

WAGI Women and Gender Institute, Miriam College. 2004. Gender socialization in Philippine child-friendly schools. In: Human Rights Education in Asian Schools vol. 7; pp. 113–127, Published on the homepage of Asia-Pacific Human Rights Information Center [HURIGHTS Osaka]. http://hurights.or.jp/hreas/7/13GenderSocialization.htm as pdf via http://www.hurights.or.jp/ pub/hreas/7/intex.html (2 nov 2006).

World Bank. 2004. Word Development Indicators. Table 2.10. Education inputs. (Data based on the UNESCO Institute for Statistics). Internet: http://www.worldbank.org/data.html#pdf (2 nov 2006).

Young, Robert J.C. 1995. *Colonial desire. Hybridity in theory, culture and race*. London: Routledge.

Korean Women as Role Models?
Gender and Ethnicity in Japanese TV Drama

Hilaria Gössmann

1   Introduction

The popular genre of TV drama has always been of special significance for the construction of gender roles in Japan. According to a public opinion poll conducted in the 1980s, women watch TV dramas not only for entertainment, but also to find advice on their own way of living.[1] Therefore, characters in TV dramas can indeed serve as role models for the audience.

This is most evident in the depictions of female Korean characters in Japanese TV dramas since 2001. At that time, a Korea boom could be observed in this genre and the number of dramas portraying Japanese-Korean encounters increased significantly.[2] This development was triggered by the Soccer World Cup 2002, which was co-hosted by Japan and South Korea.

The Korea boom in Japan was also the topic of a research project on 'Japan's Turn towards Asia in Literature, Popular Culture and Media' which was based at the Department of Japanese Studies at the University of Trier.[3] Through content analysis of TV dramas depicting Korean characters, the research project elaborated on major patterns in the construction of Korean characters in Japanese TV dramas. In all cases under examination, the role of the female Korean characters seems to be strongly appropriated in order to suit their counterparts, i.e. the (female) Japanese characters. The Japanese characters thus remain the central characters in the plot and therefore the main identification models for the predominantly female Japanese audience. The following five patterns of the construction of Japanese-Korean encounters in TV dramas[4] emerge:

1. Korea is constructed as a country where Confucian traditions play an important role in people's everyday lives. In contrast, Japan is constructed as a country without any major Confucian influence.
2. All Korean characters are presented as family-oriented, whereas Japanese characters, whose relations to their family are of lesser importance, appear rather individualistic.
3. The lethargy and aimlessness of the Japanese characters is countered by the energy and determination of the Korean characters.
4. The Korean characters express their opinion very frankly and criticise the behaviour of the Japanese people.
5. The Koreans are constructed as role models or are even utilised as 'saviour figures' of the Japanese. The encounter with the 'Korean Other' thus results in a 'healing experience' for the Japanese characters.

The analysis of the dramas shows that the categories of gender and ethnicity are equally important. It is significant that these categories do not operate independently, rather it is their intersection which gains enormous importance. This shall subsequently be substantiated in one example dealing with a Japanese-Korean encounter.

2   The TV Drama 'Kankoku no obachan wa erai!' (Korean Aunties Are Admirable!)

2.1   Limits on female self-fulfilment: Experiences of a female Japanese career woman in Korea

The drama 'Kankoku no obachan wa erai!' (Korean Aunties Are Admirable!) was aired in 2002 as a New Year's drama (*oshōgatsu dorama*) by the public broadcasting station NHK and was very freely adapted from a book by Watanabe Mayumi. The title of the drama itself already illustrates how Korean women are appropriated as role models within the plot. In this drama the main character is a Japanese mother in her early thirties who is also a working woman. Her professional career is very important to her, but she will be made to realise the significance of family during her stay in Korea.

Contrary to pattern no. 3 (see above) which prevails in dramas depicting younger Japanese women (in their early 20s), the main Japanese character, Rie, is by no means lethargic, but has already managed to achieve her life's dream – she is a renowned illustrator. When her husband, a journalist, is transferred to Seoul, he leaves Japan without his family. Convinced that she will be able to continue her work on a freelance basis, Rie decides to follow her husband and moves to Seoul with the whole family.

Right at the beginning of her stay in Korea, she has to realise that this country's traditions are diametrically opposed to her own professional ambitions. This becomes obvious in two consecutive scenes at the beginning of the drama: In the first scene, Rie's husband Yōsuke, who always used to express his acceptance of her work, now abruptly changes his attitude. One evening, when he is heavily drunk and his colleagues call Rie to come and drive him home, his Korean colleagues confront her with the question of why she has left him alone in Seoul for such a long time and why she could not have come to Korea earlier. In this scene, her husband displays uncommonly harsh behaviour, which another Japanese colleague only comments on with the words: 'In Korea, men have to show off.' Eventually, her husband states explicitly: 'I always wanted to tell you... Do stop working!' When Rie confronts him with this statement the next morning, he has no recollection of this incident whatsoever. Rie, however, remarks that drunkards always speak their mind.

In the next scene, Rie, along with her family, visits the home of an elderly Korean lady, who is called Omoni (the Korean word for 'mother') by everyone. Omoni *(the Japanese katakana transcription as given in the subtitles)*, who learned Japanese during Korea's colonisation times, owns a little boarding house where Rie's husband used to live while he was studying in Seoul. Omoni is portrayed as a very traditional person. Her attitude towards working mothers is revealed in the following conversation between Omoni, her daughter Sohi, and Rie. Yōsuke translates for his wife.

Yōsuke (to Rie):	Omoni will arrange Korean lessons for you.
Rie:	Sorry, what did you say?
Omoni:	You have to be able to speak Korean, or you won't be able to cope here.
Rie:	Omoni, I really appreciate your kindness, but I don't have the time to learn Korean. I have to do my sketches.
Omoni:	Yōsuke has a job. Why do you have to work so much?
Rie:	It has always been my dream to work as an illustrator. That's why I used to stick up for my profession so much myself after my graduation from the Academy of Arts. Sometimes it wasn't easy, but I did manage to overcome all difficulties in the end. I wanted to realise myself *(jiko jitsugen)*. That's why I continued working after the birth of my children and managed to reconcile both family and work.
Omoni (in Korean):	I seem to have forgotten some Japanese words. What does *jiko jitsugen* mean?
Yōsuke:	*Jiko jitsugen* means to look for a way of living which is best for oneself and then to live it.
Sohi (in Japanese):	I do understand a little Japanese. And I think you're right!
Yōsuke (to Rie):	This is Sohi, Omoni's daughter.

Sohi says something in Korean which is not translated by subtitles.

Rie:	What did she say?
Yōsuke:	She says, that being mother and wife is not the only way of life for women.
Omoni (in Korean):	Women did always work. But not for themselves. (in Japanese to Rie) You always say I, I, I…
Rie:	To like oneself is always a good start, isn't it?
Omoni:	I don't understand. For us women, there is no 'I'. We have always worked for the sake of the family, for the sake of the children…
Sohi:	You're old-fashioned. Times have changed.

As these two scenes demonstrate, we meet representatives of various positions with regard to women's roles in society. Aside from the two poles – affirmation of professional self-fulfilment for women on the one hand, and the assumption that a woman primarily has to care for the family on the other hand, this drama also shows an 'in between' position, an outward affirmation of 'modern values' while more traditional attitudes prevail inwards (see Fig. 1).

A vigorous proponent of the 'modern' position in favour of the professional self-fulfilment of women is of course the Japanese main character Rie herself. But, this drama also presents a female Korean character in favour of this attitude, namely Sohi, Omoni's daughter, who is divorced from her husband. She runs a little booth at the market and dreams of opening a shop of her own. Sohi, however, remains the only female Korean character who explicitly supports the choice of women's self-fulfilment.

All other – married – women are presented as living in accordance with their roles as wives and mothers. This, of course, is a rather lopsided construction of the situation in Korea. Changes in women's roles which are also evident in Korea are not mentioned in the drama.

Figure 1: **Positions of Japanese and Korean characters with regard to women's roles**

In favour of professional life and self-fulfilment for women	Modern attitude on the outside, rather traditional position inside	'It is a woman's duty to dedicate herself first and foremost to her family'
Young Japanese woman: Main character Rie, illustrator, married, two children	Elder Japanese woman: Rie's mother	Elder Korean woman: Omoni
Young Korean woman: Sohi, Omoni's daughter, divorced	Young Japanese man: Yōsuke, Rie's husband, journalist	Young Korean men: Yōsuke's colleagues, Sohi's son

In this TV drama, the attitude that a woman has to dedicate herself solely to her family, can only be found on the Korean side and is expressed mainly by Omoni, but also by Yōsuke's Korean colleagues. Since Omoni's daughter assumes a rather modern position, the pattern 'Japan equals modernity, Korea equals tradition' is dissolved – at least to a certain extent. Belonging to a certain culture is therefore not essential to assuming a certain attitude toward women's roles. Gender as well as age seems to play a decisive part, too.

The 'in between' position is adopted by two Japanese characters: outwardly they advocate modern attitudes (as it is said in the drama, they submit themselves to the current '*zeitgeist*' in contemporary Japan), while deep inside they seem to be upholding traditional values. Rie's mother, who lives as a farmer in the Japanese countryside, seems to be particularly split in her attitudes: On the one hand, she indirectly supported her daughter's professional life – while Rie was still living in Tokyo and had to work late at night, she read books to her grandchildren over the phone, which Rie did not know until then. On the other hand, when she comes to Korea, she and Omoni like each other right from the beginning. She vehemently agrees with Omoni's view that for a woman, her family has to come first. In Korea, she opens herself up to her daughter; for the first time ever, she will speak her mind to her daughter.

This is also true for Yōsuke, who, however drunk he may have been, all of a sudden tells Rie to stop working. Encouraged by their Korean surroundings, these two characters are finally able to advocate their traditional attitude – an attitude they did apparently not dare to voice in Japan. Interestingly, during their stay in Korea, they adapt to a common cliché about Koreans in Japan, namely that Koreans are 'outspoken' and always express their opinion freely. Thus, these two Japanese characters are appropriately modeled according to the features of Korean characters described in pattern no. 4. Therefore, to some extent, these two characters appear 'Koreanised'.

As a reaction to the above mentioned two key scenes in the plot, Rie now starts to actively resist her integration into Korean society: She leaves the house hiding her eyes behind dark glasses while listening to loud music through her walkman earphones. Omoni, however, holds this behavior against her, and blames her for not 'opening herself to Korea'.

In this drama, Rie's behavior is presented as objectionable; she is the total opposite of '*erai*' (admirable), because she does not seize the opportunity to become acquainted with Korea, its people and customs.

However, against the backdrop that the people surrounding her constantly counter Rie's professional self-realisation with their reproaches and lack of understanding, Rie's conscious or unconscious rejection of all things Korean can also be interpreted as a form of self-protection. Her integration into the Korean environment would only be possible at the expense of her professional self-fulfilment. Thus, she does not only experience a culture shock because of her daily life in Korea, but also because of the diverging constructions of gender in Korea and Japan. For her, this means that she is suddenly expected to succumb to the restrictions of a life as wife and mother. She is forced to live a 'traditional' life as a woman.

Despite all the efforts to deprive her of her professional orientation, Rie – insulated by her behaviour of those surrounding her – puts all her energy into a new job and sends a new sketch to her office in Tokyo. When this sketch is declined, a process of change slowly starts taking place in Rie. Comforted by Omoni, she enthusiastically starts to learn Korean and takes care of her household and children. Now, the focus of the drama shifts to Rie's life with the children, how she enjoys spending time with them and how she integrates herself into the neighbourhood. Her work is no longer mentioned at all. While she previously had been presented as a woman struggling to reconcile her work and her duties within the family, she now appears as if a burden has been lifted from her shoulders.

The last sequences of the drama show how Rie opens herself up to her Korean environment, how she learns the language and how she finds new – Korean – friends. It is significant that this immersion into her Korean environment goes along with her transformation into a happy wife and mother. The more she opens herself up to Korean life and society, the more she is able to accept her role as a mother. The last scene of the drama consequently shows her dressed in traditional Korean attire: The family spends New Year's Day in Korea eating Korean food. A video record of their celebrations is sent to Rie's mother in Japan.

This 'Koreanisation' of Rie's symbolises her change of attitude toward family and her role as a mother. Thus, this scene conveys the impression that Rie uses the video to show all these changes to her mother. As a result of her encounters with Korea and Korean women, first and foremost with Omoni, who are presented as '*erai*' – admirable, wonderful and thus worth imitating – Rie seems to have become 'chastened'.

Rie herself is well aware of how much she has changed. Finally she tells her husband: 'Alright, now you've taken me in after all…' When he asks her: 'Do you regret it?,' she answers: 'No, I'm grateful.' Again, as in many other examples, the encounter with Korea is constructed as a 'healing experience' for the main female Japanese character. In other dramas depicting Japanese-Korean encounters, the unmarried, young female Japanese characters meeting young Korean women are virtually torn out of their lethargy, and are encouraged to find a life dream for themselves. In this drama, a successful married Japanese woman is forced to reflect upon her attitude toward her family – and eventually to change it.

3   On the Reception of this Drama in Japan

The development of the main character in this drama conveys the impression that, since the landmark work conducted by Muramatsu Yasuko in the 1970s, nothing seems to have changed at all in regard to gender roles in Japanese TV drama. As Muramatsu Yasuko's analysis put forward, at that time, it was typical for married women to be presented as happy while others, working outside the family, were always shown as extremely unhappy.[5] Thus, these dramas conveyed the message that a woman's true happiness is only to be found in marital bliss. Although the drama analysed above was produced roughly thirty years later, this message seems still applicable.

During a seminar on gender and ethnicity in Japanese media at a Japanese women's university, I conducted a survey on the possible message of this particular drama among 100 female students attending my classes. First, I had them answer the question concerning which message this drama conveyed in regard to women's roles. Then, I transcribed the most common answers and had them discuss in work groups. Finally, I counted the statements which found the most supporters. They are listed below according to rank (i.e. the first point met with the most supporters):

1. Women have to make household chores and the education of their children the centre of their lives.
2. The message is neither that Omoni's lifestyle is wonderful nor that women in principle are not supposed to think about themselves. This drama, however, issues a warning to all those women who have lost contact to their societal environment.
3. In contemporary Japan, the notion that women should work and become independent prevails. The drama is supposed to encourage a reconsideration of this attitude. This is made obvious in the plot, when the main character comes to Korea and, through Omoni's influence, decides to make motherhood her priority.
4. The professional life of women is presented in a rather negative light. Only when they have managed to cope with their household chores and their children, are women free to do 'other things'.
5. In Japan, an increasing number of women decide against marriage and children while they submit themselves solely to their professional lives. Those women are made to think about the aptness of their lifestyle; they are motivated to reflect whether they have 'forgotten' to attend to something very important in their lives.

Thus, the majority of the students was of the opinion, that the drama does indeed convey the message that women should put household duties and family at the centre of their lives. As answer no. 2 shows, another common opinion held was that the message was not that Omoni's life was 'wonderful' and that women should not think only of themselves. According to the student's impression, this drama rather sends out a 'warning' to all working women who are under an enormous pressure and consequently only concentrate on their professional lives – often to such an extent that they lose track of what happens around them. This drama is thus exclusively a plea not to commit oneself to professional life, and not to lose track of what is 'essential' to life.

In contrast to all other Korean characters in Japanese dramas, Omoni is not a perfect 'role model' for young Japanese women because she is presented as too selfless and sacrificing.

As statements 3-5 illustrate, the presumption prevails among female Japanese students that through the encounter with Confucian Korea, a reconsideration and discussion of 'working women' is incited. In the accounts of the female students it became very clear that they really seemed to seek out advice for their own way of life in the TV dramas. One student wrote explicitly, that she initially had planned to work continuously after graduation. This drama, however, had indeed made her re-think this decision.

When I mentioned these reactions of the female students during an interview with the (male) director of the drama, he was extremely surprised that his drama had apparently conveyed to its audience such a negative notion about working women. According to him, it remained open whether Rie might think about her time in Korea merely as a 'creative break' from her work, a 'time out' in which she is able to recover from the pressure upon her. She could maybe 'just enjoy' being with her family. He said, that it wasn't even mentioned whether the contact with the women in Korea eventually leads to a fundamental change in her attitude towards wives and mothers – let alone a change of attitude towards her own professional self-fulfillment.

4   Conclusion

In this article, I have presented an analysis of one example of a TV drama in which gender and ethnicity interconnect most evidently. For the main character Rie, Korea becomes the symbol of everything opposed to her self-fulfilment as a woman. She consequently closes herself off from all things Korean. The common stereotype that Korea is a Confucian country in all spheres is perpetuated rather than questioned. Japan, however, appears as a country where women are able to pursue their career and find recognition as working women. After all, the first scene of the drama shows Rie accepting an award for one of her sketch creations.

Here, a typical tendency within the genre of TV drama becomes evident: Despite all the 'progress' that is visible in other examples of TV dramas – for instance by featuring men who take over roles as house-keepers – ,[6] in this genre, the family still has a high significance, especially for married women. The encounter with Korea is thus a welcome possibility to encourage the women – didactically, as it is also typical for this genre – to rethink their own lifestyles. In a drama aired during the New Year's break and thus consumed by the whole family, the upholding of traditional values does not entirely come as a surprise. What does come as a surprise, however, is how the drama deals with the book it was actually adapted from. In this book, which has the same title as the drama and was written by the Japanese illustrator Watanabe Mayumi, the author describes her own experiences in Korea. These experiences and those of the main character of the drama have very few things in common. Unlike Rie, the narrator in this book is very open-minded towards Korea and makes friends right from the beginning, especially among Korean women.[7] The metamorphosis from a self-centred working woman to a family-centred wife and mother, which is inherent in the plot of the drama, is not at all brought up in the book. Watanabe Mayumi emphasised during an interview with me that, despite their common title, the book and the drama have nothing in common and are two entirely different, independent works, (which is why she refused to say anything about the TV drama).

In the transformation process that the story undergoes on the way to being adapted as a script for a TV drama, typical elements of popular culture, which mostly is progressive, but seldom radical, become evident. Considering the audience, which comprises more age groups than usual on such a holiday, this drama sings praise to the importance of 'the family'. In order to appeal to younger audiences – and to not scare them away, it remains open whether Rie will eventually quit working or whether she will use her time in Korea as a 'time out' in her career. It would be a time during which she is able to gather new strength while enjoying time with her family – in accordance with the lifestyle of the female Korean role-models.

In this context, it is particularly interesting that only very positively connoted female Korean characters appear in Japanese productions. These characters either enter into a love affair with a Japanese man – or a friendship with a female Japanese character. In contrast to those productions, the three Japanese-Korean co-productions aired between 2002 and 2004 dealt with love stories in which Japanese *women* fell in love with Korean *men*. The male characters in these dramas contributed significantly to the popularity of Korean actors in Japan. This anticipated the boom surrounding the first Korean series ever aired in Japanese terrestrial television, 'Fuyu no sonata' (A Winter Sonata), which was broadcast by NHK in 2003.[8] The main male character and most notably the actor who played this role (Bae Yong Joon, called Yon-sama by his Japanese fans) immediately became the incarnation of the 'ideal' man and lover. As he is the antithesis of a partriarchal man who expects his wife to serve him, this idealization can also be interpreted as a criticism of Japanese men.

To sum up, concerning gender relations and interculturality in TV dramas aired in Japan, the following can be stated: In Japanese TV dramas, Korean women who are depicted as rather 'traditional' are idealised and appropriated as role models. In these dramas, which are mostly produced by men, the female Korean characters therefore serve as a means to convey traditional gender values to the mainly female Japanese audience. The male hero in this drama, written by two young female scriptwriters, is very different from the common Japanese stereotype of Korean men as it is depicted in Japanese TV dramas. He is idealised as a 'modern' man who is very caring and sensitive towards women. Thus Japanese women discovered their concept of an 'ideal man' in the male 'other', the hero of a Korean drama. Again, the amalgamation of gender and ethnicity becomes evident and it will be interesting to observe how this nexus develops in future drama productions.

Notes

[1] Masumedia bunka to josei ni kansuru kenkyūkai 1986, p. 109. This notion was also underlined by a poll I conducted among 100 female students during summer 2003. See Section 3 of this article.

[2] See also Gatzen/Gössmann 2003, Gössmann/Kirsch (forthcoming) and Iwata-Weickgenannt (forthcoming)

[3] This project was conducted under the guidance of Hilaria Gössmann and was sponsored by the Deutsche Forschungsgemeinschaft (DFG; German Research Fund).

[4] For a short description of these dramas, see the list of analysed dramas in the appendix.

[5] Muramatsu Yasuko 1979. For an analysis of women's roles in Japanese TV dramas of the 1990s, see Muramatsu and Gössmann (1998) and Gössmann (1998).

6   One example is the TV series *At Home Dad* in which two fathers renounce their own career in
     favour of that of their wives in order to take over household duties and raise the children. This
     drama was first aired in 2004 and re-broadcast in January 2006.
7   See Yamauchi 2000 and Nagai 2001.
8   On the reception of this famous Korean drama in Japan, see Hayashi 2005.

References

Gatzen, Barbara und Hilaria Gössmann (2003): Fernsehen als Spiegel und Motor des Wandels? Zur
     Konstruktion von China und Korea in japanischen Dokumentarsendungen und Serien. (Televi-
     sion as Mirror or Motor of Change? The Construction of China und Korea in Japanese TV Do-
     cumentaries and TV Serials). In: Hilaria Gössmann und Franz Waldenberger (ed.) *Medien in
     Japan. Gesellschafts- und kulturwissenschaftliche Perspektiven* (Media in Japan. From a Social
     Science and Cultural Studies Perspective). Hamburg: IFA, pp. 244-279.
Gössmann, Hilaria (ed.) (1998): *Das Bild der Famile in den japanischen Medien.* (The Image of
     Family in Japanese Media) München: iudicium.
Gössmann, Hilaria and Griseldis Kirsch (2007): 'Nostalgia for 'Asian' Traditions and Energy. En-
     counters with Chinese and Koreans in Japanese TV Dramas.' In: White, Bruce (ed.): *Japan's
     Possible Futures.* London: Routledge. (forthcoming)
Hayashi Kaori (2005): *'Fuyusona' ni hamatta watashitachi. Jun'ai, namida, masukomi... soshite
     kankoku.* (About us Fans of the TV drama 'Fuyusona'. True Love, Tears, the Mass Media
     and Korea.) Tokyo: Bungei shunjū
Iwata-Weickgenannt, Kristina (2007): Nah und fern zugleich? Konstruktionen südkoreanischer und
     japankoreanischer Figuren in japanischen Fernsehdramen (2001-2002): (Near and at the same
     time distant? Constructions of South-Korean and Japanese-Korean Characters in Japanese TV
     Dramas). In: Hilaria Gössmann (ed.) *Interkulturelle Begegnungen in Literatur, Film und Fern-
     sehen. Ein deutsch-japanischer Vergleich* (Intercultural Encounters in Literature, Film and Te-
     levision. A German-Japanesese Comparison. München: iudicium (forthcoming).
Muramatsu Yasuko (1979): *Terebi dorama no joseigaku,* (A Women's Studies Approach to TV Dra-
     mas) Tokyo: Sōtakusha.
Muramatsu Yasuko und Hilaria Gössmann (ed.) (1998): *Media ga tsukuru gendā. Nichidoku no danjo
     kazokuzō to yomitoku.* (Gender as a Construct of Media. Analyses of Women, Men and Family
     in Japan and Germany) Tokyo: Shinyōsha.
Masumedia bunka to josei ni kansuru kenkyūkai (1986): Masumedia bunka to josei ni kansuru ken-
     kyūkai (Research on Mass Media Culture and Women). Tokyo: Tokyo-to seikatsu bunka-kyoku.
Nagai Asami (2002): Mom's Story of settling into Seoul community. In: The *Daily Yomiuri*, April 13.
Watanabe Mayumi (1999): *Kankoku no oba-chan wa erai* (Korean Aunties Are Admirable!) Tokyo:
     Shōbunsha.
Yamauchi Toshinori (2000): Mayumi Watanabe: Japanese Women Chronicles her Time in Korea. In:
     Pacific Friend, March 2000, vol. 27, No. 11.

List of dramas analyzed

*   *Mō ichido kisu (One More Kiss, NHK 2001)*

Male Japanese main character (20): university drop-out looks for a goal in his life, finally starts working as a composer
Female Korean main character (24): professional pop singer, dreams of spending her life with the man of her dreams

- *Shijō no koi (Highest Love, NHK 2001)*
  Male Japanese main character (in his 40s): suffers from a divorce, gains a more positive worldview due to the encounter with the Korean character
  Female Korean main character (in her 20s): constantly believes in the good of the world, sacrifices herself to save the life of the Japanese main character's daughter

- *Faitingu gāru (Fighting Girl, Fuji TV 2002)*
  Female Japanese main character (19): university drop-out starts a profession as fashion designer
  Female Korean main character (24): escapes a marriage of convenience in Korea, wants to work in Japan

- *Kankoku no obachan wa erai (Korean Aunties Are Wonderful, NHK 2002)*
  Female Japanese main character (in her 30s): works as freelance illustrator, rethinks her position within her family
  Female Korean main character (in her 50s): considers 'family first' as basic duty for women

- *Friends (TBS, KBS 2002)*
  Female Japanese main character (in her 20s): unsatisfied with her job, starts learning Korean and finds a dream for herself
  Male Korean main character (in his 20s): dreams of making films, wants to fulfil the expectations of his father, finally able to fulfil his dreams

Results Concerning Gender Dynamics in Globalisation

Susanne Kreitz-Sandberg

1 Gender as a Unifying Perspective

Gender provides a unifying perspective for researchers from different disciplines. This is the central lesson from this edited volume, where authors from sociology, political and educational science, history, literature and media studies have presented their research on a wide range of subjects. Edited volumes provide results on different aspects of one common topic. In the case of this book all authors relate their research questions to gender dynamics in Japan. In this final chapter, I will summarise the results and propose an interpretation, as to how we can combine these results to a common account on gender dynamics in a globalized world.

Here the relevance of gender as an essential perspective will be discussed. One perspective cannot grasp the whole reality, but innovative perspectives can provide us with an insight into new realities. 'It is probably because we want so desperately to know that what we believe is true that we cannot face the fact that whatever we know must be seen only as a truth gained from a certain perspective' (Charon 2006: 4). The claim is that a gender-perspective is significant because it determines the reality of social life – a fact often being ignored within Japan-related research.

This book presents a selection of Japan related gender studies, which have been developed in the context of Social Sciences and Cultural Studies. After a decade of Workshops on Gender Studies taking place in combination with the annual conference of the German Association for Social Science Research on Japan[1] we decided to host a whole conference on the topic of Gender and, thus, invited presenters from ten different countries. The papers in this book are – as mentioned in the introduction – a selection from this conference. Most of the contributors to the volume are working or educated in Germany, but it was a very conscious decision to present our research here in the *lingua franca*. We left it open to the authors if they felt more comfortable with British or American English and hope that native speakers are generous and accept some "creative" use of their languages. The intention of this book is – as indeed it was in the conference – to open up our discussions to the much bigger community of researchers in Gender Studies as well as Japanese Studies around the globe.

As a conscious decision we chose gender as our research perspective and experienced that this facilitated an interdisciplinary approach to a variety of topics. Gender plays an immanent role in all disciplines and many social sciences and cultural studies apply actively a gender perspective in their analysis. The need of taking context into account opened our eyes for a neglected topic. In the case of Japan, Asia can be describes as a relevant context. Research on Japan in Asia became popular during the last decade. However, a gender perspective had only been applied in very few cases up to now. When reflecting on our results against the background of the social and historical constitution of the Japanese society the transformation in the role of gender under changing historical and social conditions becomes obvious (Section 2).

Gender can be understood as a key organisational principal during modernisation. In the context of globalisation, civil society defines itself less through nationality and its own culturality, and gender roles are diversifying. In Japan the term *jendā* is connected to a sense of discrimination and disadvantage, even if definitions relate neutrally to aspects of socially and culturally constructed difference. The gender concept is to be understood in the context of its social and cultural setting. For example, the expression *gender-free* is used in a similar meaning as gender-sensitive or gender fair in other cultural contexts. However, globalisation of gender norms during the 1990s influenced not only developments in Europe but also in Japan and Asia. Concepts of gender mainstreaming provide us with a tool to understand developments concerning gender in different countries. Local conditions obviously shaped the respective realisation of laws and other formalised gender norms within different national contexts in East Asia (Section 3).

Actors influence gender norms and gender norms bear consequences for all actors, no matter if women or men. Addressing gender contains obviously more than engaging in women's equal rights. It relates to both men's and women's situations. In this volume light was shed on notions of hegemonic masculinity; and it was demonstrated how masculinity and men's studies can contribute actively to the process of degendering. Both tendencies of hegemonic and innovative approaches can be observed in mass communication. Combining results of articles in this book on these innovative fields of research could contribute a better understanding of pattern of male domination and difficulties for women to make their voices heard. Interestingly, progressive gender notions for men do not seem to share the same problem (Section 4).

The choice and combination of various dimensions of difference in research helps us develop a deepened understanding of a society. Applying an intersectionality approach, which includes also other dimensions of power and influence into the analysis seem fruitful for a further development of gender studies. Self-critical consideration on how we can develop our thinking across such boarders supports us on our way towards globalising gender studies. Taking not only gender and class, but also ethnicity into account provides such a profound comprehension. A sensibility towards matters of ethnicity seems to be relevant for Japan's way towards better integration into the Asian community (Section 5).

Obviously the division in this book between concepts of gender and gendered identities, on the one hand, and actors within a gendered space of society, on the other hand, serves a purpose but does not aim at describing these areas as separate from each other. Several of the contributions in this volume touch on both areas and I shall provide a short summary of the context and central results of the articles in this publication in the following.

2 Japan within the Asian Context

The perspective in this book of presenting Japan *within* Asia is one approach of taking the country's geographical, cultural, social, political and also economic context into account. For a long time it has been difficult to define Japan's position in the world. Japan was often the non-Western exception among modern industrialized nations, allied with the United States and therefore defined as part of the so-called First World.[2] Many Japanese thinkers identified Japan as a Western nation in connection with modernisation from the Meiji period (1868–1912). However, since the 1990s, Japan reconsidered its position in relation to the neighbouring Asian countries who had experienced the so-called East Asian economic boom and started redesigning their mutual relations, for example through intensive cooperation of the ASEAN states. In connection with the burst of the *bubble economy*, various political scandals and the need of economic, political, administrative and social reforms, Japan was forced to search for its new role within Asia (Blechinger/Legewie 1998:15; Derichs/Hüstebeck/Lukner 2006).

This process has inspired extended research, for example in a project on 'Japan in Asia' by the German Institute of Japanese Studies (DIJ, internet a). A variety of conferences and publications covered areas like history, history of thought, political science as well as economy, management and business studies. Gender aspects were touched upon in connection to historical questions (Germer 2003) and historiography (Liscutin, forthcoming). However, in other disciplines gender questions were widely ignored. This is not so surprising if we take into account that many of the studies focussed on Japan's economic position in relation to other Asian economies (Hilpert/Haak 2003). Economy and business studies are subjects, which at least in the German language research, have not yet opened their discussions to gender topics within their Japan related work. Gender-sensitive contributions on the Japanese labour market come from sociology (Lenz 1987, Weber 1994, 1997, 1999, Shire 2000).[3] How interesting this field can be for a critical analysis is understood when we think of Baier's interviews (in this volume). One of her Japanese interview partners quoted other Asian Women during the parallel forum in Huairou, which took place at the same time as the Fourth World Conference on Women in Beijing in 1995. They expressed their concern that working conditions in their countries might increasingly discriminate against women with the introduction of Japanese style employment practices. Such discriminating employment practices are only one of many topics touched upon in this volume from an international gender perspective.

A gender perspective on *Asia* is relevant because gender roles are constantly produced and reproduced in daily life, as Manzenreiter in this volume shows for the area of sports. He demonstrates how practices in schools and associations reinforce a dominant gender order, sometimes under the cover of emancipating practices. Other contributions give examples of a gradually changing gender order (Schad-Seifert, Kreitz-Sandberg, Tanaka/Hong).[4] They also demonstrate the need to overcome a dichotomizing notion of Japan versus "Western nations". Investigating gender relations in a wider context of Japan *and* its neighbouring nations can be seen as one step towards taking Japan's closer geographic, economic and political context into account.

3   The Role of Gender Concepts in Modernisation and Globalisation

Modernisation processes in Japan were closely connected to a reinterpretation of concepts of nation, culture and gender (Mae 2002). While national and cultural identity was interwoven with so-called traditional gender roles during the early modernisation process we can observe how this culturally and nationally determined gender order dissolves with the shift from nation-state to global society. Trends towards pluralization, individualisation, destandardisation and a strengthening of civil society can be observed but are also accompanied by conservative backlashes, which find their expression in a wide range of publications and also in political declarations, as Mae elaborates on in this volume.

In line with Mae's description, Lenz argues that the national hegemonic gender order is shaped during the first and second phase of Japanese modernisation, the 'civil national' and the 'organised national phase' from the second half of the 19th century. Gender as a key organisational principle structured the national order and the enterprise society emerging from the 1950s. Lenz's analysis is based on the work of the German sociologist Ulrich Beck and thoughts Beck developed together with Anthony Giddens in the early 1990s. In Japan, like in other nations, the national hegemonic gender order is currently eroding and, in the shade of demographic change, gender contracts need to be discussed and redeveloped now, during the third 'reflexive phase of modernization' (Lenz).

In Japan the term gender (*jendā*) has played an increasingly important role as key paradigm in social sciences from the 1990s. The term itself is a loanword and its use is until today highly political. While prominent feminists like for example Ueno Chizuko reframe international discussions on gender equality, and political advisors like Ōsawa Mari contribute with their analysis of asymmetric power relations to the development of increasingly gender fair policies, many unnamed gender activists are fighting daily for a realisation of gender equality in companies and social institutions, as Baier has illustrated in her presentation.

Gender in its Japanese pronounciation *jendā* is to be understood as 'socially and culturally constructed difference between men and women'. This is a definition from the major Japanese encyclopedia *Kōjien*, which Schad-Seifert cites in her article. Global and structural changes are influencing international knowledge systems and international change of values is entering a new stage. While Japan's neoconservative forces try to uphold a national hegemonic gender order, the development towards gender fairness is steadily going on. The amendment of the Basic Law for a Gender-equal Society and other laws concerning equal rights in the late 1990s fuelled developments towards a more equal status between men and women. This provoked a lively discussion on the role of legislation for a new gender order (Osawa 2000).

Mae in this volume illustrated this by the example of the *Basic Law for a Gender-equal Society*[5] from 1999. She herself simply calls the law 'Participation Law' as the direct translation of *Danjo kyōdō sankaku shakai kihonhō* is 'Basic law on equal participation of men and women'. This element of participation is, however, no longer visible in the official English translation. The term *danjo kyōdō sankaku* has been criticised from many sides. Feminists disapprove of the term because it was employed instead of the more precise term of 'equality' (*byōdō*) and conservatives rejected the expression, because of 'their fear that "gender equal participation" entailed the gender-free concept which they understood as a fundamental negation of gender differences.' (Mae)

The Gender-free Concept

One of the central concepts in Japanese gender discourse is connected to the term gender-free. *Jendā furī* is – even if it is a loan word – a very Japanese term. How can one imagine something being gender-free? The answer lies in an understanding of *jendā* in terms of discrimination, division or disadvantage based on the differences between men and women. Osawa (2000:6) provides us with the following explanation: 'By "gender-free", I mean a society, where the fact of being a man or woman has no effect on the options available to people as they make their way through life' (quoted by Schad-Seifert in this volume).

Against the background of this understanding it becomes obvious why the term gender-free plays such an important role in schools and education. Gender-free education (*jendā furīna kyōiku*) became a catchphrase in 1995. It is connected to discussions on gender equality, which builds on equal rights, duties and possibilities for male and female pupils. Discourses on gender and education, which were very actively carried on, for example in the Japanese Society for Educational Sociology, were addressing the situation of boys and girls in school and education. Hereby they can be distinguished from earlier studies, where focussing on sex differences was automatically associated with problematizing or idealising the situation of women or girls in education. The aim of gender-free education is emancipatory. However, a closer look at aims of gender-free education programs leaves no doubt that the situation in schools is far from gender "free", as I describe in my comparative approach. Many gender stereotypes and segregation between boys and girls are prevailing, in daily routines in the school, in general, and in physical education classes in particular (Manzenreiter). However, nowadays it is more difficult to grasp the specific differences, as formal conditions like number of classes or expectations to engage wholeheartedly in activities are very similar for boys and girls.

In a historical perspective it becomes obvious that nowadays differences in expectations towards men and women have undergone a diversification process. The controversy triggered by the gender-free concept contains a twofold gender problem. While on the one hand the gender order of the first phase of modernisation refers to a society which defines itself in terms of nationality and its own culturality, the gender-free concept, on the other hand, is linked to a society based on individualization and transculturality, i.e. a civil society which has stopped defining itself through nationality and its own culturality (Mae). This might partially explain why the topic is still enough to provoke all kinds of political disputes.

In an international comparative perspective we might want to question if the character of 'gender-free' is programmatically different to what is described as a 'gender-sensitive' praxis, for example in the Philippines (Kreitz-Sandberg). Gender-free might be characterised as a local expression for changes in the gender order. Or, as Schad-Seifert states (in this volume), Japanese politics of realising a gender-free society can be understood in the context of global politics for gender mainstreaming.

Gender Mainstreaming

During the late 1990s the Japanese government started designing reform programs aiming at building 'a gender-equal society' (Schad-Seifert). Why was it just in the late 1980s and the 1990s that Japan experienced such a push concerning more gender-equal standards and norms? The economic crisis and reforms (Foljanty-Jost 2004, Bosse/Köllner 2001), demographic developments (DIJ, internet b) and post-modern value change (Möhwald 2002, Klein/Lützeler/Ölschleger 2002) are some of the aspects, that can be mentioned to describe the situation during the 1990s, which contributed to substantial changes in gender norms in Japan. Several articles in this book mention, however, the Fourth UN World Conference on

Women in Beijing in 1995 as the crucial trigger for massive mobilisation and changes in attitudes and organisations (Baier, Tanaka/Hong, Schad-Seifert, Lenz). Building an increasingly gender-equal society in Japan might be described as a reaction to globalising gender norms.[6]

Baier presents sources speaking of 5,000 Japanese women attending this conference and the parallel meeting for non-governmental organisations, the NGO Forum in Huairou. The Japanese women's movement and women's networks experienced a massive upswing and emphasized political activities and, thus, influenced legislation (see Lenz 2000). Baier contributes, with her case study on the Working Women's International Network (WWN) in Osaka, a concrete example of how women were fighting in the court for the realisation of equality in the context of insufficiently realised rights through the Equal Employment Opportunity Law (*Danjo kōyō kikai kintōhō*, EEOL).

However, can grass-root movements like these implement such massive changes? We have to take into account that every step forward provoked also answers from actors who were less in favour of gender equal norms. For example the introduction of the EEOL in 1985 led, as Baier brings forth in her contribution, to the introduction of specific employment patterns, which in reality were almost exclusively addressing men *or* women. General occupation in a company known as *ippanshoku,* and career tracks, alias *sōgōshoku,* are only extreme examples of how women and men are channelled into specific tracks of occupations with different chances for training, promotion and thereby wages. This has been described in detail before. However, new to an international audience is how Japanese women are organising themselves and how they could achieve gradual results towards better employment practices through networking and international cooperation. The Working Women's (International) Network (WWN) provides a very illustrative example of how global gender norms could be used in the fight towards gradual achievement of more equality within the Japanese employment system.

Therefore, as a first result in this field, we can state that equal opportunities were not automatically granted to women, they needed to be realised through a quite systematic fight against discrimination. At the same time, and this might be seen as a second result or as the flipside of the coin, global gender norms, like for example political declarations and laws ratified by the government, formed the basis for this struggle for equal opportunities.

Tanaka and Hong analyse the role of different local actors in interpreting global norms for two national contexts by the example of the implementation of the UN Convention on the Elimination of All Forms of Discrimination Against Women (CEDAW). Japan first signed this convention in 1980, and then ratified it without reservations in 1985. South Korea ratified it in 1984 with reservations regarding several articles of the convention. Tanaka and Hong apply an international comparative approach and distinguish development over time. Obviously the realisation of global norms depends on the national context. A detailed analysis of interactions between the respective governments and feminist mobilization in three different stages – the pre-ratification, the signing and ratification and the post-ratification stage – provides an important contribution in the under-researched area of effects of global norms, like those represented in the CEDAW, on the local context. In the case of Japan, Tanaka and Hong write, '[a]ll the policy debates in the process referred to pre-existing political issues.' The role of the convention was often to re-activate already existing political debates. In South Korea, in contrast, feminist mobilization was almost non-existent before the ratification.

Globalising gender norms affected a wide range of areas. Article 10 of the CEDAW declares equality of both sexes in education. Japanese public schools are since 1947 co-educative. However, home economics for both sexes had been a controversial topic from the 1970s onward. Teachers were divided about the topic and there was a lively debate both in media and education science circles. Finally, the Minister of Education accepted co-education in all subjects, in order 'not to hinder the ratification of the CEDAW' (Tanaka/Hong). Also in this policy making process feminist groups played an important role on the way towards realisation.

This whole process can be understood in the context of gender mainstreaming.[7] The impetus for a coordination of change towards more equal opportunities came at the same time in Asia, and especially in Japan, as in the European Union. The Fourth UN Women's Conference in Beijing became an important turning point towards gender mainstreaming. Ehrhardt (2003: 19) describes gender mainstreaming as a top-down process, depending on an explicit political will. However, the actual formation of laws depends much on diverse actors. Women Power Machineries, from feminist experts over female lawyers to grassroot activists, influence the implementation process, as Tanaka and Hong exemplified by the legislation process in Japan and Korea. Relevant here is that gender mainstreaming promotes sustainable development for women and men.

4   Actors, Gender Norms, and Social Change

Changing gender policies can be understood at a certain point as a functional answer to social change. In the context of an aging society, with a decrease in the number of children and an increase in the percentage of elderly people, encouraging men to take part in child care and elderly care fits into a set of looking for creative solutions. This is the understanding I gained from Schad-Seifert's article in this volume. Japan is regarded as a male-dominated or male-centred society. Sometimes this is described as a result of Confucian ethics and a moral codex of samurai culture. However, it is the 'modern patriarchy' with full-time housework and child education as the responsibility of women and the breadwinner role and lifetime employment for men, which has shaped a dominant division of labour, for such a long time characteristic of the Japanese society.

Masculinity and Men's Studies

These characteristics underwent a significant change during the previous decade. Men 'have come under pressure due to the so-called restructuring process of Japanese economy' (Schad-Seifert). Many permanent working positions have been substituted by unstable employment as temporary workers or so-called *furītā*. These flexible working patterns, which are sometimes described as an expression of idealistic value change, are undermining possibilities of supporting the whole family. Many men come to a point where they reflect critically on their male gender identity. Schad-Seifert writes: 'The fundamental process of economic restructuring and the demise of employment practices which supported male full employment and the male wage earner model have ongoing consequences on the paradigm of gender in Japanese society.'

The breadwinner role men are expected to fulfil seems to be more and more questioned by men of the younger generation. Male responsibility included an economic responsibility for the whole family. During the 1960s and 1970s the "company warriors" were the stereotype of male role models, slowly coming under critique for workaholic habits. The growing consumer society triggered this process further during the 1970s, with many families being in dept for buying real estate. The dominant gender discourse focused on the situation of women, who did not get access to permanent working positions, but it often neglected the fact that men were under massive pressure to live up to social expectations (Schad-Seifert). The most recent critique of the husband-breadwinner model comes, not only from men's liberation movements or from organisations representing family members of those who had died of overwork (*karōshi*), but ironically also from company managements, who are no longer able to support their employees as extensively as they used to do during the period of rapid economic growth.

Against the background of this process of social and organisational change men's studies and men's liberation movements have gained much attention. Training business manners with a strong focus on working against sexual harassment is only one example. Others are checklists for men (or their spouses) for investigating whether a man is able to care for himself. Provoking a smile with statements like 'knowing at least one problem in the neighborhood' or 'knowing where to find your shoes and socks,' Itō Kimio introduces us to the world of men rediscovering their independence in a private world highly domi-nated by women. Young males obviously know that they can win in the context of their search for new identities, but Schad-Seifert's analysis shows that in the present situation a liberation from traditional gender roles also bears a high risk and demands a preparedness to face an insecure outlook on one's future life.

How can, on the other hand, prevailing hegemonic patterns of masculinity be de-scribed? This question, which is actively discussed in men's studies (Con-nel/Messerschmidt 2004, Hearn 2005, Meuser 2006), is also relevant for Japan-related research. The Japanese example can contribute a differentiating view on stereotypes, which often still dominate the understanding of the Japanese society. The article on physical edu-cation and gender reproduction provides a valuable source for this. In the field of sports, familiar stereotypes are being communicated with sports being seen as a natural domain for men. Many of the statements by Manzenreiter (in this volume) leave, however, no doubt that the analysed trends are transnational, and that many of the patterns are typical not only for Japan. Physical education is described 'as a projection screen for the symbolic display of gender order'. Examples of this can be found not least in the media representation of sports, with specific social expectations towards men and women as athletic achievers. While male athletes were typically shown in action, female ones were often presented in a domestic context.

Hierarchies in school sports clubs are very obvious. Possibilities for girls are limited; if girls participate in traditional male dominated sports like baseball they have supportive functions as club managers, roles otherwise taken by boys in lower ranks. Some of the clubs have opened their doors to girls who, however, cannot join in tournaments. Girls compete more often in other fields of sports, like for example volleyball. Participation in public and private sports clubs is even stronger dominated by male youngsters than in school clubs. Manzenreiter's research in this volume shows also the wide range of possible reasons for these prevailing patterns, from a shortage of female trainers to a repelling character of unattractively male-dominated sports games. Most of the arguments are extracted from Japanese research, for example in the Journal for Sports and Gender Studies. At least, we cannot criticise the discourses for being gender-blind. Further research into the classroom or sports arena on how gender is being created and what specifics – if any – we may find in the Japanese context in comparison to other nations would without doubt be very welcome in the research community.

The number of research projects focussing on or including studies on masculinity is increasing in Japanese studies (see Roberson/Suzuki 2003). One example is the study by Sabine Frühstück (2004, 2007), on the organisational identity of the Japanese Self-Defence Force as well as the masculinity of their service members, all constantly under reconstruction. It is to be expected that Japan related gender studies receive much further input from masculinity research (e.g. Gaens 2004).

Gender and the Media

Media influence modern identities strongly and can contribute to changing as well as reinforcing gender roles. We still know little about the perception of media and how they actually influence identity. A first step in this direction is the survey, which Gössmann conducted with her Japanese students on messages they deduced from a certain TV-drama. More common, at least in the Japan related media research, is content analysis concerning specific patterns of gender representations. Schoolbooks, novels, commercials, newspapers or TV-drama are only some examples of media, which can be analysed as to a certain understanding of gender ideals and realities.

Media products present reality in a specific perspective. This is the case for print media in general and newspapers in particular. It is actually people who compose these products and stand for the respective contents. In the case of the sports writers' world, the circle is almost completely closed for women. Manzenreiter presented case studies where less than five percent of the newspaper writers were women. This can contribute among others to the presentation of women, which not always works to the women's advantage; not seldom does it disclose the female body to the male gaze.

Case studies in the field of media studies show that a certain difference in the reporting strategies of different nationally distributed newspapers can be observed, but that these differences are rather gradual than programmatic (Rechenberger 2004). Examples from the coverage of the 'comfort women issue' show more than anything else how male domination in the Japanese news media causes difficulties for women to make their voices heard. Engaged female journalists could make a change, as in the case of Matsui Yayori, a famous activist in the 'comfort women issue' who wrote many articles in Asahi Shinbun. As a result Asahi Shinbun reported more diverse positions concerning the trials seeking retribution for former so-called 'comfort women'. Yomiuri Shinbun almost ignored the whole case.

The media with a rather 'female' connotation – not least in terms of reception – are TV dramas. But do they provide their audience with a somehow more gender progressive message? The answer we have do draw from Gössmann's study is definitely negative. Role models presented in dramas have for over three decades been rather gender conservative. Modern patterns of professional women searching for individual identities are being portrayed increasingly often, but traditional patterns depicting being a mother as the most important responsibility of women prevail. This is the role where women in dramas finally find their happiness.

This selection of studies illustrates that women have difficulties entering the media with gender progressive news or programs. The under-representation of women in the media plays a central role in this respect. We might wonder how this is related to the analysis of men's liberation movements, where mass media like TV played a very important role in communicating their messages to a broad public (Schad-Seifert). Structure and content cannot be separated, and the examples presented in this volume leave me with an impression that structure has a stronger impact than content. Media studies will also in the future yield interesting results on gender, and the question how male (physical) domination determines, who can make his or her voice heard, and questions around gender progressive or conservative contents might be only few of many interesting topics.

5   Dimensions of Social Difference and Influence

Some authors in this volume mentioned an imbalance of perceptions of and realities within the Japanese society. Dimensions of social difference and influence deserve more attention. For example, Manzenreiter speaks of 'the myth of the classless society', which hints at the need to include class into this differentiation. In the three introductory contributions on gender concepts, the authors mention that, in addition to the obvious gender dualism, class was receding in Japanese public and academic discourses. It is only a very recent phenomenon that social differences and questions of class difference are (re)entering public attention in Japan. The phenomenon goes under the term *kakusa shakai* was coined for this phenomenon (Ishida 2006). However, it will be important for future research not to subsume all analyses to this rediscovered dimension of differences of class, but to interconnect the different categories in order to gain a realistic picture of the complexity within the Japanese society.

The contributions on gender in Japan in this volume connect gender to other dimensions of difference, as can be exemplified for the topics of class and ethnicity. Recent social science and cultural studies discussions bring forth the connection of different dimensions of social discrimination under the term 'intersectionality'.

Intersectionality

Ideas of intersectionality are up to now seldom applied in the context of Japanese Studies. However, I will argue that the articles in this volume build a good foundation for further intersectionality studies in Japanese society. Lenz wrote in her introductory chapter that gender was emphasized while class was receding during the organised national modernisation from the 1950s onward. How can we extend our fruitful analysis from gender as the central category of distinctions towards an intersectionality approach, in which gender, class, ethnicity and possible other dimensions of difference are integrated?

For this we need to acquaint ourselves with the background of the debate. Intersectionality has its roots in the late 1970s when black feminists and feminists belonging to minority groups entered the political arena. It is influencing present feminist debates and we can find different positions. Many have lost their original political sharpness but, as an effect, discussions on many types of 'differences' influencing social power relations are very present. Gender, class, ethnicity and others are being approached as a set of possible forms of multiple discriminations. Yuval-Davis (2005) points out that these social differences are also constructed and interwoven and influence subjective and political constructions of identity.

In order to develop my thinking towards a better understanding of how we could include intersectionality into Japan related social sciences, I will take a self-critical view on my own research presented in this volume. The contribution investigated aspects of national influence on gender patterns by contrasting results from a Japanese school study with results from a study in another Asian country, the Philippines. Both studies were concerned with gender in primary school education. A strong international convergence of topics being addressed within gender education became obvious. The representation of female and male characters and their implicit hierarchies in teaching materials, or gender specific choice of subjects are only some of the topics touched upon in different studies. Obviously international discourses influence national school and research cultures and we witness increasingly globalised gender norms. At the same time some topics are taking more space in Japanese schools, like for example discussions concerning gender segregation and gender stereotypes (Kreitz-Sandberg). However, the analysis of secondary data also made clear that focussing on external specifics, like age-group, is not necessarily sufficient. The schools under survey in Japan and the Philippines had different populations in accordance to class, a topic not obvious at the fist glance, which however deserve more attention in future comparative studies in education. Relevant, according to the intersectionality approach, is to understand hierarchies and catch power related factors of difference in this analysis. Being different is not the central problem, but having access to education, political influence, and social and economic resources are relevant dimensions for analysis.

Ethnicity

Discussions on gender are obviously related to other factors of 'difference'. One of them is the dimension of ethnicity. It is entering works presented in this volume (e.g. Gössman), sometimes in connection to concepts of nationality (Wöhr, Mae) or the relation to international comparisons (Kreitz-Sandberg, Tanaka/Hong). Ethnicity can, similar to gender, be described as a factor influencing the individual identity. More than that, these concepts are also constructions, which are actively formed and developed. The situation in Japan is specific in that ethnic differences have been ignored during the national phases of modernisation. 'Ethnicity was integrated in the hegemonic gender order in a double way: Japanese ethnicity was homogenized and highly valued by conservative political leaders and mass media and linked to a supposedly unique Japanese culture.' (Lenz)

Now, with globalisation and prevailing trends of a so-called reflexive modernity, ethnicity becomes an increasingly important topic. For example, Japan experienced a Korea boom in connection with the World Cup for Soccer in 2002, which was hosted together by Japan and Korea. The number of TV-dramas for example, depicting Japanese-Korean encounters rose significantly during that time. However, introducing ethnicity, and portraying people of different national origins, does not automatically lead to more progressive messages in the drama. Korea is constructed as a country where Confucian traditions play an important role. 'Korean characters are presented as family oriented while Japanese characters […] appear rather individualistic. The lethargy and aimlessness of Japanese characters is countered by the energy and determination of the Korean characters.' (Gössmann) And finally, the encounter with the Korean 'other' results in a kind of healing experience for the Japanese. In the analysed examples the primarily Japanese audience is confronted with stereotypes about the Korean reality. Obviously, introducing Korean protagonists is less aiming at understanding ethnically different people than at constructing and reinforcing a specific gender model "in crisis".

Another topic, where ethnicity and nationality plays an important role is the debate on so-called 'comfort women' – a euphemism for forced prostitution during World War II. Feminists in intellectual circles and non-governmental organisations (NGOs) brought up the highly political topic in the 1990s. This led to transnational cooperation of feminists in various countries demonstrating almost unknown solidarity between neighbouring Asian nations (Mae).

Leading history and sociology researchers engaged into discussions on forced prostitution. Wöhr illustrates in this volume, through text interpretations of the diverse positions, the complexity of the issue. While some authors apply gender as a dimension with a potential to overcome national divisions, others do not necessarily consent with this approach. Obviously there is a fear to address the suffering of Japanese war prostitutes and compare it with the exploitation of Korean and other ethnical divergent victims of the colonial war machinery. While gender has the potential to unify over borders, ethnicity is, in this case, the category to exemplify the difference. However, Wöhr's discussion also points out how important it would be to include the dimension of class, as far as poverty is one of the central factors for women "choosing" the occupation as sex workers to support themselves in the lack of any other possibilities.

The discussion whether the situation of gender suppression, and especially violence against women, would serve as a unifying factor is still at its beginning. Different positions concerning these matters are not necessarily dictated by the nationality of the scholars. Implicitly present is the question of how identity is formed by these historical and political conditions. Wöhr's contribution in this volume provides us with a very detailed insight into academic feminist discussions, mainly within history departments, and we can understand that the debate in Japan is wide and diverse. However, this diversity cannot necessarily be found in public debate. The importance of integrating ethnicity into an understanding of the hegemonic gender order becomes obvious for Japan's image in Asia.

6 Globalising Gender Studies

In this contribution I described several relevant areas for a better understanding of gender dynamics in globalisation. The arguments are borrowed and the examples are chosen from studies on gender in Japan with a selection of articles in political and educational science, sociology, media and cultural studies, as well as history. In summary, these results allow some generalisations on how globalising gender studies can function as a model for interdisciplinary research.

International discussions on the political arena point in the direction of transculturality, when feminists around the world travel across boarders to join hands and discuss questions closely related to their identity as men or women (Mae, Schad-Seifert). Exchange of potentially controversial positions can be seen as a step towards transnational understanding

(Wöhr). Research on hegemonic gender patterns shows that descriptions resemble each other over national boarders (Manzenreiter).

Lenz argues that backlashes concerning gender equality bear the danger that this could rather isolate Japan from, than integrate her into the bigger East Asian community. Not only in Japan, but also in other Asian nations relevant changes of the gender order are taking place. International networks play an important role (Baier, Kreitz-Sandberg). The introduction of the Equal Employment Opportunity Law in Japan influenced the Equal Employment Law in Korea. Here Japanese feminist policy had an obvious impact on that of South Korea (Tanaka/Hong). The revision of the Nationality Law in both countries is another example. What started as gradual changes entered quickly into a central paradigm shift. Obviously the transcultural developments which Mae mentions can be traced in the implementation process of gender laws in East Asia. A need to take the transcultural situation in our societies into account becomes obvious.

Notes

[1] Special thanks for the initiative to organise these workshops to Ilse Lenz and Michiko Mae. Up to date information about workshops and conferences is available at www.vsjf.net.

[2] Ulrike Wöhr applies these terms in her chapter and provided me with applied definitions on the terms First, Second and Third World, see URL: http://www.nationsonline.org/oneworld/third_world_countries.htm (January 12, 2007).

[3] This is the case for the German language discussion and also in Scandinavia, as exemplified in the comparative volume by Tsukaguchi-LeGrand/Le Grand (2003) on Gender and Work in Japan and Sweden, which also has a strong sociological focus.

[4] References to chapters in this volume quote only the author's name. I do not in every case include all the relevant secondary sources presented in the book. For this I invite the readers to (re)read the respective chapters.

[5] For reference via the internet: http://www.gender.go.jp/index2.html

[6] Global gender norms became a standard to which private companies and national agencies have to apply in the process of gender mainstreaming. Gender mainstreaming should not substitute women's policies but add to equality through this additional perspective. Promotion of women aims at reducing discrimination on the basis of measures, laws and political strategies. The whole organisation is meant to change and qualitative changes towards equality are followed up by evaluation and control (von Wrangell 2003).

[7] 'Gender mainstreaming is the integration of the gender perspective into every stage of policy processes – design, implementation, monitoring and evaluation – with a view to promoting equality between women and men' (European Commission, internet). It is – as opposed to women's policies – not aiming at supporting only one sex but, rather, at contributing to the process 'of articulating a shared vision of sustainable human development and translating it into reality.' (ibid.) Gender mainstreaming became a key category in international debates from the Fourth Women's Conference in Beijing in 1995. The states of the European Commission were obliged to apply the gender mainstreaming principles by signing the Amsterdam Treaty in 1997 (Ehrhardt 2003). The Amsterdam Treaty protects fundamental rights within the European Union, such as equality between men and women, non-discrimination and data privacy. It is available online: http://europa.eu/scaplus/leg/en/lvb/a09000.htm#a09002 (January 22, 2007).

Susanne Kreitz-Sandberg

References

Blechinger, Verena/Legewie, Jochen (1998): Japans neue Rolle in Asien [Japan's new role in Asia]: Einleitung. In: *Japanstudien* 10, pp. 15–25.

Bosse, Friederike/Köllner, Patrick, eds. (2001): *Reformen in Japan* [Reforms in Japan]. Hamburg: IFA.

Charon, Joel M. (2006, 1st 1992): The Nature of Perspective. In: Charon, Joel M.: *Symbolic Interactionism. An Introduction, an Integration, an Interpretation*. Upper Saddle River, N.J.: Pearson Prentice Hall.

Connel, Robert and J.W. Messerschmidt (2005): Hegemonic Masculinity: Rethinking the Concept. In: *Gender & Society*, 19:6, pp. 829–859.

Derichs, Claudia/Hüstebeck, Momoyo/Lukner, Kerstin (2006): Japans Rolle in der Welt [Japan's role in the world]. In: Piazolo, Michael, ed.: *Macht und Mächte in einer multipolaren Welt*. [Power and Powers in a Multi-Polar World]. Wiesbaden: VS Verlag, pp. 141–183.

DIJ German Institute for Japanese Studies (internet a): Completed Projects: Japan in Asia. http://www.dijtokyo.org/?page=project_detail.php&p_id=1&lang=en (January 16, 2007).

DIJ German Institute for Japanese Studies (internet b): Focus of Research: Challenges of Demographic Change. http://www.dijtokyo.org/?page=activities.php (January 16, 2007).

Ehrhardt, Angelika (2003): Gender Mainstreaming – wo es herkommt, was es will und wie es geht [Gender mainstreaming – where it comes from, what it wants and how to do it]. In: Jansen, Mechthild M./Röming, Angelika/Rohde, Marianne (eds.): *Gender Mainstreaming. Herausforderung für den Dialog der Geschlechter* [Gender mainstreaming. Challenge for the dialog between men and women], Munich: Olzog, pp. 13–33.

European Comission. Employment, Social Affairs & Equal Opportunities. Gender Equality. Gender Mainstreaming. General Overview http://ec.europa.eu (March 23, 2007)

Foljanty-Jost, Gesine, ed. (2004): *Japan in the 1990s. Crisis as an Impetus for Change*. Münster: Lit.

Fruhstuck, Sabine (2007): *Uneasy Warriors: Gender, Memory, and Popular Culture in the Japanese Army*. Berkeley: University Presses of California, Columbia and Princeton.

Frühstück, Sabine (2004): Engendering the Military – Militarizing Japan. Abstract for Presentation at the Conference: Gender Dynamics and Globalisation. Comparative Perspectives on Japan and Asia. Berlin. JDZB, 19-21 November 2004.

Gaens, Bart: The (R)emasculation of the Sararīman "Shima Kōsaku's Equation for Success" as Manual for Contemporary Japanese Businessmen. Presentation at the First Conference of The Nordic Association fort he Study of Contemporary Japanese Society in Gothenborg, 22-24 August 2004.

Germer, Andrea (2003): Feminist History in Japan: National and International Perspectives. In: *Intersections: Gender, History and Culture in the Asian Context*, 9, August 2003. 20 p. http://wwwsshe.murdoch.edu.au/intersections/

Getreuer-Kargl, Ingrid (1997): Geschlechterverhältnis und Modernisierung [Gender relations and modernisation]. In: Lenz, Ilse/Mae, Michiko (eds.): *Getrennte Welten, gemeinsame Moderne? Geschlechterverhältnisse in Japan* [Separate worlds, a common modernity? Gender relations in Japan] Opladen: Leske + Budrich, pp. 19–58.

Hearn, Jeff (2005): From Hegemonic Masculinity to Hegemony of Men. In: *Feminist Theory*, 5:1, pp. 49–72.

Hilpert, Hanns Günther/Haak, René, eds. (2002): *Japan and China. Cooperation, Competition and Conflicts*. Basingstoke, New York: Palgrave.

Ishida, Hiroshi (2006): The Persistence of Social Inequality in Postwar Japan. In: *Social Science Japan Newsletter*, 35, pp. 7–10.

Klein, Axel/Lützeler, Ralph/Ölschleger, Hans Dieter, eds. (2002): *Modernization in Progress. Demographic Development and Value Change in Contemporary Europe and East Asia*. Bonn: Bier'sche Verlagsanstalt.

Lenz, Ilse (1987): The Gender Factor in Industrial Employment and the Impact of Microelectronic Technology: Preliminary Remarks on the Case of Japan. In: Bergmann, Joachim/Tokunaga, Shigeyoshi (eds.): *Economic and Social Aspects of Industrial Relations. A Comparison of the German and the Japanese Systems*, Frankfurt, New York: Campus, pp. 129–151.

Lenz, Ilse (2000): What does the women's movement do, when it moves? Kommunikation und Organisation in der neuen japanischen Frauenbewegung [Comunication and organisation in the new Japanese women's movement]. In: Lenz, Ilse/Mae, Michiko/Klose, Karin (eds.): *Frauenbewegungen weltweit. Aufbrüche, Kontinuitäten, Veränderungen* [Women's movements worldwide]. Opladen: Leske + Budrich, pp. 95–132.

Liscutin, Nicola (ed.): *Making History: Feminist Interventions in the Historiography of World War II, Japan and Germany* (forthcoming).

Mae, Michiko (2002): Öffentlichkeit und Privatheit im japanischen Modernisierungsprozess [The public and the private in the Japanese modernisation process]. In: *Japanstudien* 14, pp. 237–266.

Mae, Michiko (2007): Auf dem Weg zu einer transkulturellen Genderforschung [Towards transcultural gender studies]. In: Mae, Michiko/Saal, Britta (eds.): *Transkulturelle Genderforschung. Ein Studienbuch zum Verhältnis von Kultur und Geschlecht* [Transcultural gender studies. A study book on the relation of culture and gender]. Wiesbaden: VS Publisher, pp. 37–51.

Meuser, Michael (2006): *Geschlecht und Männlichkeit: soziologische Theorie und kulturelle Deutungsmuster* [Gender and masculinity: Sociologic theories and cultural interpretations]. Wiesbaden: VS Publisher.

Möhwald, Ulrich (2002): *Changing Attitudes Towards Gender Equality in Japan and Germany*. Munich: iudicium.

Osawa, Mari (2000): Government Approaches to Gender Equality in the mid-1990s. In: *Social Science Japan Journal*. Vol. 3, No. 1, 2000, pp. 3–19.

Rechenberger, Daniela (2004): The 'Comfort Women' and Their Coverage in Japanese Newspapers. Presentation at the Conference: Gender Dynamics and Globalisation. Comparative Perspectives on Japan and Asia. Berlin. JDZB, 19-21 November 2004.

Roberson, James E./Suzuki, Nobue (2003): *Men and Masculinities in Contemporary Japan: Dislocating the Salaryman Doxa*. London/New York: Routledge.

Shire, Karen A. (2000): Gendered organization and workplace culture in Japanese customer service. In: *Social Science Japan Journal*. Vol. 3, No. 1, pp. 37-58.

Shire, Karen A./Imai, Jun (2000): Flexible Equality: Men and women in employment in Japan. *Duisburg Working Papers on East Asian Studies*. No. 30, 2000.

Tsukaguchi-LeGrand, Toshiko/LeGrand, Carl, eds. (2003): *Women in Japan and Sweden. Work and Family in Two Welfare Regimes*. Stockholm: Almqvist & Wiksell International.

von Wrangell, Ute (2003): Gender Mainstreaming, Frauenbeauftragte, Gleichstellungsbeauftragte – wie passt das zusammen? In: Jansen, Mechthild M./Röming, Angelika/Rohde, Marianne (eds.): *Gender Mainstreaming. Herausforderung für den Dialog der Geschlechter* [Gender mainstreaming. Challenge for the dialog between men and women], Munich: Olzog, pp. 49–75.

Weber, Claudia (1999): Frauenerwerbsarbeit in Japan [Women's employment]. In: JDZB (ed.): *Beziehungen von Bildungs- und Beschäftigungssystem in Japan in vergleichender Perspektive* [Comparative perspectives on education and employment systems in Japan] (JDZB Publication; vol. 39). Berlin: Japanese German Center Berlin, 1999/08, pp. 88–98.

Susanne Kreitz-Sandberg

Yuval-Davis, Nira (2005): Gender mainstreaming och intersektionalitet [Gender mainstreaming and intersectionality]. In: *Kvinnovetenskaplig tidskrift* 2-3.05, pp. 19–30.

About the Authors

Maria Sachiko Baier, M.A.

studied Japanese studies, political science and social & cultural anthropology in Vienna/Austria and Leiden/The Netherlands. She was the editor of the VSJF-Newsletter (01/2004-12/2006). Currently she is working as an assistant with "Jugend am Werk" (Youth at Work) in Vienna, and on her Ph.D. thesis in political science. Her special fields of interests include: social change, social movements, gender, and political theory.

Claudia Derichs

is professor for political science at the University of Hildesheim, Germany. She did her PhD in Japanese studies and is also a translator for Arabic and Japanese. She has published numerous books and articles on Japanese and Southeast Asian politics, among them an introductory textbook on political systems in East Asia (ed. with Th. Heberer, 2003). She is currently the Vice Chairwoman of the German Association for Asian Studies (Deutsche Gesellschaft für Asienkunde, DGA).

Hilaria Gössmann

is a professor of contemporary Japanese studies at the University of Trier in Germany, where she supervised a research project on representations of "Asia" in Japanese literature, media and popular culture. The research project was sponsored by the Deutsche Forschungsgemeinschaft (DFG). Her research interests include: contemporary Japanese literature, popular culture and media, with a focus on gender and interculturality.

Mihee Hong

is a lecturer in gender studies at Sookmyoung Women's University in Seoul, South Korea. She completed her PhD at the University of Bochum, Germany, on the women's movement and gender relations in South Korea. Her research interests include women's movements, feminist policy and social policy.

Susanne Kreitz-Sandberg

is senior lecturer at the Department of Behavioural Science and Learning at the University of Linköping, Sweden. Her PhD in education (University of Bielefeld, Germany) was based on youth studies in Japan and entered into a research position at the German Institute for Japanese Studies in Tokyo and later into teaching modern Japanese society at the University of Düsseldorf. Her research interests and publications cover comparative education, intercultural competence, youth studies and gender.

Ilse Lenz

is professor for social structure and gender studies at the University of Bochum, Germany, and currently Dean of the Faculty of Social Science. She is the coordinator of the Marie Jahoda chair, a guest professorship for international gender studies. Her research areas include: globalization and transnationalism, feminism, social movements and institutional change. Presently, she is finishing a research project on the German and Japanese new women's movement with Michiko Mae.

Michiko Mae

is professor of Japanese studies at the University of Düsseldorf. She is specialised in Japan-related gender studies and cultural studies. Her main research fields are: Inter- and transculturality, cultural identity, the public and the private sphere, concepts of subjectivity in modern Japan, women's movements and civil society. Her publications include works on transcultural gender studies, women's movements and gender relations in Japan.

Wolfram Manzenreiter

is associated with the Department of East Asian Studies at the University of Vienna where he teaches modern Japanese society. His research work is mostly concerned with social aspects of sports, popular culture, technology and labour in a globalising world. As visiting professor, he has been invited to universities in France, Germany, Japan and Turkey. He is the author of several books and articles on popular culture, leisure and sport in Japan.

Annette Schad-Seifert

is professor at the University of Düsseldorf in Germany. Her main fields of research are the history of social ideas in modern Japan, social science research and contemporary cultural and gender studies of Japan. She has published on Fukuzawa Yukichi and on Cultural Studies in Japan. She is currently preparing a book on the discourse of masculinity and men's studies in modern Japan.

Hiromi Tanaka, M.A.

is a doctoral candidate in social sciences at the University of Bochum, Germany. Her research fields include globalization and transnationalism, comparative gender politics and Japanese society. She has just completed her doctoral dissertation on women's networks as an organizational frame for gender equality mobilization in a global era.

Ulrike Wöhr, Ph.D.

is professor at Hiroshima City University where she teaches gender studies and Japanese studies. Her main area of research is the history of women and feminism in modern Japan, with a focus on the relationship of gender and nation, or ethnicity. Currently, she is doing comparative research on gender in the wartime histories of Japan and Germany.

Gender-Diskussion

Marianne Heimbach-Steins;
Bärbel Kerkhoff-Hader; Eleonore Ploil;
Ines Weinrich (Hg.)
Strukturierung von Wissen und die symbolische Ordnung der Geschlechter
Gender-Tagung Bamberg 2003
Es bedurfte der Kategorie *Gender* als einer Disziplinen und Diskurse übergreifenden Meta-Kategorie, um die Polarisierung zwischen der nota bene „normalen" Männerperspektive und einer besonderen, für viele männliche wie weibliche Wissenschaftssubjekte suspekt bleibenden Frauenperspektive aufzubrechen und feministische Kritik aus der Nische des Partikularen herauszuführen. Gender fungiert als *Wahrnehmungs- und Analyseinstrument* für gesellschaftliche Geschlechterverhältnisse, die sich in vielfältigen kulturellen Ausdrucksformen und gesellschaftlichen Ordnungen verfestigen und sich mit Hierarchisierungen und Machtasymmetrien verbinden. Der vorliegende Band dokumentiert die Beiträge der Tagung „Strukturierung von Wissen und die symbolische Ordnung der Geschlechter", mit der die Frauenbeauftragten der Universität Bamberg das Jubiläumsjahr 2003 „*100 Jahre akademische Bildung von Frauen in Bayern*" eröffneten: Die Hauptbeiträge präsentieren aktuelle Grundlagendiskussionen und exemplarische Anwendungsfelder des Gender-Diskurses in den Bereichen Medienwissenschaften, Soziologie, Geschichte und Ethik. Workshop-Berichte ergänzen das fachliche und thematische Spektrum und geben Einblicke in die Vielfalt innovativer Genderforschung von der Frühgeschichte/Archäologie bis zur Sozialpolitik, von der alttestamentlichen Exegese bis zur historischen Musikwissenschaft. Drei Beiträge zur Frage von Gender Mainstreaming, zur Ehrenpromotion von Elisabeth Gössmann, zum Stand der geschlechterspezifischen Situation an der Bamberger Universität sowie eine Zukunftsvision über die Hochschulen nach weiteren hundert Jahren weiblicher Präsenz runden den Band ab
Bd. 1, 2004, 200 S., 15,90 €, br.,
ISBN 3-8258-7251-3

R. Johanna Regnath; Mascha Riepl-Schmidt; Ute Scherb (Hg.)
Eroberung der Geschichte
Frauen und Tradition
Mit dem Titel „Frauen und Tradition" präsentieren 15 Autorinnen konkrete und ideelle weibliche Denkmalsetzungen und deren symbolische Wirkung: Vielfältige Formen des Erinnerns und des Verschweigens prägen unsere Gesellschaft und machen oft weibliche Traditionslinien, Erinnerungsorte und „Frauen"geschichte(n) unsichtbar. Die Auseinandersetzung mit „Tradition" offenbart die Brüchigkeit weiblicher Rollenzuschreibungen und zielt auf deren Veränderung genauso wie das Netzwerk „Frauen und Geschichte Baden-Württemberg e.V.", dessen Tagung „Eroberung der Geschichte – Frauen und Tradition" dieser Band dokumentiert.
Bd. 3, 2006, 304 S., 24,90 €, br.,
ISBN 3-8258-8953-x

Christine Künzel; Gaby Temme (Hg.)
Täterinnen und/oder Opfer?
Frauen in Gewaltstrukturen
Die kollektive Zuschreibung der Frau als Opfer gesellschaftlicher, männlicher Gewalt verstellte lange Zeit den Blick auf die Rolle von Frauen als Mittäterinnen in sozialen und kulturellen Gewaltstrukturen und auf Fragen der Verantwortung. Der folgende Band ist dazu angelegt, Zuschreibungsprozesse von Täter und Opferpositionen in interdisziplinärer Perspektive zu analysieren. Dies geschieht anhand einer Fokussierung auf die Themenkomplexe: Nationalsozialismus, Krieg, Terrorismus, Prostitutionsmigration, Mädchengewalt, häusliche Gewalt, mediale Diskurse und Gerichtsurteile.
Bd. 4, 2007, 272 S., 24,90 €, br.,
ISBN 3-8258-8968-8

LIT Verlag Berlin – Hamburg – London – Münster – Wien – Zürich
Fresnostr. 2 48159 Münster
Tel.: 0251 / 620 32 22 – Fax: 0251 / 922 60 99
e-Mail: vertrieb@lit-verlag.de – http://www.lit-verlag.de

Maria Buchmayr; Julia Neissl (Hg.)
work-life-balance & Wissenschaft – ein Widerspruch?
Die Vereinbarkeit von Beruf und Privatem gewinnt mit der Verankerung der Strategie Gender Mainstreaming innerhalb der Organisation Universität zunehmend an Bedeutung. Die Thematik der Vereinbarkeit wird großteils in Bezug auf Frauen diskutiert. Dies spiegelt sich in zahlreichen Vereinbarkeitsmodellen wider, die sich an Frauen richten und letztendlich zur Reproduktion der geschlechtsspezifischen Arbeitsteilung beitragen. Der Band befasst sich vor allem mit bestehenden beruflichen Rahmenbedingungen im universitären Kontext und innovativen Überlegungen, diese klaren Rollenzuteilungen im Berufsbild WissenschaftlerIn aufzulösen.
Bd. 5, 2006, 152 S., 14,90 €, br.,
ISBN 3-8258-9525-4

Focus Gender
hrsg. vom ZIF – Zentrum für Interdisziplinäre Frauen- und Geschlechterforschung der HAWK/FH Hildesheim/Holzminden/Göttingen und der Stiftung Universität Hildesheim

Waltraud Ernst; Ulrike Bohle (Hg.)
Geschlechterdiskurse zwischen Fiktion und Faktizität
Internationale Frauen- und Genderforschung in Niedersachsen, Teilband 3
Dieser Band untersucht Geschlechterdiskurse in Texten und Bildern zwischen Fiktion und Faktizität. Kritische, insbesondere feministische KulturwissenschaftlerInnen der letzten Dekade konnten zeigen, dass künstlerische Ausdrucksformen gesellschaftspolitische Realitäten oftmals in einer Art und Weise reflektieren, die diese entlarvt und damit „Wirklichkeitstreue" gerade herstellt. Zugleich wurde Geschichtsschreibung und mediale Berichterstattung auf ihren suggestiven Charakter und ihre realitätskonstituierende Wirkung hin untersucht. Die Arbeiten weisen darauf hin, dass Geschlechterbilder einen zentralen Bestandteil jeglicher kultureller Produktion darstellen.

Jedoch gerade weil sie nicht eindeutig sind, ständig neu festgeschrieben werden. Genau dadurch entsteht Raum – nicht nur in Kunst und Kult – für einzelne Subjekte und ganze soziale Bewegungen, sich in mehr oder weniger schmerzhafter und individueller Weise selbst zu gestalten.
Bd. 6, 2006, 248 S., 24,90 €, br.,
ISBN 3-8258-9237-9

Astrid Franzke; Helga Gotzmann (Hg.)
Mentoring als Wettbewerbsstruktur für Hochschulen – Strukturelle Ansätze der Implementierung
Der Band vermittelt vielfältige Einblicke in neuere Forschungen zur Implementierung von Mentoring an Hochschulen aus dem deutschsprachigen Raum und in Erfahrungen von hochschulpolitischen Expertinnen. Mentoring wird dabei als Instrument zur Geschlechtergleichstellung, zur Förderung des studentischen und wissenschaftlichen Nachwuchses sowie zur Personalentwicklung und Qualitätssicherung thematisiert. Die zentrale Fragestellung lautet: Wie gelingt der Übergang vom Projektstatus in die regulären Hochschulstrukturen? Dazu werden schwerpunktmäßig folgende Fragen untersucht: Was passiert innerhalb von Organisationen, wenn neue Instrumente implementiert werden? Welche unterschiedlichen Ansätze und Überlegungen zur Implementierung von Mentoring existieren? Wo befinden sich dazu an den Hochschulen Ressourcen? Wie lässt sich personelle und strukturelle Unterstützung mobilisieren? Welche institutionellen Orte für die Platzierung von Mentoring bieten sich in den Hochschulen an? In den Buchbeiträgen sind dazu innovative Antworten und kreative Anregungen zu finden.
Bd. 7, 2006, 232 S., 19,90 €, br.,
ISBN 3-8258-9569-6

LIT Verlag Berlin – Hamburg – London – Münster – Wien – Zürich
Fresnostr. 2 48159 Münster
Tel.: 0251 / 620 32 22 – Fax: 0251 / 922 60 99
e-Mail: vertrieb@lit-verlag.de – http://www.lit-verlag.de